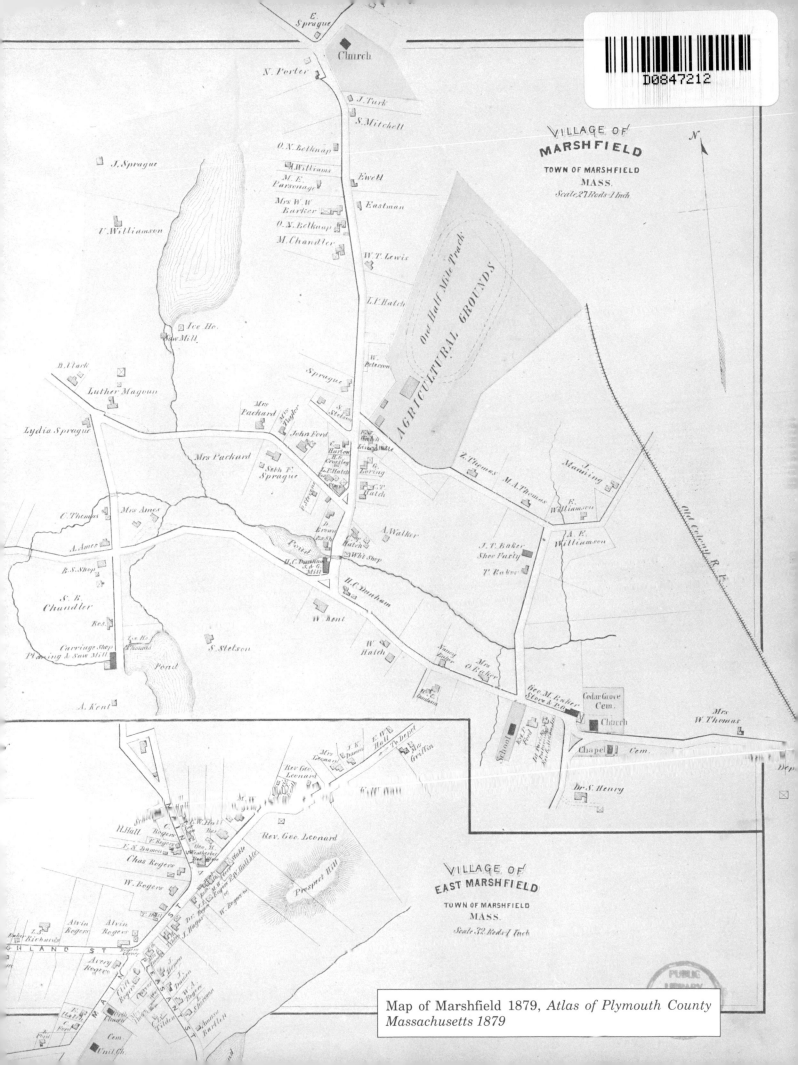

Map of Marshfield 1879, *Atlas of Plymouth County Massachusetts 1879*

Marshfield 1640-1990

Marshfield

A Town of Villages   1640-1990

Cynthia Hagar Krusell
Betty Magoun Bates

Historical Research Associates
Marshfield Hills, MA
1990

© 1990 by Historical Research Associates. All rights reserved
Published by Historical Research Associates, Marshfield Hills, MA 02051
Printed in the United States of America
ISBN 0-9627871-0-8

Frontispiece: *Bluefish Rock, about 1880*

Illustrations by Anne Philbrick Hall — gold-leaf seal on hard cover; pp. vii, 3, 12, 15, 22, 25, 39, 45, 49, 54, 57, 77, 85, 86, 94, 96, 114, 121, 122, 123, 135, 145, 149, 152, 155, 159, 171, 183, 185, 199, 202, 203, 205.
Photographs by Cynthia Hagar Krusell — pp. 4, 5, 11, 12, 13, 14, 35, 36, 38, 65, 66, 70, 75, 82, 83, 84, 87, 93, 113, 127, 133, 140, 141, 177, 182, 186, 195, 200, 202, 204.

Daniel Webster, 1852
Lithograph by Joseph Alexander Ames
Courtesy of Robert W. Davis

*It is wise for us to recur to the history
of our ancestors. Those who do not look
upon themselves as a link connecting
the Past with the Future, do not perform
their duty to the world.*

— Daniel Webster

Contents

Foreword

THERE is a flavor to New England town histories as distinctive as of Baldwin apples plucked from old trees after frost. The most wonderful is William Bradford's *Of Plymouth Plantation*. It is in the King's English as spoken in the reigns of Elizabeth I and James I.

Who can ever forget, who has heard it but once, "As one small candle may light a thousand, so the light here kindled hath shone unto many, yea in some sort to our whole nation," and "So they left that goodly and pleasant city which had been their resting place near twelve years; but they knew they were pilgrims, and looked not much on those things, but lift up their eyes to the heavens, their dearest country, and quieted their spirits." These lines were written about 1640.

The same language was still spoken by the countrymen who blasted the British regular army back to Boston along the battle road of April 19, 1775. In a Lincoln town history published at the turn of the present century, the vivid account of Amos Baker, one of the last survivors of the famous day, was presented to posterity: "Major Buttrick said 'Will you stand here and see them burn the town down?' And the order was given to march and we all marched down without further argument." It tells of the skirmish at Concord Bridge, of the retreat of the British, of the running fight along the road till nightfall and concludes with a classic understatement worthy of the heroes of antiquity. "I verily believe that I felt better that day, take it all the day through, than if I had staid at home."

Marshfield is one of the earliest offshoots of the Pilgrims' Plymouth. Its history, in careful detail, from 1640 to 1990 tells much about the development and character of the United States from small beginnings to the mechanized, industrialized complications of contemporary society. Detailed study is the foundation of scientific projection. Planners for the future will learn and profit from this careful examination of amoebic villages that grew to be a big town - the Town of Marshfield.

— Thomas Boylston Adams
Chief Trustee of the Adams Papers
President of the Massachusetts
Historical Society 1957-1975

Acknowledgments

THE AUTHORS are grateful to the following people who have contributed valuable information toward the completion of this history of Marshfield on its 350th anniversary:

Eleanor Adler, Elsie Keene Almeida, Beatrice Gonsalves Amado, Robert Ames, Steven Anstatt, Robert Archer, Jeannette Hixon Avery, Evelyn Duddy Babcock, Edward Bangs, Jr., Esther Bartlett, Walter Bartlett, Margaret Beals, Joseph Beals, Constance Anderson Benzaquin, Eileen Biagini, Joseph Biagini, Karen Biagini, Bradford Blackman, Lawrence Bonney, Marjorie Bournazos, Mildred Bratt, David Brega, Bruce Brigell, Clara Brown, Margaret Brown, Lilian Bullock, Allen Burchell, Margaret Cain, Margarite Cappelo, Barbara Henderson Chandler, Carleton Chandler, Lois Hubbard Chandler, Russell Chandler, Jane Clough, Katya Coon, Dennis Corcoran, Roger Crawford, James Cunning, Anne Davenport, David Davenport, Brian Doherty, David Ellis, Ruth Alexanderson Emery, Doris Goodwin Ewart, Alan Feinberg, Robert Feinberg, Richard Frisbee, Judith Francis, Manuel Francis, Ray Freden, Carol Funderburk, Frederick Gibson, Barbara Graham, James Haddad, Donald Hagar, Edith Culver Hagar, Frederick Hagar, Anne Philbrick Hall, Priscilla Rogers Hall, Richard Hall, Stephen Hall, Heather Hanson, George Harlow, Ann Hayden, Natalie Staples Henderson, Wilfred Henderson, Francis Houghton, Pauline Hunt, Nancy Huntley, Faith Penniman Jean, Joanne Henderson Josselyn, Kenneth Joy, Raymond Joyal, Wilfred Keene, Leo Kelley, Herbert Kendall, Eula Langille Kroupa, Leonard LaForest, Olga LaForest, Constance Keene Lambert, Barbara Lincoln, Natalie High Loomis, Ethel Banner Macomber, Eleanor Magoon, Tracy Magoun, Muriel MacKay, Joan Mahoney, Elizabeth Sherman Hatch Martinson, Lois McDaniel, Joseph McDonough, Ann McGowan, Helen Seaverns Melvin, Carol Arrigo Michener, James Mullen, Nancy Mullen, John Nangle, Jr., Charles Najum, Doris Toabe Nectow, Faith Newton, Phyllis Nielsen, Susan Prouty Norris, Bertram O'Donnell, Shirley O'Donnell, Virginia Babcock Ortiz, Thornton Oxner, Edwin Parsons, Janet Whitaker Peterson, Hope Poor, Philip Randall, Margaret Roswell, Joan Scolponeti, Edith Magoun Shepherd, Charles Sinnott, Ruth Baker Sinnott, Anna Myrle Snow, Susan Spencer, Maeve Sullivan, John Taylor, Edward Therrian, Beverley Thomas, William Thomas, John Tilley, Shirley Trout, William Vaughan, Christopher Waitkus, Catherine Whalen, Leonard Williams, Dorothy Youmans, M. Sugar Young.

For anyone whose name has been omitted, we thank you, too. We are particularly grateful to the Ventress Memorial Library for the use of the Trustees-Historical Room and for the kindness of the staff. We especially appreciate Esther Coke's help in computerizing the design and layout of the book. Finally, it is impossible to give sufficient thanks to our untiring editor and special friend, Frances Downing Vaughan, whose humor and support carried us through the difficult process of refining the manuscript for publication.

Introduction

AS THE SUN rises out of the sea to bring the light of another day to Marshfield, it casts shadows over the hills and valleys of a landscape that has known such mornings for many thousands of years. After the final glacier retreated, there was the era of the caribou herds. Then the Eastern Woodland Algonquins came and built their summer shelters by the sea and the rivers, fished along the shore, and raised their crops of maize. They developed a network of woodland footpaths and landmarks known only to themselves.

Europeans first came to America to fish the coastal waters and trade their worldly goods for highly valued furs brought down the rivers by the Native Americans. As European wars increased and timber supplies decreased, the English, French, and Spanish began looking westward from Europe to new horizons. They traveled with the rising sun and found, not gold or riches, but woodlands filled with timber for ships and waters with a wealth of fish. In time, Plymouth Plantation was established, and soon the settlers looked about for outlying farm land. One of the places they found was Marshfield.

Geography greatly influenced the settlement pattern of Marshfield. Easily reached by water within the sweep of the bay of Plymouth and Duxbury, the southern lowlands and river valleys drew the first tide of settlers. The fertile valley of the tidal Green Harbor River offered some of the richest farm lands to be found in Plymouth Colony. Settlement spread northward to take advantage of the broad valleys of the North and South rivers, with their salt meadows and easy access to the sea at the old river mouth, where Rexhame beach is today.

The South River, with its major tributary the Furnace Brook, provided water power for the first Marshfield gristmill built at what is today the Veterans' Memorial Park. Later this convenient water-power site was used for a saw mill and a cotton mill. Deposits of bog iron in the Furnace Brook valley attracted men to operate an iron furnace.

The North River, biggest of Marshfield's three rivers, provided a major passageway along the northern border of the town. The surrounding uplands and hills produced the great stands of white pine and hard white oak necessary for a thriving shipbuilding industry. Soon shipyards sprang up along the upland areas adjacent to the river. Mills were established on the brooks that flowed into the river. The families at the north end of the town took advantage of the fertile fields along the river's edge for farming and cut the salt hay on the river meadows for cattle feed.

For the first comers, Marshfield began in metes and bounds, rods and degrees. These were the measurements by which the land was laid out and granted by the Plymouth Colony Court and later by the proprietors of the town, after its founding in 1640. The settled area of the town grew as land was granted, piece by piece, with each grantee getting some tillage, pasturage, wood lot, and salt hay meadow. Each separate part of Marshfield began to develop its own distinct character, and the town became a collection of dispersed villages. It is these villages, each different and identifiable to this day, that are the principal subject of this narrative.

The families who settled these villages, and the people who followed in their footsteps, are the cast for our story of Marshfield. The settlers cleared and tilled the land, built homes, mills, and churches. They all by necessity were farmers, and some were also fishermen, millers, shipbuilders, store owners, blacksmiths, and cobblers. Over the years, as the town became more populated and complex, other people took their places and pursued other occupations and activities. Indeed, the people of Marshfield have guided her destiny to the present time. We who live here today are a part of a continuing story, a story started even before the first settlers.

There have been several turning points in Marshfield history, when the course of events has been dramatically changed. These include the arrival of the settlers, the departure of the Loyalists after the American Revolution, the coming of the railroad, and the extension of the present Route 3 to the town's doorstep. The story of Marshfield cannot be understood without recognizing these pivotal moments in the course of events.

As we celebrate Marshfield's 350th birthday, we look back at what has been our past and forward to what shall be our future. We hope that this narrative history of Marshfield will excite the reader about the story of what has happened here and inspire the people of the town with pride in our heritage and faith in our future.

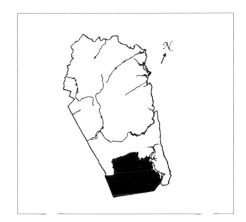

Green Harbor Village

WILLIAM GREEN guided his small boat up the narrow marsh creek from Plymouth. To the northwest stretched a low-lying range of hills; to the east, a rise of dunes and a ribbon of white beach. Beyond lay the sea. He had been to this area before, while exploring the extent of Plymouth Bay with his fellow Plymouth Colony settlers Myles Standish and Edward Winslow. Green was determined to establish a fishing station here. Separated from the nearby upland by a broad tidal creek and marsh, the beach offered not only protection from Indian attack, but also excellent fishing in both the river and the sea.

It was the spring of 1623. Only the soaring gulls and the flashing flocks of returning sandpipers and plovers inhabited the shore. The incoming tide was beginning to flood the marsh, lifting Green's boat and enabling him to land at last on the beach. Disembarking, he strode to the top of the sand dunes and looked out over the blue stretch of Cape Cod Bay. Turning, he gazed upon a land of gently undulating hills skirted with flat fertile fields, tidal marshes, and the broad expanse of the Green Harbor River valley. Thus may William Green have first seen the area we now call Marshfield.

Green started a small fishing station here at what became known as Salt House Beach. He set up fish weirs on the river, fished off the beach, and dried and salted his fish at the edge of the sea. Salted New England codfish was much in demand in European markets, and Plymouth Colony needed the revenue from this lucrative trade. How long William Green remained at this place is not recorded. Plymouth Governor William Bradford mentioned William Green only once in the journal he wrote about the early years of the Plymouth Colony. Green does not appear in any Marshfield records, but his name was used as the first name for the area, Green's Harbor. The term is still used to designate the south part of Marshfield and the river that flows through it.[2]

Some ten years later, in 1632, there arrived on these same shores a man who was to found the town of Marshfield and whose family was to feature for two centuries in town affairs. Edward Winslow was granted land in the fertile area at the north end of Plymouth Bay "at a place general [sic] called Green's Harbor, where no lots had been allotted in the former division." Winslow eventually took title to some twelve hundred acres of land granted to him by the Plymouth Colony Court for his service to the colony. Winslow's land lay along the edge of what became known as the Careswell Marsh from the Duxbury line to Green Harbor River. He built a dwelling house at the marsh's edge, cleared the land for extensive farming, and brought others to settle near him in this place at the edge of the bay.[4]

Winslow had come with the Pilgrims on the *Mayflower* to Plymouth in 1620. He was one of the group of English religious exiles who voyaged to America intent on establishing a colony free of Anglican church authorities. The term *Pilgrim* was later attached to this group to convey the idea of wanderers or travelers. They did not call themselves Pilgrims. They were Separatists, a liberal faction of the Puritan movement of seventeenth-century England. They believed in total separation from the Anglican church. The more conservative Puritans wished to purify the established church of its corrupt practices, but remain within mainstream Anglicanism. It was the Puritans who settled Massachusetts Bay Colony in 1630 under Governor John Winthrop, but it was the Separatists who came to Plymouth. Only about one-half of the passengers on the *Mayflower* came for religious reasons. The others came as merchants for economic reasons, or as hired hands or servants.

Edward Winslow, a printer, joined the Separatists during their years of exile in Leyden, Holland. Born in Droitwich, Worcestershire, England, in 1595, Edward grew up in a well-to-do landed family, whose ancestral home stood south of the city of Worcester in the small village of Kempsey. The Winslow family homestead still stands today and is called *Kerswell*, a name Winslow used for his Marshfield estate. Over the years the name evolved into *Careswell*, origin of today's Careswell Street. Edward Winslow's father, Edward Winslow, had moved from Kempsey to the area of Droitwich, where he managed a large sheep farm and owned an interest in a salt works. Salt was used for preserving sheep hides to produce leather which was in demand by printers and bookbinders, who sold and bartered their books and publications in the churchyard and nave of St. Paul's Cathedral in London.

Edward made frequent trips with his father to London. He became interested in the printing business and was apprenticed to a printer in the

Kerswell, *Edward Winslow's ancestral home in Kempsey, Worcestershire, England*

London publishing district at the foot of Ludgate Hill. He joined the Separatist congregation at St. Bride's Church on Fleet Street. It was to this church that the exiled Separatists in Leyden, Holland, turned in search of a printer for their religious treatises. Edward Winslow responded to this call and went to Holland in 1617. So it was that he was among the Separatists on board the famous voyage of the *Mayflower* to America.

Winslow was a leader at Plymouth Colony. He became a personal and respected friend of the local Wampanoag Indian chief, Massasoit. It was due to Winslow's diplomatic abilities that, in 1621, a treaty was drawn up between Plymouth Colony and the Wampanoags. This was kept for fifty-five years until the outbreak, in 1675, of the New England Indian war, known as King Philip's War.

King Philip was the English name given to Massasoit's son Metacomet. Massasoit asked the English to suggest names for his two sons, and the Greek warrior names of Philip and Alexander were thus bestowed upon them. The Wampanoags, a subtribe of the larger New England Algonquins, had been severely decimated by an illness which struck them prior to the arrival of the English settlers. The tribe at Patuxet (Plymouth) had only a single survivor, Squanto, who became a good friend of the Pilgrims shortly after their arrival. The reduced number of Native Americans left in the vicinity of Plymouth was an important factor in enabling the English to establish and maintain their settlement.

Edward Winslow also served the Pilgrim group as ambassador to England, making four voyages to the mother country to obtain money and goods for the settlers at Plymouth. It was Winslow who brought the first cattle to the Plymouth Colony in 1624. Asked to serve the Puritan cause under Protector Oliver Cromwell, Winslow returned for the last time to England in 1646. He served as a commissioner to assess the value of Spanish ships seized by the English and to evaluate royal estates taken to finance the Commonwealth. In 1655 he was sent as a commander with Admiral Robert Venable on an expedition to drive the Spanish from the West Indies. Winslow became ill and died on shipboard between Haiti and Jamaica on 8 May 1655. He was buried at sea. His death was a great loss to the Plymouth Colony and to Marshfield.[6]

Marshfield as we know it today began with the arrival of Edward Winslow in 1632. He regularly came to his Green Harbor farm during the summer but returned in the winter to Plymouth, as Governor William Bradford wished. In an effort to keep the church members together and the church strong, Bradford required all the settlers of the outlying towns to return to Plymouth to live during the winter until 1636. It was in that year that Winslow settled as a permanent resident at his Green Harbor farm.

A number of 100-acre land grants from the Plymouth Colony Court were made to other settlers in 1637 along the Neck Road (Ocean Street/Route 139 running easterly to Fieldston). Grants were also made near the present Training Green and Town Hall.

The southern border of Marshfield was easily accessible from Plymouth by way of the marsh creeks of the Duxbury Bay area, but by 1633 a water passage to the Green Harbor River estuary had been created. In 1636 it was ordered by the Plymouth Colony Court that "the cut at Green's Harbor for a boat passage shall be made eighteen foot wide and six foot deep." This waterway connecting Duxbury Bay with the Green Harbor River was perhaps the first canal dug in America. It created an inland water route from Plymouth via the Duxbury creeks and the Green Harbor River, through a narrow creek to the South River estuary, and up the North River to the

Green Harbor Canal, looking south from Canal Street. The canal was dug in 1636 to create a continuous waterway from Plymouth to Marshfield.

Green Harbor Path (Pilgrim Trail). Along this path the early settlers came to Marshfield.

present town of Hanover. In 1843 a bridge, known as Rainbow Bridge, was built over the canal at today's Canal Street. A granite marker, placed on the west bank of the canal at the bridge by the Marshfield Historical Commission, notes this historic spot.[6]

Soon needing an overland route along which to drive their livestock from Plymouth to Marshfield, the settlers began to use an ancient Indian way that led along the edge of Plymouth Bay. It followed the beach in North Plymouth through present-day Kingston, crossing the Jones River at the old Wading Place near Rocky Nook, and continuing through Duxbury west of present Route 3A/Tremont Street, to enter Marshfield at the Duxbury line at Careswell Street. This old way continued through Marshfield, crossed the South River at a narrow place known as the Valley Bars, and ran along the foot of Snake Hill to a ferry crossing of the North River near the present Humarock Bridge. This early road was recognized and formally designated by the Plymouth Court on 10 May 1637. It was, quite possibly, the first court-ordered road in America. It was called the Green's Harbor Path, since it led to Green's Harbor. In Marshfield it was often referred to as the Plymouth Path or the Scituate Path, depending on which direction the traveler was headed.

The Green Harbor Path was used for many years as the main road to Marshfield from Plymouth. The present Careswell Street causeway near Duck Hill was not built until 1836, when Daniel Webster was granted a permit by the Plymouth County commissioners to improve the cart path that led from the 1699 Winslow House to the Duxbury line. When the Duxbury and Cohasset Railroad Company acquired a right of way through Marshfield in the late 1860s, the course of the Green Harbor Path, laid out originally as a "way forever," was altered.[7]

A controversy arose over this in 1917, spearheaded by Elizabeth Paulding Eames, who lived by the side of the path near the Duxbury line. She researched the exact course of the old trail as it ran through Marshfield. In a continuing correspondence with the New York, New Haven and Hartford Railroad Company, she sought to have the trail either bridged or tunneled. Her efforts were futile at that time, but her research became extremely valuable, since it has served as the basis for current efforts to redefine the exact course of the path.

Today it is called the Pilgrim Trail, honoring the early settlers. The Marshfield Historical Commission is currently concerned with preserving the Green Harbor Path along its southerly course from the Duxbury line to the old Winslow Burying Ground. Preservation covenants have been procured from some owners of land along the path in hopes of opening it once again as a continuous walking way.[8]

Another early road, much used by those traveling from Plymouth to Boston, was the so-called Bay Path. This was the term commonly used in the colonial period for any road leading to the Bay Colony at Boston. An easterly branch of the Bay Path from Plymouth led through Marshfield paralleling the Green Harbor Path in the southwestern part of the town, but following more nearly the later route taken by the railroad southwest of Black Mount. Crossing the Green Harbor River at today's Webster Street, it followed that street to Ocean Street, then took approximately the course of Main Street/Route 3A today northerly to the old Vassell's ferry crossing of the North River at the present site of Little's Bridge to Scituate.

The first settled part of Marshfield was Green Harbor. This area is comprised of about three thousand acres of land lying south of the Green Harbor River. The river flows into Marshfield on the Moraine Street line

Elizabeth Paulding Eames

1847-1933

She belonged to a bygone generation. In height she barely reached five feet, but she was as straight as the broomstick she held behind her back each morning to improve her aging posture.

Elizabeth Paulding Eames, my great aunt, was born in the front room of her family home that stood on a small knoll near the old Green Harbor Path (Pilgrim Trail) off Careswell Street. Her early school years were spent at the little Winslow district school, and later she walked six miles a day to attend Partridge Academy in Duxbury for her higher education. For many years she taught in the Marshfield schools.

She became interested in local history and wrote a number of essays on familiar landmarks and historic occasions. These she shared with her friends and neighbors at the meetings of the Marshfield Historical Society. Some of these essays were carefully put away in a small black box that was discovered in 1968, thirty five years after her death. The box, filled with poems, diaries, essays, and dusty letters, was returned to Marshfield by a relative with instructions to "do what you want with the remains of Aunt Lizzie."

In the box was an essay which told of a very early path that passed through the west side of Aunt Lizzie's property.

She wrote that she often walked along the old path "with glimpses of Plymouth, dear old historic Plymouth, in the distance, all covered by a beautiful blue haze. . . . A long time I gaze and so many thoughts and memories with so much of early history crowd into my mind. While I gaze the pail and berry-picking is well nigh forgotten . . . with an effort I turn my back on this most beautiful scene and hie me to the berry patch. . . . I wondered if years ago the Indians with birch baskets instead of tin pails picked berries on this very spot. . . . following along the trail. . . . [I] reached the Hewitt place. In front of that place reached by going down a steep incline is a wonderfully sheltered valley . . . at the present time deer can often be found there enjoying its shelter and seclusion . . . the Indians undoubtedly used it for various relics have been found."

There were also many letters written to the New York, New Haven and Hartford Railroad Company in 1917 requesting that the company bridge the break in the old Green Harbor Path made by the building of the railway in 1871. From her great love of nature and her resolve to save this historic landmark, Aunt Lizzie amassed a body of research material that now enables the Marshfield Historical Commission to carry her work forward and fulfill her dream to preserve the Green Harbor Path forever.

— Betty Magoun Bates

near the present Garretson cranberry bogs and meanders through the bogs to flow under Webster Street near the present Green Harbor Golf Course. Before the dyke was built in 1872, the river was brackish as far inland as Webster Street. West and inland of the Webster Street underpass the river was fresh water and referred to as the Green Harbor Fresh. The river continues through the widening marshes at the present Daniel Webster Wildlife Sanctuary. It once flowed out to sea just south of Cut Island at the Duxbury line near Canal Street, Green Harbor. The old mouth of the river was closed by a violent storm about 1806. For four or five years there was no outlet to the sea. The river became stagnant, having as its only course the narrow marsh creeks of Duxbury Bay.

A Green Harbor Canal Company was formed in 1806 for the purpose of draining the marshes and building "crossways and bridges, and for digging a canal or canals for the water to pass into Plymouth and Duxbury Bays." A new canal was dug behind Green Harbor beach. It connected with the old 1636 canal at the Duxbury line. This waterway is known today as the Cut River. The present entrance to the Green Harbor River was opened up by the sea in 1810 and further cut through by forty local fishermen, under cover of night, to widen the entrance for their boats. The outlet between Bluefish Rock and Green Harbor beach is known as the Narrows.[9]

The southern half of the Green Harbor area (that is, all the land lying around the present Winslow House) was granted by the Plymouth Colony

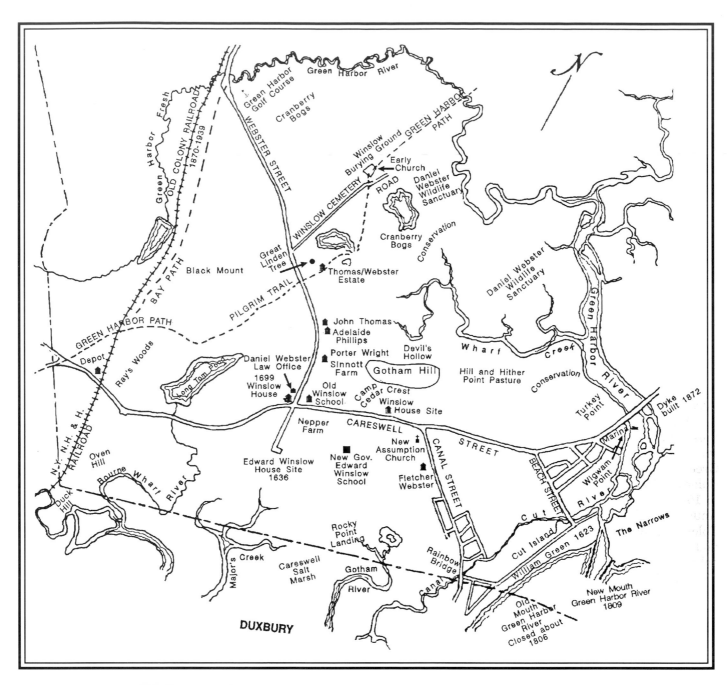

Green Harbor area

Court largely to Edward Winslow. The northern half (that area which later became the Daniel Webster estate) was granted to William Thomas. A piece of land between these two large parcels was granted first to Robert Carver, then given to John Thomas in exchange for land on Parsonage Street. (John Thomas came as a servant of Edward Winslow and was no relation to the William Thomas mentioned above.) Edward Winslow, William Thomas, and John Thomas built the first three homesteads in Green Harbor. They cleared the land for tillage and pasturage, planted orchards, set aside wood lots, and established paths and ways between their farms and fields.

Other, smaller grants followed. Some of the first grantees never lived on their land, but either sold it or exchanged it with others. Sometimes land was granted with the provision that the grantee had to settle on it or it would revert to the town. The first grants in Marshfield were made by the Plymouth Colony Court. After the town was incorporated in 1640, the Marshfield proprietors, or settled freemen of the town, were responsible for granting land within the town. *Freemen* were defined as male inhabitants who were church members and in good standing in the community. Edward Bumpus was given a piece of land at Oven Hill Point (Duck Hill). John Rouse had land at Careswell Creek near the Winslow property. James Pitney received a grant which he sold to James Lindall in 1646. Pitney's daughter, Sarah, married John Thomas, and the Thomas family lived for many generations at the old homestead. Sarah Pitney Thomas was honored by her descendants who erected a statue in her memory and in memory of all the early colonial women of Marshfield. The statue is in the possession of the Historic Winslow House Association today.[10]

When Edward Winslow arrived in Marshfield, he was accompanied by his wife, Susannah White, and their three children. He had married Susannah as his second wife 12 May 1621, she being the widow of William White. Both had lost their spouses during the illness that struck the Pilgrims the first winter at Plymouth. Theirs was the first marriage ceremony held at Plymouth Colony. Susannah brought to the marriage her two sons, Resolved and Peregrine White, who were about eighteen and sixteen years of age in 1636 when the family came to Marshfield. In addition, the Winslows had a son of their own, Josiah Winslow, born in 1629 in Plymouth. Josiah was seven years old when he came to Green Harbor. A daughter, Elizabeth, born during the 1630s, completed this "first family" of Marshfield.[11]

Edward Winslow was active in the affairs of both colony and town and must have had little time for his family and his farm. The Winslows had servants and farmhands to help with the hard work of pioneering in early Green Harbor. Winslow, having served a term as governor of Plymouth Colony in 1633, began another term in 1636 and was to hold this office again in 1644. When not governor, he served as assistant governor almost continuously. Winslow worked on the 1636 revision of the laws of Plymouth Colony. He served as a member of the General Court at Plymouth until 1646 and was one of the so-called Undertakers, or those responsible for the colony debt, until 1641. He was commissioner to the New England Confederacy in 1643 and 1644. He traveled to Maine to set up trading posts on the Kennebec and Penobscot rivers, and to Connecticut and the Aptuxet Trading Post in Bourne to trade with the Indians.[12]

In addition to his many duties with the colony, Winslow encouraged people to settle at Green Harbor so that the town might qualify for incorporation. In Plymouth Colony, a town could not be incorporated until it reached a certain population and had a minister and parsonage. The town was incorporated on 2 March 1640. The church and town were one, and early town meetings were held in the church. At a Marshfield town meeting in 1645 one of the first publicly funded schools in the colonies was established.

Having traveled to England in 1624, 1631, and 1634, Winslow returned again in 1646. It was to be his last trip. Away from his home at Marshfield for the remaining nine years of his life, he was destined to die in the service of Puritan Oliver Cromwell in the West Indies campaign of 1655.[13]

Edward Winslow's son Josiah was seventeen when his father left for England the final time. Josiah's half-brother Resolved White had left home in 1640 at the time of his marriage to Judith Vassall, daughter of the ferry-keeper at the North River, and half-brother Peregrine White was to marry Sarah Bassett in 1649 and move to her family land on the banks of the South River, across from the old North/South River mouth.[14]

When Josiah married Penelope Pelham of a prominent Boston family in 1651, the couple returned to London for the marriage ceremony in St. Bride's Church, the very place where Edward Winslow had joined the Separatists before coming to America. Edward was back in London at the time, serving Cromwell. Oil portraits of Edward, Josiah, and Penelope were painted by Robert Walker of London. Edward Winslow's portrait, now at the Pilgrim Society in Plymouth, is the only likeness of any *Mayflower* passenger that exists today.

It seems probable that Josiah Winslow and Penelope, upon their return from London, began to build their own home adjacent to the original Winslow house. Josiah's mother, Susannah, must have been living in the old homestead. Two cellar holes were discovered later, indicating the existence of two houses at the original Winslow site (marked by a granite stone off Perryn Way across Careswell Street from the 1699 Winslow House). Susannah died sometime before 1675, having outlived her husband, Edward Winslow, by some 20 years.[15]

Josiah followed in the footsteps of his father and assumed a variety of civic responsibilities. He was a delegate to the Plymouth Colony Court, a commissioner to the Confederacy for New England, and governor of Plymouth Colony from 1673 until his death in 1680. Although not a military man by nature, he was made commander in chief of the colonial forces during the 1675 King Philip's Indian War. When Plymouth authorities seized Wampanoag Chief Massasoit's son Wamsutta (Alexander) for questioning, they brought him to Winslow's Green Harbor home. Alexander became ill at Careswell and died on the way back to his people at Titicut (Middleborough). His death was blamed directly on the Winslow family and was one of the precipitating causes of the ensuing war. Josiah Winslow led the troops in the decisive Great Swamp fight in Rhode Island on 19 December 1675. This battle broke the strength of the Indians and led to their ultimate surrender in July 1676. Josiah was destined to live only four more years.[16]

Josiah and Penelope Winslow had two children who lived to adulthood: a daughter, Elizabeth, born in 1664; and a son, Isaac, born in 1670. It was Isaac who built the present so-called Historic Winslow House in 1699, a year before his marriage to Sarah Wensley. Again, in the public-service tradition

of the Winslow family, Isaac attained numerous prominent positions, both military and civil, in the colony. He served as judge of the Probate Court at Plymouth, chief justice of the Court of Common Pleas, and president of the Council for the Province of Massachusetts Bay. He was known in Marshfield and in the colony as the Honorable Isaac Winslow.[17]

1699 Winslow House in winter. This home of the Winslow family for over a century was restored in 1920 by the Historic Winslow House Association.

Isaac Winslow and Sarah Wensley were married by the Reverend Cotton Mather in Boston on 11 July 1700. Sarah Wensley was the daughter of Samuel Wensley and Elizabeth Freeman Paddy Wensley, whose portrait hangs with other Winslow portraits at the Pilgrim Society in Plymouth. Reproductions of the Winslow family portraits are to be seen at the 1699 Winslow House. Isaac and Sarah Winslow had six children, all of whom lived to adulthood. This was the largest family to live at the 1699 Winslow House. Their first child, another Josiah, born in 1701, was a young man of only twenty-three when he was killed by the Indians in May 1724 at the battle of St. George River in Maine. A daughter, Penelope, married James Warren of another *Mayflower* Pilgrim line. A son, Edward, married Hannah Howland, descendant of Pilgrim John Howland. Edward was a prominent Plymouth Loyalist at the time of the American Revolution and was forced to leave Plymouth by the Patriots.

It was the Honorable Isaac Winslow's son John, born in 1703, who brought wide-spread fame to the Winslow family of Careswell in Green Harbor. John had an outstanding military career in the French and Indian War and made a name for himself in the so-called Acadian campaign. He was sent in 1755 by Governor William Shirley of Massachusetts to be second in command under Lieutenant Colonel Robert Monckton of the colonial

Winslow Family Crest
*Pen and ink drawing by Anne
Philbrick Hall, 1990*

*Sampler stitched by Deborah Winslow,
descendant of Kenelm Winslow, from
collection of Historic Winslow House
Association*

Debe Winslow is my name
English is my nation
Marshfield is my dwelling place
Christ is my salvation
When I am dead & in my grave
& all my bones are rotten
When this you see remember me
Let me not be forgotten
Lord if I live, let me be thine
And also if I die
Come life come death
Let me ever be thine
Amen amen say I.

Deborah Winslow did this
in the 14th year of her age 1757

*Door handle on the front door of
the 1699 Winslow House*

troops in an all-out attempt to oust the tenacious French population from British-owned Nova Scotia. General John Winslow and Lieutenant Colonel Monckton seized the French fortress, Beauséjour, at the head of the Minas Basin, then overtook and conquered Nova Scotia. The French inhabitants were asked to leave their farms and to gather at the small church in the village of Grand Pré, where they were ordered to abandon their homes and their country.

The subsequent deportation of the French Acadian population, and their ultimate dispersal along the Atlantic coast of the American colonies as far as present New Orleans, Louisiana, became the subject of Henry Longfellow's epic poem *Evangeline*.

It was a "loathsome" task for General Winslow whose heart was with the French peasants. In his kindness he brought a number of French people back to Marshfield. The town took on the responsibility of housing and caring for them. Marshfield town records for 1757 refer to "the use of the schoolhouse for the French people brought into the town." The Massachusetts State Archives contain a reference to the French families of Charles Mieuse and J. Mitchel as living in Marshfield. One of these families was still being mentioned in the 1778 town records, not by a family name but as a "French family."[18]

Window in the 1699 Winslow House

General John Winslow served in the 1756 Lake George campaign of the French and Indian War. He died in 1774, just before the outbreak of the American Revolution. Had he lived, he doubtless would have been one of Marshfield's Tory sympathizers.

It was left to General John's son, Dr. Isaac Winslow, age thirty-five at the time of his father's death, to carry on the Winslow family destiny in Marshfield. He, though a Tory sympathizer, was so beloved by the people of Marshfield and renowned for his experimental work with smallpox inoculation, that his house was not confiscated by the Great and General Court of Massachusetts.

The old Winslow family holdings in Marshfield were divided, for the first time, in 1761 by General John Winslow. The Winslows had been living continuously on their original land grants for one hundred twenty-five years. General John Winslow deeded fifty acres of "upland and meadow in Marshfield at a place called and named by names Wigwam Point and Turkey Point" to his son Pelham Winslow. In 1769 General John deeded another fifty-two acres of land to his son Isaac, being "that part of my homestead in Marshfield whereon I now dwell known by the name of the Hill and Hither Point Pasture." In 1773 General John deeded "all my real estate both upland and meadow containing about 700 acres . . . it being the homestead farm on which I now live" to sons Pelham and Isaac as tenants in common for four thousand pounds. General John also sold to his two sons his cattle, horses, sheep, swine, and other livestock; all carts, plows, and implements; and his household furniture and personal estate. Since this transaction took place just prior to the Revolution, the sale of all of General John's estate suggests his concern with the threatening circumstances in the American colonies. His sympathies with the British were evident in his long years of service as a military officer in the French and Indian War campaigns. Realizing the possibility of the seizure of his property by the Patriots in the case of a British defeat, General John secured his property for his heirs by these transactions one year before his death in 1774.[19]

It is interesting to note that on a 1784 map made ten years after General John Winslow's death, there appear two Winslow houses at Green Harbor. The one standing at the location of today's 1699 Winslow House was marked

Monument in memory of the early settlers of Green Harbor, located in the Winslow Burying Ground. This cemetery is the site of Marshfield's first church and the tomb of Daniel Webster.

"Gen Winslow." The other, placed northeasterly along present Careswell Street near Gotham Hill, was marked "Dr Winslow." This suggests that either Dr. Isaac Winslow or his brother Pelham, sons of General John, built a house of his own or moved to an already standing house. Dr. Winslow married Elizabeth Stockbridge in 1768, and Pelham Winslow married Joanna White of Plymouth in 1770. Both were married before the death of their father, General John, and would have needed a place of their own to live. There is a tradition that a Winslow house, perhaps the one at Gotham Hill, was sold to Bildad Washburn of Kingston about 1795. It was taken apart and transported by boat and oxcart to Washburn's lot on Main Street, Kingston. This may have been the other Winslow house on the 1784 map. There is also a legend of a tunnel that ran between the present Winslow House and Gotham Hill, maybe to this other house.[20]

Although the Winslows must be called Marshfield's "first family" of the colonial period, the Thomas family was equally landed, well-to-do, and important in town affairs. William Thomas came to Marshfield as early as 1638 and settled in 1645 on his 1500-acre estate (later Daniel Webster's) north of the Winslows, at the edge of the Green Harbor River. He was of Welsh descent and had arrived in Plymouth Colony in 1637. Receiving a grant of land at Green Harbor in 1641, he gave one hundred acres between present Parsonage Street and the Green Harbor River to the town for a parsonage and "ministerial lands". Land at Winslow Burying Ground was given to the town by the colony, with an additional parcel given by William Thomas "for the maintenance of religious institutions."

Marshfield's first church, used for religious services and town meetings, was built at Winslow Burying Ground. The minister of the church in 1641 was Richard Blinman, who came to Marshfield with his fellow Welshman William Thomas. Both were said to have come from the area of Wales around Monmouth and the Severn estuary. (There is a Marshfield, Wales, near Cardiff, and this is probably the origin of our town's name. Located in the Borough of Newport, County Gwent, the parish of Marshfield "lies in a lowland area between Cardiff and Newport, close to the Severn estuary. More than half of it is less than thirty feet above sea level. . . . The area is drained by a complex system of narrow watercourses." This seems an apt description of our Green Harbor landscape.) Later the first school sessions were held in the church. The Thomases served the town and colony in many capacities over the next one hundred fifty years as assistant governors, representatives to the General Court, judges, and selectmen of Marshfield. But they left their greatest mark on Marshfield history during the revolutionary era.[21]

Nathaniel Ray ("Nat Ray") Thomas, fifth in descent from the settler William Thomas, built an elegant new house on the site of the old family home at Green Harbor just prior to the American Revolution. It was "the largest improved estate in the county" with many outbuildings, including a barn and stable, blacksmith shop, smoke house, bake house, harness shop, a tannery, and counting house. Nat Ray Thomas had seventy to eighty head of cattle, sheep, and hogs. The Thomas place might well have been compared to George Washington's Mt. Vernon in Virginia. The only other comparable estate in the area south of Boston was the Peter Oliver estate in Middleborough. Nat Ray Thomas became the leader of Marshfield's heavily Tory population, the largest on the South Shore. The concentration of Tories was due to the number of "landed gentry" here who were either serving the British in the government or in the military affairs of the colony. Thomas accepted the position of mandamus councillor for the British colonial government in Boston in 1774, thereby incurring the wrath of the local patriots.[22]

Some members of Tory families in Boston were sent to relatives' homes in the country for protection. Anna Green Winslow, wife of Joshua Winslow of the Boston branch of the Winslow family, was sent to stay with the Thomases in Marshfield. Anna Winslow wrote about her experiences in a diary that she kept from January to May 1773. She described life at the Thomas estate, frequent teas at both General John Winslow's and at Dr. Isaac Winslow's, and visits to the home of Colonel Anthony Thomas. She wrote on 14 May 1773, "The hill[s] are covered with verdure, the mowing grass promises food for the cattle & all the fields promise plenty of corn — Lord suffer no frost to nip our grain & fruit in the bud or deadly blast to fall on the ripening ear."[23]

Tension grew between the Tories and Patriots of Marshfield. The Patriots staged a "Tea Party" on 19 December 1773, when they stole tea from Bourne's ordinary and burned it at Tea Rock Hill. Nat Ray Thomas requested British troops to be sent from Boston to protect the Tories. British General Thomas Gage at Boston dispatched one hundred fourteen of the King's Own 4th Regiment to Marshfield. They arrived on 23 January 1775, marched through the center of the town, and took up residence at Nat Ray's estate. Their presence caused great alarm through the whole area as they harassed and frightened the surrounding neighborhood.[24]

Patriots of neighboring towns gathered their forces at the home of Colonel Anthony Thomas, descendant of John Thomas (497 Parsonage Street). They plotted an attack on the Nat Ray Thomas place to force the departure of the British troops. Intimidated by the British cannon, they hesitated to attack. Word came of the battle of Lexington via a messenger who rode through the darkness of night to Marshfield. On the morning of 20 April 1775, Captain Willie Thomas, cousin of Anthony Thomas, climbed to the top of Ward's Hill (Pudding Hill) and fired three shots to alert the town that war had begun. The British troops quickly made their escape from Marshfield on two sloops waiting off Brant Rock, but not before taking two Patriot sentries, Jacob Dingley and Blanie Phillips of Duxbury, hostage. Dingley was released unharmed within a few hours, and Phillips immediately escaped. Nat Ray Thomas leapt on his black horse and rode across the marshes, fording the rivers and riding the beaches to Hingham, where he boarded a packet for Boston. In the meantime, the Patriots marched from Anthony Thomas's over Black Mount, bearing a casket for the hated Nat Ray Thomas, to find only his wife, Sarah Deering Thomas, to greet them at the door.[25]

Mrs. Thomas stayed in Marshfield during the remainder of hostilities, retaining her one-third dower right in the homestead. The rest of the estate was confiscated. It was a formidable task caring for a farm and a family of seven children, aged three to twenty. In 1781 Sarah Thomas and six of their children joined Nat Ray Thomas in exile in Windsor, Nova Scotia, where they spent the remainder of their lives. The Thomas property was taken by the state. Nat Ray Thomas died in 1787 at Windsor. His wife continued to live in Nova Scotia with some members of the family until her death in 1810.[26]

Their son John Thomas remained in Marshfield and, tradition says, espoused the patriot cause. He successfully petitioned the state to get his mother's one-third dower rights of the estate returned to him. He married Lucy Baker, raised a family, and farmed the land. It was he who sold what

There's a good many high-flyers travellin' about to see the Webster place.

— Maria Louise Pool[28]

Daniel Webster, the Farmer of Marshfield

Engraving from an oil painting by Joseph A. Ames, 1852, from collection of Massachusetts Historical Society

remained of the old Thomas farm to Daniel Webster on 23 April 1832 for $3,650. It was, at that time, an estate of only 160 acres.[27]

Daniel Webster first saw the Thomas place in 1824 while traveling with his wife, Grace, from Sandwich to Boston. They fell in love with it at once and soon arranged with John Thomas to purchase it, with the provision that Thomas could live in the house until his death, which occurred in 1837. Webster was to live in Marshfield for twenty years, from 1832 until 1852. His impact on his Green Harbor land and on Marshfield was so great that these years may truly be called the Webster Era.[29]

Daniel Webster moved into the John Thomas house in 1832 with his second wife, Caroline Le Roy Webster, and his three children by his first wife, Grace Fletcher Webster, who had died in 1828. His son Daniel Fletcher was nineteen; his daughter, Julia, fourteen; and his son Edward, twelve years old when the family arrived at Green Harbor. Daniel Webster, although internationally famous as a statesman, was at heart a farmer. His frequent letters from Washington to his farm hands at Green Harbor, the name by which he always referred to his Marshfield estate, are filled with detailed instructions and elaborate plans concerning his land and livestock.[30]

Webster changed the face of the land at Green Harbor and, in some sense, changed the people and the town of Marshfield during the twenty years he lived here. Webster farmed on a grand scale. He put large acreages under cultivation in the fertile Green Harbor River valley, planting onions, turnips, potatoes, and squash on the low-lying land between his house and the river. He rotated crops to increase the productivity of the soil and used menhaden and kelp for fertilizer. To the north of the house he planted rye, oats, and beans. He set out apple, peach, and pear orchards and laid out avenues bordered with a great variety of imported tree specimens, including elm, chestnut, English linden, tamarack, ash, and hickory. Descendants of these trees can still be found in many areas of the old Webster farm today. (An English little-leaf linden tree on the estate has been declared a Champion Tree by Dr. Francis Holmes, director of the Shade Tree Laboratory at the University of Massachusetts. It is 74 feet high, has a spread of 84.5 feet, and a circumference of 180 inches. The tree is thought to be around two hundred fifty years old.)

Webster created a series of little spring-fed ponds where he kept flocks of ducks and geese. Along the flanks of Black Mount there were grazing fields for his numerous cattle, oxen, horses, sheep, swine, poultry, and even llama. He experimented with breeding livestock and encouraged local farmers to raise fine animals and to produce high-quality fruits and vegetables. His interest in agriculture, horticulture, and animal husbandry was the inspiration for the Marshfield Agricultural Fair, which, although incorporated in 1867, fifteen years after Webster's death, was the direct result of his encouragement of local farmers.[31]

With the Green Harbor River at his garden wall and the ocean within sight, Webster loved hunting in the river valley and fishing the open sea off Brant Rock. He had a dock and boathouse located at the end of Careswell Street in what is today Green Harbor village, as well as a gunning shack on an island in the middle of the Green Harbor River. One of his boats was named the *Calypso* and another, the *Lapwing*. He took his neighbor and boatman, Seth Peterson, with him on fishing and hunting expeditions. Neighbor Charles Porter Wright was employed from youth on Webster's farm and served as manager for the last eight years of Webster's life. Another Marshfield friend and farmhand was John Taylor, who lived north

of Webster's farm (555 Webster Street). Webster appointed John Taylor as overseer of his family farm at Franklin (Salisbury), New Hampshire.[32]

Daniel Webster, born in Salisbury, New Hampshire, 18 January 1782, graduated from Dartmouth College and began his career as a lawyer in New Hampshire. He served as a representative from New Hampshire to the United States House of Representatives and later, after he set up a law practice in Boston, he was elected to the United States House of Representatives from Massachusetts. He became a senator from Massachusetts in 1827, a post that he held at the time he moved to Marshfield in 1832 and continued to hold until 1840. He served again as senator from 1845 to 1850. Webster first became the secretary of state under President William Henry Harrison in 1840, and continued from 1841 to 1843 under President John Tyler. He was appointed secretary of state again in 1849 under President Millard Fillmore and was serving in this capacity at the time of his death in 1852.

Government officials from Washington and foreign dignitaries came to Marshfield to visit the famous statesman and orator. When Webster was at Green Harbor, everyone in Marshfield was aware of the presence of this magnetic figure whom the Reverend Sydney Smith, English author and clergyman, referred to as "a small cathedral by himself."

Webster arose early each morning and went to his law office or library, which was located in a small separate building near the house. Here he attended to his official correspondence and kept his farm records. He is said to have been writing a natural history of Marshfield at the time of his death. It was in this law office that in 1842 Webster conferred with England's Alexander Baring, Lord Ashburton. They agreed on the boundary between the United States and Canada along the Maine border, a line which remains today part of the bound between the two countries.[33]

Webster was deeply saddened during his life by the deaths of several family members. His first wife, Grace Fletcher Webster, died, as noted, in 1828. His brother Ezekial Webster's death occurred the following year. Two of his children died in infancy. His youngest son, Edward, was killed in the

Mexican War on 23 January 1848, and his daughter, Julia Appleton, died three months later on 28 April 1848. Webster was especially fond of his daughter, who had drawn the plans for the library wing addition made to the Webster house in 1842. Webster was stricken by these deaths of his beloved family members and planted two elm trees on the lawn of his estate in memory of Edward and Julia in 1848. These he called the brother and sister elms.[34]

Daniel Webster made his last public speech upon his return to Marshfield from Washington on 25 July 1852. He addressed a crowd of admirers and fellow townspeople from Cherry Hill, a small eminence east of his mansion. His health failed rapidly after this great oration, and he died at his Green Harbor home on 24 October 1852. He had requested to be buried in the ancient Winslow Burying Ground at Marshfield, declining a state funeral and burial in the National Cemetery at Washington. A great gathering of nearly three thousand people attended his funeral. Some came by boat from New York and Boston, sailing up the Green Harbor River to land at the wharf near the house. Others arrived by horse-drawn carriage from the Kingston railroad station along the old Green Harbor Path. A continuous line of carriages came down over Marshfield Plain. It was said that the dust rising from the roads could be seen for miles in all directions. Webster's body was laid out in state under the great linden tree that still stands on his estate. After the funeral, the long procession of mourners solemnly walked to the simple graveside services at Winslow Burying Ground. Ralph Waldo Emerson remarked that "America and the world had lost the completest man."

Mention should be made here of the respect that Webster paid to his horses, which he was said to have had buried standing up in their halters and shoes. The truth of this tradition was borne out by the discovery in 1979 of the grave sites of three horses by Frank Lachima while excavating for the foundation for the house of Stephen and Elizabeth Pineault on the ridge above Devil's Hollow on Gotham Hill. The bones, identified by Anne

Philbrick Hall as those of riding horses, proved to be in the precise order for upright burial.

Following the death of the great leader, the Webster Era in Marshfield came to a close. Webster's widow, Caroline Le Roy Webster, moved to New York City where she lived for the next thirty years. His son Fletcher and daughter-in-law, Caroline White Webster, lived at their home on Canal Street, but by the time of Fletcher's death in 1862, they had moved back to the Webster mansion on Webster Street. Fletcher served as a colonel in the Union Army during the Civil War and raised a company of volunteers, known as the Twelfth Regiment of Massachusetts, in April 1861. Colonel Fletcher Webster was killed at the Second Battle of Bull Run on 30 August 1862.[35]

The old Thomas/Webster house burned on 14 February 1878. It was replaced by the present Victorian house, built in 1881 on the old foundation. This house was designed by Boston architect William Gibbons Preston for Fletcher Webster's widow, Caroline White Webster. At the time the house was being built, she is thought to have lived at the 1699 Winslow House, owned by the Webster heirs. Thus once again were the old Winslow and Thomas estates woven together in the fabric of Marshfield history.

Webster accumulated a total of some twelve hundred acres of land during his Marshfield years. He had wanted to acquire all the Marshfield land that had been owned by the Winslows and the Thomases. After his death, over one-half of Webster's land was sold at auction in 1855.

In August 1884 the house and the remainder of the estate was bought by Walton Hall and his wife, Ella Lincoln Hall, of Marshfield. Walton Hall, son of Tilden Hall and Mehitable Jones, was from a Marshfield Hills family. He paid three thousand dollars for the property and four hundred fifty dollars for some personal belongings of Daniel Webster.

Walton Hall acquired additional land and established cranberry bogs both west of the Winslow Burying Ground and northeasterly of the house. In the 1898 Valuation of Marshfield, Hall owned over five hundred acres of

The tree-lined avenue leading to the Thomas/Webster estate follows the course of the Green Harbor Path (Pilgrim Trail).

land, including thirty acres of homestead land, plus mowing and tillage, orchard, woodland, pasture, dyke land, and cranberry meadow. He was a leading citizen of Marshfield, being a founder of the Marshfield Savings Bank and an administrator of a trust fund established by his neighbor Edwin Phillips. Walton Hall died on 17 December 1927. The Hall family maintained the estate much as it had been in Webster's time until the 1940s. Part of the 1940 Marshfield Tercentenary celebrations were held at the Walton Hall estate, then owned by his son Lincoln Hall.[36]

The estate remained with the Hall heirs until about 1950 when it was purchased by Vincent Cohee. He founded the Daniel Webster Camp, which was subsequently owned by James and Phyllis Anderson from 1966 to 1986, then acquired by William Last (North Star Realty). Mr. Last, a local developer, presented plans for a subdivision of the estate. The 1988 Marshfield town meeting approved a zoning change that allowed elderly housing under a special permit in a residential zone. The Marshfield Historical Commission tried unsuccessfully at two separate town meetings during 1989 to have the town purchase the 18-acre estate. Mr. Last, after considerable effort, was granted a permit under the new zoning bylaw, with an agreement to certain conditions and covenants established by the historical commission and the planning board that would preserve the historical integrity of the property. These covenants concern the Pilgrim Trail, the mansion, the great linden tree, and the original site of the Law Office.

A nonprofit organization, the "Daniel Webster Preservation Trust," was established by James Cantwell and Michael Donohue in January 1990. The goal of the organization is to raise funds for the purchase of the land and building, and for the restoration and preservation of the Webster mansion and existing estate. This effort to acquire and preserve the old Thomas/Webster place is the fourth such attempt since 1906 to save this valuable piece of Marshfield history.[37]

The Winslow property at Careswell passed out of the family after the death of Dr. Isaac Winslow in 1820. It was later bought by Daniel Webster. In 1879 the house was owned by Nathan Holbrook, whose agent at the time was Porter Wright, son of Daniel Webster's overseer. In 1903 Oscar Weston was living in the old Winslow house, and it was from him that the house was bought in 1919 by Edgar B. Sherrill, John Gutterson, and Edward C. Ford, who deeded it to the Historic Winslow House Association in 1920. The association was responsible for the restoration of the house, an undertaking financed through the operation of a tearoom in the newly built ell during the 1920s and 1930s. This was at first run by Edith and Bradford Sargent and then by Gretchen McMullen.

The 1699 Winslow House was restored to represent two periods of occupancy, the colonial period of Isaac Winslow and the 1750 Georgian period of General John Winslow. It represents the aristocratic element of Plymouth Colony and remains in the most original condition of any of the old homes of the descendants of the Pilgrims. The 1699 Winslow House still stands at the corner of Careswell and Webster streets, a reminder of Marshfield's prominent founding family and of the continuing dedication of the Historic Winslow House Association to the preservation of this ancient house.

The old 1699 Winslow House has gathered unto itself other buildings related to Marshfield history. First came Daniel Webster's Law Office, moved from the Webster estate in 1965, restored, and dedicated in 1970. It is owned by the Marshfield Historical Commission and maintained by the Historic Winslow House Association. A Massachusetts Historical Commission grant in 1988 enabled further restoration of this building, including an authentic reconstruction of the old chimney. Daniel Webster's Law Office was designated a National Historic Landmark in 1974.

1842 Daniel Webster Law Office, moved from his estate to the grounds of the 1699 Winslow House in 1965

In that same year the historical commission moved an old shed from the Josiah Winslow home site on Old Colony Lane near the present airport. It was the gift of Peter Rinaudo, owner of the property at the time. The shed was remodeled as a blacksmith shop, with the help of a matching Bicentennial grant, and is now owned by the Marshfield Historical Commission. Frank Simmons donated blacksmith equipment that had once belonged to blacksmiths Charles Church and Joshua T. Paulding. Bellows and tools have been contributed by various people. The Blacksmith Shop is under the care and maintenance of the Marshfield Historical Society.

A carriage shed on the grounds of the 1699 Winslow House contains three magnificent carriages. These include Daniel Webster's phaeton, gift of Torrey Little to the Historic Winslow House Association; a Concord coach originally sold to Charles T. and Franklin W. Hatch in 1854; and a brougham. The carriage shed was built by students of Marshfield High School in the 1970s.

The Concord coach was used to run the stage route between Marshfield and Cohasset, and, after 1871, to transport people from the Marshfield railroad station to the hotels at Brant Rock. The coach line was owned and operated by John H. Flavell after 1900. The Concord coach was restored with part of a $20,000 fund established by the late Doris Boylston, granddaughter of Charles T. Hatch. The restoration was done by the Edward Rouse Company of Louden, New Hampshire, in 1982. It was coach No. 42 in a series of numbered custom-made Concord coaches. The coach was restored with great attention to authenticity, using the velvet upholstery made by the original company and replicating the old leather work. It was returned to Marshfield, and dedication ceremonies were held

Concord Coach
Pen and ink drawing by Anne Philbrick Hall, 1990

James Keith, blacksmith, working in the Marshfield Historical Society Blacksmith Shop on the grounds of the 1699 Winslow House

at Marshfield Town Hall on 24 October 1982, the 130th anniversary of Daniel Webster's death in Marshfield. The coach is owned by the Marshfield Historical Commission.

The Peter's-style brougham (made by Chauncey Thomas) belonged to Samuel Fayette Curtis, president of the Old Colony Railroad Company. It was given to the Marshfield Historical Society by Curtis's granddaughter, Mary Woodworth.

The Historic Winslow House Association, the Marshfield Historical Society, and the Marshfield Historical Commission have cooperated in bringing together this collection of buildings and objects. In doing so, they have created a unique historical complex.

Across Webster Street from the 1699 Winslow House stands the 1857 Winslow School, Green Harbor's district school until 1910 and now the home of the Marshfield Historical Society. The old Winslow School was one of twelve district grammar schools in Marshfield. The historical society acquired the building and the land in 1925. During the 1920s and 1930s, Edward C. Ford, president of the Marshfield Historical Society for many years, operated an antique business, called the Careswell Shop, in the school building, which he rented from the society. The old Winslow School is the only district school in the town still very much in its original condition. It was renovated with a bequest from Edward C. Ford, and opened as the headquarters for the Marshfield Historical Society on 11 October 1969. As our first settlers gathered together for church services and town meetings, so our historical organizations come together and cooperate today in their dedicated efforts to preserve the traditions of Marshfield.

Old maps of Green Harbor give an idea of how the area changed over the years. A map made of the 1822 division of the Winslow land holdings gives a detailed picture of what existed on some of the land originally granted to Edward Winslow in 1636. The only buildings shown are the 1699 Winslow homestead, a barn, and a cider house. The rest of the six hundred acres is pasturage, orchard, tillage, or wood lot. Names used to designate localities on the estate include Wigwam Point, Turkey Point, Rocky Point, Oven Hill, Hither Point, Hither Point Pasture, and the old Landing Place.

By 1838 the William Ford map shows sixteen houses in the whole area of the old Winslow and Thomas estates south of the Green Harbor River. Seth Weston, a tenant farmer of Daniel Webster, was living in the 1699 Winslow homestead. Daniel Webster lived at the William Thomas place, and Asa Hewitt resided at the old John Thomas farm between the Winslow and Thomas lands.

In the period between the 1838 and the 1879 maps of Green Harbor there occurred many important changes in the area. Two homes, the Fletcher Webster place and the Adelaide Phillips home, both renovations of already existing houses, came to vie in beauty and elegance with the old Winslow and Thomas places.

On 1 June 1849 Daniel Webster purchased 160 acres of land with a house on Canal Street for his son Fletcher. The house had belonged to Charles Porter Wright, Jr., and had been built by his sister's husband, Daniel Glass. Webster created an English manorial estate. He planted English oaks and lindens, laburnums and hawthorns. From a number of springs he created a 5-acre pond where pink water lilies floated. The pond still can be seen behind the present Our Lady of the Assumption Church on Careswell Street. Nearby, in a woodland clearing, a dance pavilion was constructed, not far from where the creek is today.[39]

Old Winslow School. *This building is now the headquarters of the Marshfield Historical Society. Etching by Margaret Philbrick, about 1975.*

You will hear just beyond the sand hills, the rush of the ocean as the tide rises.

— Maria Louise Pool[38]

Fletcher Webster's financial problems had forced him to mortgage the property in 1854. The mortgagee foreclosed on the property and it was sold at auction in 1857. The family moved back to the old Daniel Webster estate on Webster Street. The place on Canal Street passed to Mrs. Harriet Sears by 1900 and in 1920 was sold to Edmund Kelley and later, to the Flaherty family. It burned to the ground in a devastating fire on the bitter cold night of 27 December 1943.[40]

The house at 14 Daniel Road, now owned by Vincent Horrigan, was Fletcher Webster's carriage house. The fence and linden trees can still be seen along Barna Road at Canal Street near the site of the old Fletcher Webster place. Development of this property began in the 1920s when it was divided into lots containing 10,000 square feet which sold for twenty-five dollars apiece. Some summer and some year-round cottages were built.[41]

Another change occurred in 1860 when Adelaide Phillips bought the old John Thomas place, owned today by Charles Hutchinson (108 Webster Street). She transformed the house (not the original, but one built about 1850) by adding a third story with a mansard roof. A fire destroyed this house 9 July 1990.

Adelaide moved to Marshfield with her three brothers, Alfred, Edwin, and Adrian; her sister, Matilde; and adopted sister, Arvilla. Adelaide Phillips was a world-famous opera singer, a protégée of the renowned Jenny Lind. The Phillipses created an elegant estate with extensive gardens and outbuildings. They employed a coachman, housekeeper, and cook. They planted asparagus beds, grew melons, and set out black apple trees. Alfred specialized in raising hay and managed to produce forty tons of hay per acre, a record quantity. This was stored in a large barn on the estate.

A letter written to Adelaide from a friend who had visited her in 1874 describes the life at the Phillipses' home in Marshfield, with their many dogs and animals and a garden conservatory where Alfred raised flowers for the Boston market. A social round of "orchard" parties, musicals, and dancing went on continuously, gracing the ancient grounds of what had been the site of the 1648 home of John and Sarah Pitney Thomas. The family was especially fond of the graceful curve in the road in front of their house on Webster Street and declared they would remove themselves from Marshfield were the town ever to straighten the road. It was to be another

Adelaide Phillips house. The statue is in memory of Sarah Pitney Thomas, wife of settler John Thomas.

one hundred years before that happened, in the 1960s. Adelaide died on 3 November 1882 at age forty-seven, while on opera tour in Germany.

Just before Adelaide's death, she set up a trust fund to care for her brothers. She had, in addition to the brothers and sisters mentioned, two other brothers, George and Frederick Phillips. Matilde, who died in 1915, was a victim of polio, and several members of the family had physical disabilities. Her brother Edwin gave money in 1919 for a home for crippled children. The money given by Edwin Phillips has grown today to a value of around $4 million.[42]

Two events greatly influenced the growth of Green Harbor in the late nineteenth century. The Duxbury and Cohasset Railroad was extended through Marshfield in 1871, and the so-called Webster Place depot was built on the north side of Careswell Street near the Duxbury line. People journeyed down from Boston and from Rockland, Whitman, and Abington to enjoy the beach at Green Harbor. Summer cottages sprang up along the waterfront and in the village, and the rural character of old Green Harbor in the days of the Winslows and Thomases was changed forever. In time, the farms, orchards, and pastures were abandoned and a new way of life came to Green Harbor and to William Green's Salt House Beach.

In 1872 the Dyke Road was laid out to connect the villages of Brant Rock and Green Harbor. Much controversy arose over the proposal to build the dyke. The fishermen of the river were opposed to the proposal while the farmers upstream were in favor of it. The farmers won the day and the dyke was built and widened to carry a road in 1879. This was originally a toll road. Before the advent of automobiles, the charge was ten cents. It is said that some people would drive around through Marshfield to avoid the toll, while others crawled under the wooden gate at night. The building of the dyke transformed the Green Harbor River valley. Freed of the daily intrusion of salt water, the valley became a rich farming area. Garden crops of onions, turnips, potatoes, carrots, strawberries, and other farm produce were raised, and either shipped by sea or transported by the railroad to the Boston market.[43]

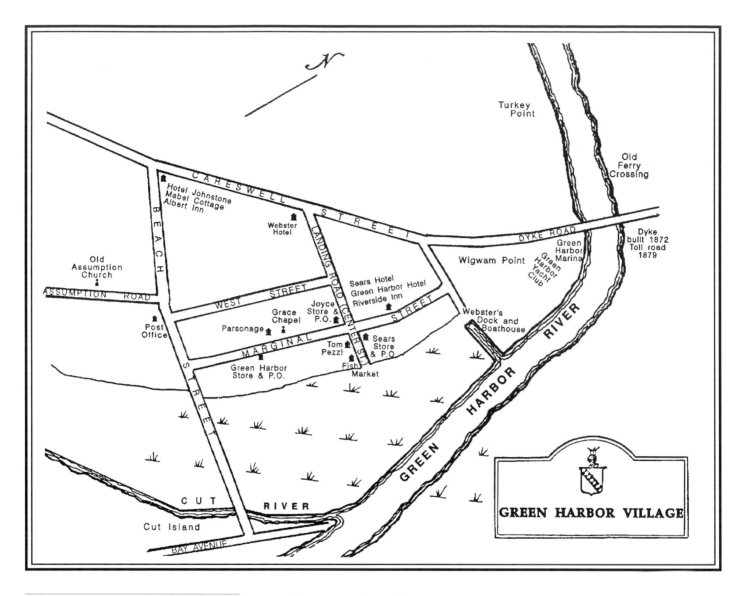

Green Harbor village

Green Harbor village became a popular place at the side of the river. By 1879 there were two stores at the intersection of Center (now Landing Road) and Marginal streets. One, on the northeast corner, was owned by Charles Sears, who operated the Green Harbor Post Office from this location. The other, on the southwest corner, was owned by a Mrs. Joyce. Tom Pezzi, a cabin boy aboard a ship that ran aground off Brant Rock, was adopted and raised by a local family. He became quite a local character in Green Harbor. He had a home and a wharf on the river end of Center Street. Pezzi is listed in the 1875 Marshfield assessors' records as having three boats, a saloon building, a fish market, and an icehouse. Over the door of his fish house was a large sign that read "Tom Pezzi Forever." He is still remembered in his adopted and beloved Green Harbor.[44]

The Webster Hotel and adjoining stable had been built, possibly as early as 1865, by Calvin Estes of Bridgewater. Located on Careswell Street at Center Street, it was a three and one-half story "small" country hotel with a mansard roof. In 1903 it was owned by the heirs of Lot J. MaDan and by 1941, by Edward Duplex. It burned on 16 November 1964. By 1879 the Sears

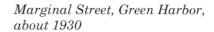

Hotel, or Green Harbor Hotel (later called the Riverside Hotel), stood on the west side of Marginal Street halfway between Center and Careswell streets.

In 1881 religious services began to be held "at the river." In April 1882 two lots of land on Marginal Street were given by Fletcher Webster's widow, Caroline Webster, for the purpose of erecting a Unitarian chapel and a parsonage. A small church was built and dedicated in October 1882. This church was named Grace Chapel in memory of Grace Fletcher Webster, Daniel Webster's first wife, and also in memory of her namesake granddaughter. A Grace Chapel Society was formed to maintain the church. The number of chapel members declined over the years and the society disbanded. The building was taken down in 1960 by Charles Brown, neighbor and long-time resident of Green Harbor. Next door to the Grace Chapel site there is the old parsonage house (47 Marginal Street). It was originally the home of Seth Peterson, Webster's gardener and boatman, and once stood on the Webster estate. It was until recently the home of the late Margaret Brown.[45]

Robert Brown and his wife, Mary Flynn Brown, came to Green Harbor village in the early 1900s from Newfoundland. They had eight children who grew up in the village. The family has been at the center of community activities over the years. Mr. Brown was a carpenter and a lobsterman. He designed boats, built houses, worked on the Ocean Bluff Casino, and constructed the bowling alleys there. His son Charles Brown, a carpenter, was the harbormaster at Green Harbor for years. Margaret, known as Libby Brown, was president of the Women's Auxiliary of the American Legion and active in the organization until her death in 1989. Elizabeth Brown Whitford, who died in 1986, was also active in the Women's Auxiliary and well known for her many other civic activities, especially her work with veterans. During the great Ocean Bluff fire in 1941, she made pies and cakes which the family took to the firemen on duty.[46]

Clara Brown remembers her childhood in the village when, as she says, "we children made our own fun and stayed together. We used to go coasting up at Gotham Hill and skating on the dyke by the island and have a bonfire on the ice. We walked everywhere. There were just a handful of people and you knew everybody. There was a spirit of helping one another. The neighborhood collected the money to rebuild George and Ida Delano's house after it caught fire from the burning Riverside Inn next door."[47]

Other members of the Brown family were Gertrude, Florence, Albert, and Herbert. Clara and Herbert Brown live in the village today. The Browns exemplify the generous and cooperative community spirit, very much a part of Marshfield's many villages.[48]

The children of Green Harbor village in the early twentieth century attended the district school at Brant Rock, across the Dyke Road. Sometimes they walked to school and sometimes they rode in John Flavell's horse-drawn carriage, known as a barge. Later, when the Green Harbor pupils went to Marshfield to high school, the trip took an hour in the barge.

Webster Hotel / House. It was built about 1865 and burned in 1964.

Riverside Hotel / Inn, formerly the Sears Hotel. It was built before 1894 and burned in 1919.

Marshfield: 1640-1990

Dan Atwood was a well-known driver at one period. The charge for the service was fifty cents per child per week, to be paid by the parents.[49]

By the turn of the century there were eighty-six houses and three hotels at Green Harbor village. These hotels were the Webster Hotel on Careswell Street, the Hotel Johnstone on the north side of Beach Street near Careswell Street, and the Riverside Inn (formerly the Sears Hotel) on the west side of Marginal Street north of Landing Road, with proprietor H.O. Chandler. This hotel burned about 1919. By 1903 the Albert Inn (13 Beach Street), named for proprietor Albert G. Flanders, and earlier known as the Mabel Cottage, was built near the site of the old Hotel Johnstone. A two and one-half story house with Queen Anne features and a fancy cupola on the top, it is today the only building remaining of the three hotels that once stood at Green Harbor village. Later Charles Flanders, a popular Green Harbor resident, owned and operated the Albert Inn, which has now been made into apartments.[50]

On Duxbury Beach (Green Harbor Beach) in 1900 there were seventy-three houses and one small hotel, known as the Winslow House, which stood at the southeast corner of Beach and Bay Avenue. This hotel burned about 1940 (and the arsonist burned with it). There was a Porter Riding School off Canal Street in 1926. Some people still remember the glorious experience of riding the length of Green Harbor beach on horseback. This beach, stretching south to the Gurnet at Duxbury, is still considered to be one of the most beautiful beaches in the world. It is a long crescent strip of unusually fine-grained sand, backed by dunes and the sweep of Duxbury Bay. Many of the Green Harbor Beach houses were severely damaged in the winter blizzard of 1978. They have since been renovated, enlarged, and modernized. Today Green Harbor Beach is an attractive year-round community.[51]

The growing Catholic population of Green Harbor was for some years served by the pastor of St. Joseph's Church in Kingston. The Reverend Andrew Haberstroh served for fourteen years and covered his large area by horse and buggy until the advent of automobiles. Mass was celebrated in a field at Green Harbor in summer and at private homes in winter. Sometimes the old Albert Inn and the old Webster House were used for this purpose. Finally, in July 1919 Father Haberstroh bought the so-called Webster Hall (dance hall) on Assumption Road at Green Harbor for eight hundred dollars. Thus began the history of the mission parish of Our Lady of the Assumption Church. From 1936 to 1939 the Reverend George Gately, pastor of St. Joseph's in Kingston, served the summer parishes of Our Lady of the Assumption and St. Ann's by the Sea at Ocean Bluff. The Reverend John Phelan followed for the years 1939 to 1951. Our Lady of the Assumption continued as a mission church until it became a separate parish in 1949. The church burned on 23 June 1981. The parishioners then went to Mass, first at St. Ann's by the Sea, then at the Governor Edward Winslow School and at the old store beside the Green Harbor Post Office, while waiting construction of the new Our Lady of the Assumption Church. The new church was completed in August 1983 at the corner of Canal and Careswell streets. The Reverend Philip McConville has been the pastor of this church since 1970.[52]

Charles W. McLauthlin opened the Green Harbor store about 1901. He had married, in 1900, Lydia Curtis Peterson, daughter of Seth Peterson, boatman and sporting companion of Daniel Webster. An ell was added to the store in 1907. McLauthlin owned and operated the store, living in the upstairs quarters until his death in 1938 at age ninety. The Green Harbor

GREEN HARBOR POST OFFICES

The Green Harbor Post Office was first located in the Sears store with Charles Sears and then William T. Sears postmasters from 1886 to 1901. In 1886 there were twenty-eight families (ninety-two people) at Green Harbor, with a summer population of three hundred and seventy-five. The location of the post office was moved to Charles McLauthlin's store in 1901, where it remained until the 1950s. For a short time around 1934 it was located at Sarah G. (Gertie) Sampson's house on the southwest corner of Landing Road and Marginal Street. In 1954 it moved to Jerry Gallant's on the south side of Beach Street at West Street, where it is today. Postmasters of the Green Harbor Post Office since the days of Charles McLauthlin have been Lydia C. McLauthlin (1915-34), Sarah G. Sampson (1934-54), Jerome A. Gallant, Jr. (1954-76), Ernest A. Chandler, Jr. (1976-78), and more recently, George R. Leaver (1986-89). Leaver is currently on detail to Scituate. The position was filled from September 1989 to January 1990 by Edwin R. Parsons, Jr., and from January 1990 to May 1990 by Phyllis N. Nielsen, member of the 350th Commemorative Trust. From May 1990 to September 1990 the position will be filled by Denise Rose.[53]

store has since belonged to Varnum E. Gratto, Dan Michellini, Michael Moss, Harry and Virginia Bruckner, and now, Joe and Jodi McDonough.[54]

In 1881 Frank Sinnott came to Marshfield. At first he sold groceries from a horse-drawn cart, but he soon bought a wagon from which he peddled meat around Marshfield for twenty-eight years. The traveling butcher shop was called Sinnott and Porter until Frank bought out Mr. Porter. By 1895 Sinnott had four meat wagons and a meat shop located on Ocean Street across from Feinberg's Department Store. He soon opened two branch stores in Green Harbor and Duxbury. He had two slaughterhouses and did his own slaughtering in the winter but purchased meat from Boston in the summer. Eventually he sold the business to Ephraim Walker. Walker, in turn, sold to Arthur Dorr and Dorr to the First National Store. Sinnott continued to work at the store and became the first manager of the Marshfield First National Store when it was located at the Feinberg building.

The Sinnott home at 88 Webster Street was built in 1843 by Charles Porter Wright on land given to him by Daniel Webster. Frank Sinnott married Cora Perry in 1897 and rented the farm from Arthur Dorr in 1899, later purchasing it and opening a farm stand. On their 13-acre farm the Sinnotts raised a variety of produce for sixty-three years. It was one of the last farms to remain operating in Marshfield.

Frank Sinnott was involved for many years in the affairs of Marshfield, serving as selectman for four terms, founder and first president of the Marshfield Board of Trade, founder of the Board of Water Commissioners in 1925 and a commissioner for over thirty years, and president, director, and manager of the Marshfield Fair. He was responsible for the construction of the two and three-quarter miles of breakwater from Brant Rock to Fieldston, for the restoration of the Winslow Cemetery, and for the plan of Route 139 in Marshfield.

Sinnott had six children, many of whom have continued to be involved in the civic affairs of Marshfield. His son, the late Frank ("Mel") Sinnott, Jr., was police chief for fourteen years, retiring in 1971. Mel's wife, Ruth ("Sis") Baker Sinnott, of the original Baker family of Marshfield, has served the town in many capacities. In the tradition of the early Winslow and Thomas families, the Sinnott family has contributed much to the town.[55]

Two summer camps have come to Green Harbor: one to inhabit the old Winslow family fields near Careswell; the other, the old grounds and house site of settler William Thomas. Large acreages of these old estates were still intact in the 1920s and provided the space and terrain for summer camp activities.

Camp Cedar Crest was started at Bournedale, Massachusetts, and moved to a 20-acre parcel of land between Careswell Street and Gotham Hill, Green Harbor, about 1922. It was established by the Immaculate Conception Parish of Everett and operated as a camp for ten weeks every summer. In the beginning there were eighty campers. It grew to accommodate 435 campers with seventy-five staff members, including counselors, kitchen workers, and grounds-keepers. Buildings for the girls were erected on Gotham Hill, while the boys lived in cabins below. There were forty-two buildings in all. The usual camp routine was followed, with crafts, games, sports, and a trip to the beach by truck for swimming. Movies and singing around the campfire ended the day. Religious services were a part of the daily program. The camp was run by Monsignor Edward M. Hartigan. Camp Cedar Crest closed in 1972, and the property was sold in 1973 to Putnam Realty Trust which developed the area for the housing on Gotham Hill Drive.

A small girl's camp was located on Bay Avenue from the 1930s to the 1950s. It was run by the Roman Catholics and was not a part of Camp Cedar Crest.

Camp Daniel Webster, still in operation, was founded by Vincent Cohee about 1950, when he purchased the Thomas/Webster estate from Walton Hall's heirs. A roller-skating rink, built at the edge of Webster Street in 1952, burned in 1958. The camp was leased and operated by James and Phyllis Anderson from 1960 to 1966, when they purchased it. When James

Green Harbor Store
Watercolor by Carolyn Harvey, 1985

The line-up at Camp Cedar Crest (Immaculate Conception Boys Camp), Gotham Hill, Green Harbor. The camp operated from 1922 to 1972.
Photograph courtesy of John A. McLaughlin

Anderson first ran the camp in 1960, there were fifty to one hundred campers with twenty counselors. By 1986 there were two hundred and fifty campers, ages five to fourteen, with sixty-five counselors. The camp today has a miniature golf course, an archery range, a target range, swimming pool, volleyball court, and baseball diamond. William Last (North Star Realty) bought the camp and surrounding eighteen acres in 1986.[56]

The Green Harbor Marina is located on the south side of the Dyke Road. It was incorporated in 1957 by Carl W. Nielsen, who had purchased the Arthur Bird property adjacent to his Green Harbor Calso gas station in the mid-1950s. Nielsen was in the outboard-motor repair business and had added a large showroom to his existing building where he sold Sebago boats (from Sebago, Maine) as well as Delano boats that were manufactured in Marshfield. Over the next several years he dredged and made a basin for the marina. Then he enlarged the facility to include a pier, ramps, and boat slips. The Green Harbor Marina became a family business with Carl's wife, Pat, and their son Carl, Jr. Pat opened a small restaurant known as Pat's Lobster Shop. The marina was sold to Larry Lovell and Robert White of Marshfield and Duxbury in 1962.

Michael Connolly of Norwell purchased the Green Harbor Marina in 1986. It provides open year-round dockage for about two hundred boats. Full service and gas are available at the dock. The boat sales of the Green Harbor Marina are among the highest in the state of Massachusetts.

The Green Harbor Yacht Club stands next door to the marina. It was started in 1960 with Frederick Meagher, a summer resident of Green Harbor, serving as first commodore. Present commodore is John Coyle, also a summer resident.

Land for the Green Harbor Golf Course was purchased from Dr. Leonard Short in 1965 by Manuel Lopes Francis and his son Manuel N. Francis. Manuel Lopes Francis came from Portugal at an early age. When

A bird's-eye view of the Green Harbor River basin, 17 October 1984
Photograph by Gerhard O. Walter

he first arrived in this country, he worked at a hat factory, then at a golf course in Maine, where he met and married Shirley Winslow. Manuel L. and Manuel N. Francis worked for ten years at Belmont Country Club, then built the course at Green Harbor together.

The Green Harbor Golf Course is comprised of 165 acres on the southern edge of the Green Harbor Fresh, east of Webster Street. It is the area where Walton Hall had built extensive cranberry bogs in the early 1900s on the northern edge of what had been the old Thomas/Webster estate.

Manuel L. and Manuel N. Francis began a turf farm on the land. Manuel L. Francis had developed a certain type of putting-green grass, known as Vesper bent grass, and is world-renowned for this special grass adapted for golf greens. This grass and regular turf were raised and sold from the farm on Webster Street.

In 1971 the "front nine" greens of the 110-acre golf course were opened and the "back nine" were built in 1977. The Francises have built a total of twenty-two golf courses in the South Shore and New England areas. The Green Harbor Golf Course services about three thousand to four thousand people of all ages every year.

*Looking across the Green Harbor
River to Green Harbor village,
about 1890*

Manuel N. Francis, the son, now manages the golf-course business. Other members of the Francis family also work at the Green Harbor Golf Course. Thus another family has charted its destiny at Green Harbor.

The Recreation Center on Webster Street is located almost on the line between the old Winslow and Thomas estates. It was built in 1967 by the Marshfield Kiwanis Club, which was given ninety-six acres of land by Allan R. Wheeler of Scituate. He placed covenants in the deed outlining certain restrictions for the use of the property. The Kiwanis Club sold eighty-three acres, including Slaughter Island and Cherry Hill, to the Marshfield Conservation Commission. A little over thirteen acres of land and buildings were transferred to the town for a youth center in 1973. The Recreation Commission took over the care, custody, control, and management of the property. They stated that it was "to be used for recreational purposes with the understanding that the Marshfield Boys' Baseball League shall have the continued use of the present Little League baseball fields and that the Youth Center not be used as a halfway house." It has also been used by the elderly for beano, whist parties, and dances. It closed about 1975.[57]

The Recreation Commission was appointed by the selectmen in 1958 with five members "for the purpose of conducting and promoting recreation, play, sport and physical education." In 1973 the commission was enlarged from five to nine members and later decreased to seven members. In 1982 the commission was nearly abolished because of lack of direction. The budget was reduced and the programs and services affected. Just four programs were offered for six- to twelve-year-olds only. But today the Recreation Commission is flourishing. It offers forty programs and has over three thousand participants ages three to seventy-five, with a staff of twenty-five workers.

In 1984 the Recreation Commission, with the help of the Rexhame Beach Association and the Sea Rivers trustees, opened and began to operate the Rexhame Beach snack bar. The commission runs programs and makes improvements at the Peter Igo Park, the Tower Avenue Park, the Daniel Webster School, the Marshfield Hills park, and the high school tennis courts. It runs programs for teens, youths, adults, and seniors, and for the mentally and physically handicapped. It also conducts summer programs, including

the canoe project at Green Harbor, a sailing program, and a sand-sculpture contest. The commission has been responsible for expanding the Camp Mardayca program for children with special needs. It also sponsors band concerts on the Training Green, after-school sports programs in the elementary school gyms for four hundred children, and the annual Rexhame Beach "rid litter days" cleanup. Fund-raisers include the annual "beach run classic" on Green Harbor Beach, the Elks "dunking booth" at the Marshfield Fair, the volleyball tournament, and beach-sticker sales.

The "new" Governor Edward Winslow School, opened in September 1970, is located just east of Edward Winslow's original Green Harbor home site at Careswell Creek on the edge of the Duxbury marshes. The district school has returned to Green Harbor, having vacated the "old" Winslow School in 1910. The crush of Marshfield's growing population necessitated the revival of the idea of educating primary-grade schoolchildren in their local areas. They arrive at school by bus, however, rather than on foot or by horse-drawn barge, and are no longer responsible for cutting and bringing in the wood for the wood stove or going to fetch water at the well.

The first principal of the Governor Edward Winslow School was Leo Dauwer, who served in this capacity until 1978. The school accommodated grades one through six. Frederick Hubbard, who had been assistant superintendent of schools from 1970, became the principal in 1979, continuing for the next ten years until 1989. The current principal is James F. Meehan and the school has kindergarten through grade 5. Enrollment in 1970 was 611 compared to today's 600. The federal government's PAC program for special-needs children is headquartered at the Governor Edward Winslow School, as is the enrichment program under the leadership of Sharon Seeg.

The Daniel Webster Wildlife Sanctuary is located on a 388-acre parcel of land lying in the heart of the Green Harbor River valley at the end of Winslow Cemetery Road. A group of conservation-minded townspeople, spearheaded by Dorothea Reeves and known as the Committee to Preserve Dwyer Farm, acquired the property from Edward Dwyer and turned it over to the Massachusetts Audubon Society in 1984. The property is now administered by Massachusetts Audubon as a part of the South Shore Audubon Regional Center.

Much of the sanctuary land once belonged to settler William Thomas and later, to Daniel Webster. After Webster's death it was auctioned off and bought by several different people, including Edward White (direct descendant of Peregrine White), Burleigh Collins, Frank Scheufele, Henry and Thomas Liversidge, and Edward Dwyer.

The Massachusetts Audubon Society has developed trails and created a wetlands for wildfowl. Bird and nature walks are conducted regularly and special programs offered from time to time. It seems appropriate that this land, so beloved by Daniel Webster who hunted and farmed here, should be preserved today as a nature sanctuary. Webster walked over these fields with John James Audubon, who is said to have drawn one of the Canada geese seen here for his now-famous bird print. Webster once remarked to a visitor that, "so far as my influence extends, the birds shall be protected." A quail poured forth his song and Webster said, "There! does not that gush of song do the heart a thousand-fold more good than could possibly be derived from the death of that beautiful bird!"[58]

The Marshfield Conservation Commission, formed in 1961, owns several pieces of property in the Green Harbor area, totaling 292 acres. Webster's Wilderness is a 124-acre parcel at the head of Wharf Creek, which includes such Webster landmarks as the Home Bog, Slaughter Island, and Cherry Hill. Wharf Creek Woodland and Estes Woods are a 90-acre piece of woodland adjacent to Wharf Creek and Green Harbor River. The Green Harbor Lots are three small lots scattered along the river. Other conservation land lies at Cut River and Duxbury Marsh. Smaller pieces include the 4-acre Crowder's Woodland (Ray's Woods) and the 16-acre King Philip's Esker along the Green Harbor Fresh southwest of Webster Street.

Although the development of summer cottages began at Green Harbor village and at Green Harbor beach as early as 1870, the beginning of what might be called modern development was the 1920 group of cottages built at the old Fletcher Webster place on Canal Street.

About 1947 came Green Harbor Park on Careswell Street at Edward Road across from today's Elsa's Restaurant, formerly Plett's Pub and Duplex's. Eddie Duplex laid a foundation for a new Webster House hotel which he never built. The foundation is still to be seen adjacent to Elsa's. A small restaurant called the Pantry Shelf (472 Careswell Street) was started in the early 1950s and owned by Sally Small and Dolly Proust. In 1960 it was operated by Edythe Puffer whose lobster rolls and homemade pies were very popular. By the mid-1960s the extensive development at Winslow Cemetery Road and along Webster Street had started. Statesman Terrace and Orchard Road were constructed and, somewhat later, Presidential Circle was built. These roads and houses began to intrude on the integrity of the old Thomas/Webster Place.

With the opening of the Route 3 expressway in 1965 and the ensuing arrival of the new Marshfield "settlers," the need for housing increased. Soon the untouched land at Webster's beloved Black Mount began to yield to roads and house lots. First came Whitford Circle in 1965. Then Roger Sealund commenced developing Black Mount Village. In the course of the years, many developers have built attractive houses on this high hill. These include William Last and David Bowering and, most recently, John Spence and David Gregory. Today this beautiful area of the old Thomas/Webster land is still being opened to new housing.

The road at Fairways Edge was constructed in 1988. This area, over-looking the Green Harbor Golf Course, has a sweeping view north across the Green Harbor River and the South River to Telegraph Hill. Presently the development is under the management of William Last.

The houses at Sea Flower Lane were built on the old Winslow land near Edward Winslow's original house site at the edge of the Duxbury marsh. The old Winslow fields and orchards are overlaid with Charles Nardone's development at Old Farm Way and Atina Road. William Tetrault of Harborside Realty began building roads and houses at Gotham Hill even before World War II. Atwell Circle at the old Rocky Point landing place was built about 1972.

A small part of the Winslow property has functioned as a farm almost continuously. The land between Perryn Way and Atwell Circle, where the Governor Edward Winslow School is now, was owned by Christian and Anna Nepper. It included the house at 585 Careswell Street. The Nepper farm was known for its apple and peach orchards, corn, and chickens.

The Nepper family ran a bakery, known as the Sweet Shop, which was famous for Mrs. Nepper's danish pastry and for their daughter Dorothy's fudge. The Sweet Shop was later replaced with a small house at 609 Careswell Street. Christian Nepper died in 1947 and the farm was sold to Donald Blunt and Vego Nielsen.

Dr. James McLaughlin bought the Nepper place in 1949. He has done extensive organic farming and raised flowers on this old piece of Winslow property for forty years. McLaughlin served as president of the Marshfield Historical Society and chairman of the Green Harbor River Commission and Green Harbor Basin Committee in the 1970s.

On the Duxbury line, near the old homesteads of Edward Bumpus and John Rouse, came two new areas of housing in the 1960s. Prince Circle was built on the site of an earlier gravel pit owned by Walter Prince of Duxbury, who sold the land to Roger Sealund about 1966. The subdivision known as Ponderosa Pines was bought by Charles Nardone and developed in the 1970s. The road that runs through this area is named Pioneer Trail and parallels the course of the old Green Harbor Path (Pilgrim Trail) as it enters Marshfield on the Duxbury line.

The influx of so many new people to Marshfield created a need to introduce them to the community. The Welcome Wagon organization was founded in 1958. Its successor is today's Newcomers' Club. In addition to the club's many social activities, it contributes funds to the YWCA,

Marshfield's Community Christmas, the Ventress Memorial Library, the Council on Aging, and local youth organizations. Recent co-presidents have been Barbara McKinnon and Roena Zink. Marguerite Lee became the president in June 1990.

It is interesting to note that the highways of transportation are the vehicles of change. The old Green Harbor Path brought about the original clearing and settling of Marshfield in the seventeenth century, while the opening of the Route 3 expressway began the modern period of intense development and change, perhaps the most drastic the town has known in its entire 350-year history. Modern development began at once to alter the landscape of this seaside town. Today a large part of what had remained well into the twentieth century of the open space on the old homestead land grants has disappeared. It behooves us to remember the old Pilgrim roads and waterways and the people who first made their way to Green Harbor by foot or boat. In today's fast-paced life of the automobile and the expressway, we are grateful for those who have come this way before us and who have built, generation upon generation, the traditions of this ancient Pilgrim town.

Laundry Day *at Bluefish Cove,*
Brant Rock
Watercolor by Dorit Flowers

A fall morning at Green Harbor
near Marginal Street
Photograph by Vin Horrigan

Assumption Church from
Flaherty's Pond
Photograph by Vin Horrigan

Sunrise at Brant Rock
Photograph by Vin Horrigan

1699 Winslow House, 1990
Photograph by David Brega

Rollers south of Hewitt's Point,
Brant Rock, 1989
Photograph by Vin Horrigan

A winter afternoon at Green
Harbor, looking toward Union
Chapel at Brant Rock village
Photograph by Vin Horrrigan

Mount Rushmore flag flown on Green Harbor Festival Day, 16 June 1990, as part of the celebration of the 350th anniversary of the founding of Marshfield. This flag has been displayed at the Mount Rushmore Memorial in South Dakota.
Photograph by Vin Horrigan

The schooner Spirit of Massachusetts *sailing to Green Harbor for the 350th anniversary celebration*
Photograph by Vin Horrigan

The Concord coach as it appeared
in the 350th celebration parade on
6 May 1990. The coach was
purchased by Charles T. and
Franklin W. Hatch in 1854 and
later became the property of the
Town of Marshfield.
Photograph by Sarah Sullivan

First Congregational Church,
built in 1838
Photograph by Cynthia Hagar Krusell

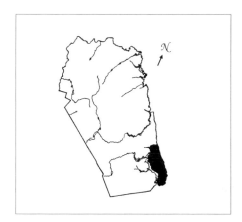

Brant Rock and Ocean Bluff Villages

It is the sea, you know, which sends us each new day. It comes in splendor over that lustrous water for leagues and leagues, growing brighter and brighter until it is one unutterable glory.

—Maria Louise Pool[1]

BRANT ROCK is the village named for the rock between the islands, the so-called Spectacle Islands. The village center is the nose bridge of the spectacles as seen by the early Green Harbor settlers standing atop Black Mount and gazing out to sea. It was, and is, the place of the brant, that small member of the goose family that has frequented the seacoast of Marshfield for hundreds of years. Hence the name Brant Rock, used from the earliest days. It was sometimes referred to as simply "the Brant," while Green Harbor was called "the Cut."[2]

There are two islands. The larger island to the north of Brant Rock village is divided between Brant Rock and Ocean Bluff today. The area south of Samoset Street is considered to be part of Brant Rock village, while the land north as far as Fieldston is called Ocean Bluff. John Bradford, son of Governor William Bradford of Plymouth Colony, saw the opportunity for rich grazing lands on this island seaward of the Green Harbor River. He was given the first grant of land here and it became known as Governor's Island. John Bradford may have lived on the island, but there is no record to prove it. Sometime after 1660 it became the property of Christopher Winter. Winter's second eldest daughter, Martha Winter, married John Hewitt in 1668 and at her father's death in 1683, his "island home" passed to her and then to his grandson Winter Hewitt. The Winters, and then the Hewitts, had a large sheep farm with a flock of at least seventy sheep on the island, called Hewitt's Island for many years. Hewitt's Point is today's reminder of this early island family.[3]

The smaller island to the south of Brant Rock village, including today's Ocean Street (sometimes called the High Road), Blackman's Point, Bluefish Cove, Branch, and Island streets, was early granted to Resolved White, brother of Peregrine White and stepson of Governor Edward Winslow. It passed to his son William White, who employed John Branch as his tenant farmer, then to John Branch in quitclaim deeds from William White in 1684 and 1687. The island today is known as Branch's Island.

John Branch married Mary Speed in 1652 and they had five children born between 1654 and 1664. There is a tradition that some later member of this family and his wife drowned while swimming their horse over Green Harbor River. It was of great interest when, on 2 April 1980, a burial site

was uncovered near Bancroft Street on Branch's Island, which revealed two Caucasian eighteenth-century skeletons, one male and one pregnant female. The remains of these skeletons, after careful examination by a University of Massachusetts anthropologist, were interred in Winslow Cemetery in December 1983 by members of the Marshfield Historical Commission.[4]

Branch's Island was deeded in the mid-1700s to Gideon Harlow of Duxbury, a cattle dealer, who pastured cattle here and built a shanty on the island. Later owners were Albert Williams and then Thomas Blackman by 1835. Thomas Blackman married Gideon Harlow's granddaughter Olive in 1845. The Blackmans had a salt hay barn which is still on their property. Bradford and Helen Josselyn Blackman, who own today's trailer park, acquired the property from Mary H. Blackman, his aunt, in 1952. The park at Blackman's Point attracted those who wanted a seaside spot for outdoor living. Today there are about one hundred trailers replacing the campground and army tents of the 1920s, when a tent site could be rented for twenty-five dollars a summer. In that era there was no electricity. Water came from a communal tap in the field and the iceman and milkman made daily deliveries. The Blackman Realty Trust was formed in 1976. Its principals are Brad and Helen Blackman and their three children. Intending to sell the property, the Blackman family is in the process of drawing up a plan for a subdivision of the trailer park into thirty-three lots. A Blackman's Point Homeowners' Association has been organized with June Donnelly serving as president. The association has been given a right of first refusal on the property.[5]

These islands, embraced by the sea, provided excellent pasturage and meadowland for the Marshfield farmers who were granted strips of land running inland from the edge of the shore. Stone walls, rail fences, and hedges were built to keep the livestock from the beach and to divide the lots. Families living across the river at the foot of Black Mount had sea pastures on the islands. In 1692 when a jury of fifteen men designated the town highways, a road was described as running the entire length of the beach from the mouth of the Green Harbor River to the mouth of the South River at Rexhame. It passed through "John Branch's Island, and along through said island as the way now lieth by the westward end of Branch's house, and so along as the way now is unto Winter's Island, and along through said Island near to the cliff on the east side thereof, until it comes to the beach at the north corner thereof, and so along the beach till it cometh to the mouth of South River."[6]

Permanent settlement on the islands was scanty, sporadic, and seasonal. John Branch, first settler, had a house on the smaller island in 1692 and was probably the first to build a year-round home, although others may have erected barns from time to time. Nearly one hundred years later, in 1785, a drawing of the Marshfield seacoast indicates the area along the beach as meadows and pastures belonging to members of the Thomas, Ford, Keene, and Sampson families. The John Ford map of 1838 shows only the location of a house that burned in that same year on Hewitt's Island and a Lobster House near the present town pier at the end of Central Street.

The Blackmans had a gunning house built in 1835 on Branch's Island. Four small houses near the Green Harbor River at what is today Bluefish Cove were erected in 1848 on land belonging to Gideon Harlow. These were used only in the summer by lobster fishermen. A "gunnin' house," used as a shelter for hunters, was built at Brant Rock in 1845. The Blackmans started a lumberyard on the east bank of the Green Harbor River in 1870, bringing lumber from Maine and the West and supplying some of the material for the summer-cottage building industry.[7]

We know that a part of Hewitt's Island (the larger island now called Ocean Bluff) had passed into the hands of Eleazer Harlow (brother of Gideon Harlow), from whom Daniel Webster purchased it in two parcels which totaled 140 acres in 1838 and 1840. In one of his letters to his farm overseer, Seth Weston, Webster instructed him to rebuild the island house that had once been there. He called the place his Island Farm. The inventory of Webster's real estate made in 1853, a year after his death, listed "the Island Farm, together with Dwelling House and all buildings thereon, containing about one hundred and forty-two acres." The parcel was bought at the sale of Webster's estate in April 1855 by Henry and Thomas Liversidge. In June 1888 the Thomas Liversidge executors sold this 140-acre portion of Hewitt's Island to Walton Hall, who acquired much of what once had been Daniel Webster's property. Later this part of the island passed to Barnabas Everson and George W. Baker. The rest of the island was acquired by Bradley S. Bryant.[8]

The small island in the middle of the Green Harbor River west of the dyke and visible from the Dyke Road needs to be mentioned here. It has a history of its own. A 1.9-acre piece of land, it does not appear on the 1795 map of the area, but is in existence by 1872. It is said to be composed of Saco soil, found only around Saco, Maine. An interesting theory is that schooners transporting lumber from Maine to T. B. Blackman's lumberyard on the Green Harbor River used the Saco soil as ballast for their ships. It is believed that the island was owned by Erastus Everson, a writer, who built a small house and was living there by 1894. When he died in 1897, the property passed to his son Barnabas Everson in 1898, and then to his grandson Sherman McClellan, who owned it for forty years. McClellan built a new cottage on the island in 1926. In 1942 he sold it for one hundred dollars to his son Edgar McClellan, who in turn sold it to his daughter Edna McClellan Blauss Howland for one dollar in 1958. The cottage burned in 1970, and Edna's son Eric Blauss built another one to replace it. This also burned. On

Erastus Everson on his island in the Green Harbor River, about 1895
Photograph courtesy of Russell Gardner

26 June 1981 Edna sold the island to her two sons, Eric and David Blauss. The family still camp on this "peaceful oasis from the fast pace of life."[9]

Cows grazing on the Dyke meadow, about 1890

Thomas B. Blackman described Brant Rock in the 1850s as a place he visited with his father to go gunning for sea ducks, find lobsters under the rocks, and gather strawberries from the pastures. There was a cartway leading south from the Neck Road (Ocean Street/Route 139) which itself ran easterly from Marshfield Center to Winslow Street. The cartway passed through four gates along the beach and islands before it reached Blackman's house (3 Ocean Street) at what is today Blackman's Point. Blackman said that "the slough [at Fieldston] had been filled with stone, and a bridge was constructed, but across the beach it was mud and sand. I have grooned thin beach when I could not go more than the length of my team at a pull." This cartway, which ran the length of the beach, was not improved and built through to Ocean Bluff until 1862.[10]

Blackman spoke of the Charity House at Ocean Bluff as being the only house north of the Brant Rock in 1850. The Massachusetts Humane Society kept a stove, some wood, and matches for the use of shipwrecked men in this Charity House. Another Humane Society shelter stood along the beach between Blackman's Point and Bluefish Cove. The house at 50 Cove Street is thought to be the building. A United States Life Saving Service station was built in 1893 on the shore front, across from today's Brant Rock Union Chapel. Captain Benjamin T. Manter, assisted by Dana B. Blackman and six surfmen, carried out the courageous duties of this early service to aid men and women in distress along the coast. The United States Coast Guard took over the Life Saving Service in 1915. The Coast Guard patrolled and guarded the beaches during World Wars I and II. The station was closed in 1947 and razed in 1967, bringing to an end a vital chapter in the history of the protection of the Marshfield coast line.

A paper written by Jeannette Hixon Avery relates her memories of Coast Guard activities about 1910 when she summered at Brant Rock in a cottage at the south corner of Ocean and Puritan streets:

Life Saving Service personnel practicing with a breeches buoy, about 1890. The lifesaving station (in the background), built in 1893, was removed in 1967.
Photograph courtesy of Harris F. Penniman

Once a month the lifesavers practiced their rescue tactics. The large boat was rolled out and rowed a short distance into the water. On land the small cannon boomed and shot a rope out to the boat. The breeches buoy was like heavy breeches of canvas attached to a ring which was suspended from a pulley running along the rope. This was pulled out, the seaman climbed into the contraption and was pulled to safety. The lifesaver or coast guardsman walked up the beach in the late afternoon until he met the patrolman from the next station.[11]

Shipwrecks were a frequent occurrence along the Marshfield coast line. One of the earliest marine disasters was the sinking of a French galleon in 1616. Her timbers were scattered between Ocean Bluff and Brant Rock. About 1880 a diver discovered this old wreck and brought up a cannon and two blunderbusses. The keel was uncovered after a violent storm in 1953, along with a grapnel, a fluke, an anchor, a helmet, pieces of eight, and a conquistador's shield. Some of these artifacts were found by Marshfield's well-known author, the late Edward Rowe Snow. Divers today still look for treasures from this seventeenth-century galleon. Fragments of the French vessel are in the possession of the Pilgrim Society at Plymouth. A record kept by Wales Tilden, Jr., coroner, tells of the 31 August 1839 wreck of the brig *Tilton* on Marshfield beach with the loss of nine lives. Elijah Ames made the coffins and Joseph Baker dug the graves.[12]

Another wreck occurred on 6 February 1854 (124 years to the day before the great storm of 1978), when the bark *Amanda* came ashore at Bluefish Cove in a violent winter blizzard. She was captained by Daniel D. Baker, a Duxbury man, who had been gone six months in the Mediterranean fruit trade. He had run into terrible gales on the trip home. A snowstorm with extreme freezing conditions turned the voyage into a struggle for survival. Finally striking rocks and shipwrecking on a beach, Captain Baker was surprised to recognize "the old fence on Branch's Island and the beaches in Brant Rock Cove." He had, by some miracle, been brought almost to his own doorstep. He was taken home across the fields by a tandem team hitched to a sled, the Neck Road being impassable.[13]

The *Chattanooga*, a 135-foot bark, was wrecked at Hewitt's Point, Brant Rock, on 25 June 1888. She was approaching Boston in a dense fog, and a strong southerly current swept her off her course. Carrying a heavy cargo of salt from Puerto Rico, she grounded and broke up at the point. The keel is still there. Men from the lifesaving station at Fourth Cliff came to the rescue and all hands were saved.[14]

In the early nineteenth century a controversy arose over whether or not to allow cattle to feed upon the beach grass. It was believed that the grass helped to prevent erosion of the sand dunes. An act was passed in February 1827 by the Massachusetts General Court, "giving the inhabitants of the town of Marshfield authority to build a sea-wall, palisades or hedge fences to preserve and secure the whole of Marshfield Beach from incursions and encroachments of the sea, excepting the seashore lying directly between Hewitt's and Branch's Islands and that no cattle, horses, sheep, etc., should be admitted to go at large on the beach." This was indeed a foresighted attempt more than 160 years ago at preservation of our fragile barrier-beach coast line, an early act of coastal zone management. An 1880 picture taken at Ocean Bluff shows a wooden sea wall. Later a wall was built in front of the Churchill Hotel along the high road at Ocean Street south of Brant Rock village.[15]

An improved road from Waterman's Causeway (Neck Road at Fieldston) to the Thomas Liversidge land at Ocean Bluff was built in 1862 and continued as far as the Pioneer Cottage in Brant Rock village in 1867. The so-called Dyke Road was built in 1872 and improved in 1879, and the extension of Ocean Street to Blackman's Point was made in 1890. Before the building of the dyke connecting the villages of Brant Rock and Green

Gathered to see the 135-foot bark Chattanooga, *wrecked at Hewitt's Point on 25 June 1888*

Arriving by Concord coach at the Brant Rock stables for a stay at the seashore, about 1890
Photograph courtesy of Harris F. Penniman

Harbor, there was for some years a ferry, established under the General Statutes of Massachusetts in 1866 "for carriage of passengers over Green Harbor River." It was operating by 1869 when William D. Baker was appointed to "keep the water ferry." This ferry ran from Liversidge landing off present Marshall Street, Brant Rock (near the present Peter Igo Park) from April to October only. A canal was dug to the landing from the main stream of the river. The fare was five cents per person.

The Duxbury and Cohasset Railroad was extended to Marshfield in 1871. The influx of visitors arriving by horse-drawn barge from the railroad depot at Marshfield increased the need for seashore accommodations at Brant Rock and Ocean Bluff. Thus many of the hotels and summer cottages were built in the 1870s. By 1879 a stagecoach business, running from Marshfield depot to Brant Rock and Green Harbor, was conducted by Franklin W. Hatch. He owned a livery stable located at the corner of North and Ocean streets in Brant Rock village. He had fifty horses and it took six of them to pull the barge which carried about fifty people. Later he sold the business to his brother Charles T. Hatch. In 1855 Charles T. Hatch bought a Concord coach from the famous Abbott Downing Company in Concord, New Hampshire, for $675. It was known about town as the "Tallyho" and was used to make the run between Marshfield and Hingham, as well as to transport children to school. The stagecoach business was later conducted by John H. Flavell from 1891 until at least 1926.[16]

A new age began for Brant Rock in the 1860s, the age of the grand hotels. After the Civil War and with the coming of the industrial age, more people had the money and leisure for a summer vacation at the seashore. In 1861 the Pioneer Cottage (304 Ocean Street today), the first of Brant Rock's many hotels, was built. This was renamed the Atlantic House by 1879. In 1866 Captain George Churchill erected the Churchill Hotel on what was then called Ocean Avenue, at the site of today's dwelling houses at 193 and 197 Ocean Street, Brant Rock. Later Dr. Archibald Davison, who lived next door and disapproved of croquet being played on Sundays at the Churchill Hotel, bought the hotel himself. It burned in 1909; there is no

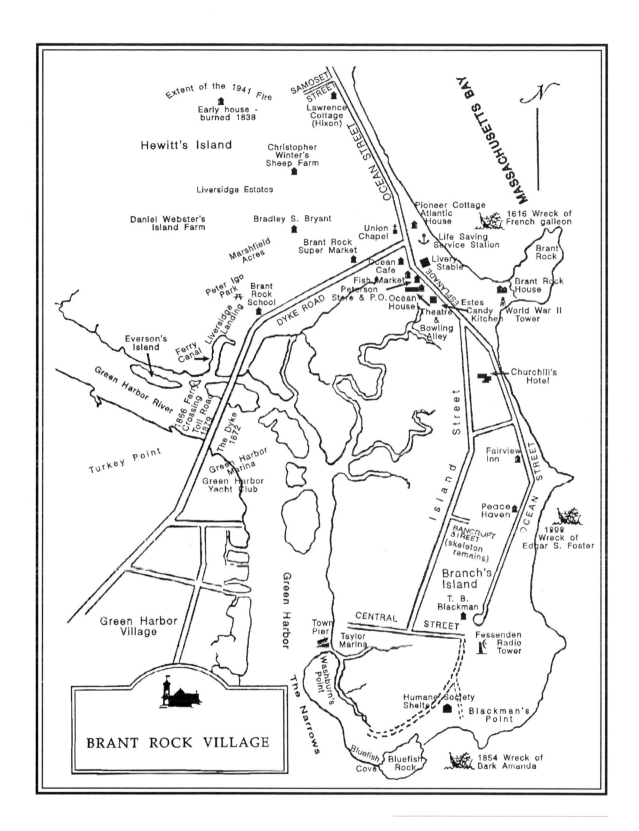

Extent of the 1941 Fire

Early house - burned 1838

Hewitt's Island

Christopher Winter's Sheep Farm

Liversidge Estates

Daniel Webster's Island Farm

Bradley S. Bryant

Marshfield Acres

Peter Igo Park

Brant Rock School

Brant Rock Super Market

Union Chapel

SAMOSET STREET

Lawrence Cottage (Hixon)

OCEAN STREET

MASSACHUSETTS BAY

N

Pioneer Cottage Atlantic House

1616 Wreck of French galleon

Life Saving Service Station

Brant Rock

Livery Stable

Brant Rock House

Ocean Cafe

Fish Market

Peterson Store & P.O.

Ocean House

Estes Candy Kitchen

World War II Tower

Theatre & Bowling Alley

DYKE ROAD

ESPLANADE

Everson's Island

Ferry Canal

Liversidge Landing

Green Harbor River

1866 Ferry Crossing Toll Road 1879

The Dyke 1872

Turkey Point

Green Harbor Marina

Green Harbor Yacht Club

Green Harbor Village

Green Harbor

The Narrows

Churchill's Hotel

Island Street

Fairview Inn

Peace Haven

BANCROFT STREET (skeleton remains)

Branch's Island

T. B. Blackman

OCEAN STREET

1909 Wreck of Edgar S. Foster

Fessenden Radio Tower

CENTRAL STREET

Town Pier

Taylor Marina

Washburn's Point

Humane Society Shelter

Blackman's Point

Bluefish Cove

Bluefish Rock

1854 Wreck of Bark Amanda

BRANT ROCK VILLAGE

Brant Rock Village

Enjoying a day of cool summer breezes at the Brant Rock House. The hotel, built in 1874, was razed about 1938.

Photograph courtesy of Harris F. Penniman

evidence that the croquet players were responsible. The Brant Rock House, which stood directly opposite the Rock, was built in 1874. Proprietor Henry T. Welch served shore dinners and rented rooms, boats, and bathhouses. This building was torn down about 1938. The Ocean House, built by Paine and Bonney in 1875 and owned for years by the Peterson family, was a familiar landmark. It burned in September 1973.

The Fairview Hotel, or Inn (133 Ocean Street), was built in 1874 by Martin Swift of Bridgewater. It is the only one of the Brant Rock hotels still standing. During the 1920s and 1930s it was owned by Dan DiCain, who called it the Como. It was an elegant and exclusive club. Patrons began the evening by dining to music of strolling violinists and later retired to the gambling tables at the rear of the inn. Later the hotel was bought by Joseph Sullivan who reinstated the name Fairview. In recent years the inn has been owned by Pat and Pota Stabile, then by Lennie and Patti Marma who sold it to the current owners, Walter T. Greaney and Michael Elms, in 1985.[17]

The Peace Haven, last and largest of the hotels, was built in 1903. It stood on Ocean Street between present Jersey and Iowa streets. It took up four lots and was capable of accommodating four hundred people. The Peace Haven Hotel Annex stood on the waterfront north of the Peace Haven (108 Ocean Street). The annex was later known as the Phillips' cottage for the Phillips family of Hanover, who still own it today. The Peace Haven, owned first by E. S. Freeman and later by Catherine Owens and her sister, was bought and torn down by Arthur Macker of Marshfield in the early 1940s. Due to the scarcity of lumber during World War II, Mr. Macker used timber from the Peace Haven to build cottages at Brant Rock and at Marshfield Acres on Hewitt's Island.[18]

In 1879 at Ocean Bluff the large Liversidge estate occupied most of Hewitt's Island. There were open fields in every direction. A small cluster of cottages, known as Abington Village, was located just north of the Liversidge place. A pond and icehouse, owned by George H. Thomas, stood between Chickatawbut Avenue and Lowell Street at Ocean Bluff. The Thomas Ice Company was formed about 1876 by Luther Thomas and his son George. The family business was still in existence in the 1950s when many of the cottages had iceboxes. If ice was needed, the cottager put an "Ice" card in the window. Leon Stetson, son-in-law of George Thomas, would deliver the ice, which was packed in straw or sawdust in the back of his truck. He passed out shards of ice to the hot, thirsty children. Familiar items of his trade were his ice pick, ice tongs, and the rubber apron he wore over his shoulder.[19]

There was a sufficient number of year-round school-age children by 1893 to warrant a district school, which was built at the corner of Marshall Avenue and the Dyke Road. After the students finished the fifth grade, they were transported by horse-drawn barge to the South Grammar School (2033 Ocean Street, Marshfield) and later to Marshfield High School (76 South River Street, then on Hatch Street) in Marshfield proper. John H. Flavell replaced his horse-drawn barge with a motorbus service by the 1920s. The Brant Rock School was in session for thirty-six years, closing its doors in 1929. The old school building was used by the police department from the 1930s until 1958 and then by the water department. It is now leased by the DAV Chapter 35.[20]

The year 1895 also saw the building of the first church in the village. The Union Chapel, at the corner of Ocean Street and Dyke Road, was the idea of Bradley S. Bryant, Archibald Davison, Charles Lawrence, Joseph Williams, and Charles Howland. They saw the need of a place for summer worship in the village. The chapel was built by Luther White with stonework done by Foster Ewell. Ewell also built a horse trough and a drinking fountain that stood on the church lawn until the 1950s. He was paid twenty-five dollars by the town for this job. The cost of the building was thirty-five hundred dollars, with an additional four hundred dollars for a belfry. It is a nondenominational church, holding services in the summers. There is an agreement in the Bryant deed of conveyance that the church must revert to the Bryant family if no longer used for religious services. The structure weathered the storm of 26 and 27 November 1898. The front lawn was frequently used as a drilling field by the men at the lifesaving station.[21]

Union Chapel, Brant Rock. The chapel was built by Luther White in 1895. Its lower portion was made of beach stones. The Life Saving Service station (on the right) became a lifeboat station of the United States Coast Guard in 1915.

On Brant Rock beach in front of the Life Saving Service station after the great storm of 26 and 27 November 1898. The action of wind and surf created high drifts of snow.

In 1982 major restoration of the church was undertaken by members of the community. By 1989 the roof had been redone, the belfry shingled, the clock faces restored, a weather vane completed, the front wall reshingled, and some of the latticed windows replaced. On 4 July 1986 the clock, so familiar to everyone in the area, began to toll the hours again for the first time since 1979. The church is being used temporarily by the Victory Baptist Church which holds services the year around. Today's pastor is the Reverend Robert Remick.[22]

The great winter storm of 26 and 27 November 1898 brought devastation to the fragile barrier-beach areas of Brant Rock and Ocean Bluff. A fifty-foot wide breach was made in the dyke. Many cottages at Brant Rock were badly damaged, washed off their foundations, or completely destroyed. Ocean Bluff was severely damaged, with only fifty out of three hundred cottages left intact. The breakwater gave way and the sea flowed through the streets. Victims of the storm sought safety in the Life Saving Service station which itself became threatened and almost washed away. People were pulled across from the station to the Union Chapel which became a haven for everyone, including the lifesaving men. There were two shipwrecks here: one, the *Edgar S. Foster* out of Gloucester bound for Newfoundland, came up on the beach by the Peace Haven Hotel; the other, the *Mertis H. Perry*, washed up at Rexhame. Fish were scattered up and down the beach and scavenged by the residents and the seagulls.[23]

By 1900 Brant Rock was a bustling summer resort. Four hotels provided accommodations for the "summer people." At the Ocean House under proprietor Walter Peterson, band concerts were held from the porch balcony. There were bowling alleys and a dining room. Souvenirs, magazines, candies, and ice cream were sold. By the 1920s moving pictures were offered upstairs, and a pool room and an ice-cream parlor were located downstairs. Frank Banzi and his son Fred bought the Ocean House about 1918 and continued the theatre and bowling alleys. The building burned September 1973.[24]

Jeannette Hixon Avery remembered:

When we grew a little older, we were allowed to go to the movies in the hall over Peterson's store. What a firetrap that was, with the wooden benches and one wooden stairway. Those were silent movies, of course, and the pictures were short. In between, the lyrics of a song were projected on the screen with still pictures. We all sang. Then back to the Perils of Pauline. *An old woman [Mrs. Cuff], at least she seemed old to me, played the piano. I admired her so much as she followed the tempo of the picture. Thinking back to it, the style was very distinctive, a sort of staccato, pattering along. It really deserved a place, however small, in the history of music.*[25]

Others cherish the memory of watching the movies, perhaps lost in a romantic love scene, to the accompaniment of the thumps and crashes of balls and pins in the bowling alley located beneath the theatre. The noise was all the greater since the bowling alleys had been thoroughly warped by the occasional inundation of the tide over the building's first floor.

In addition to the Ocean House, the Petersons ran the Brant Rock Cafe and the grocery and variety store in the building next door. The Brant Rock Post Office, which in 1879 had been owned by B. White and located near the Hatch livery stables, had moved to the Ocean House by 1894. The postmaster was Walter Peterson. Later postmasters and postmistresses were Julia Peterson, Margaret Fletcher, Althea F. Staples, Edward Fonseca, Ernest Chandler, Jr., and Diane Cook.

Jeannette Hixon Avery described the store and post office:

The old general store was a marvel. They stocked everything, sneakers, hardware, dress goods, groceries, and cough syrup. The penny candy counter was a magnet. You really could buy a 'penny's worth.' On top was a round glass bowl full of 'picklelimes.' The clerk would ladle out one, hand it to you as is, and you would suck on it while you waited for the mail to be sorted. Also there was a large music box with the flat metal disks. Someone always had a nickel to start that. The post office was a very crowded social spot when the mail came in.[26]

Brad Blackman remembers "the pot-bellied wood-burning stove in the store around which the locals gathered to tip back their chairs, warm their

Gentlemen of 1890 at the Pool Room in Brant Rock. Band concerts were held on the Ocean House porch balcony next door. Photograph courtesy of Harris F. Penniman

feet, gossip, and tell lies." In the 1930s, 1940s, and 1950s, the present Brant Rock Post Office building was used for beano games. The post office remained at Peterson's until about 1961 when it was moved to the southwest corner of Ocean Street and Dyke Road.[27]

Later, Peterson's store was bought by Edward Theran, who sold it to Fred Battie. Wilfred ("Biff") Henderson bought the store at public auction in 1957. He and his brother Russell ran the Henderson Bros. Plumbing and Heating Company until 1987 when the business was liquidated and the building sold to Arthur and Pat D'Allessandro.

Truc Ebenezer Estes had opened the doors of his famous Candy Kitchen by 1900. Here one could buy vanilla, chocolate, molasses, and checkaberry popcorn bars; salt-water taffy kisses of all varieties, chocolate fudge, walnut creams, ginger candy, stuffed dates, caramel corn brittle, roast peanuts, spanish peanuts, white and pink mints, hand-dropped chocolates, and molasses peppermints. A huge copper popcorn popper stood in the corner and the candy cases were a delight to young and old alike. There was an iron hook in the wall where the taffy was hung and pulled. This was replaced in later years by a taffy pulling and wrapping machine. Faith Jean recalls that "the puller strung it out like a rope and the wrapper cut, spun, and wrapped the kisses. Each batch made twenty-eight pounds of candy. They made three batches each week of fourteen flavors. The candy cost [thirty] cents per pound and popcorn ten cents per bar [or five and ten cents for rabbit-ear bags of popcorn]. A seaplane flew in once to pick up a load for the Hotel Fontainbleu in Florida."[28]

Estes owned the store from 1900 to 1930 when he sold it to Leslie Clark. Clark ran it until 1946 when it became the property of Stuart and Edna Studley. They passed it on in 1965 to their son Stuart, Jr., otherwise known

Pool Room and shooting gallery, the Ocean House, and Peterson's store with the horse-drawn barge that transported people to the beach from the railroad station at Marshfield. The barge also carried Brant Rock and Green Harbor children to school.
Photograph courtesy of Harris F. Penniman

as "Bump" Studley. The store burned on 8 August 1971, a Sunday, taking with it some of the sweetest memories of Brant Rock.[29]

Another Brant Rock landmark, the fish market, was first owned by Fred Keene of Green Harbor who moved the building to its present location. By 1894 H. C. (Henry) Phillips was the owner. He died in 1933 and was succeeded by his two sons, Albert and Harry Phillips. Harry was a Class B checker champion of New England and an algebra teacher. He always had a checkerboard at the fish market and would challenge anyone who entered. Most of the time, however, Harry played checkers with his nephew Parker Phillips. Harry also ran a business renting dories at the beach for two dollars a day. Subsequent owners of the fish market were Fred Staples and Harold Bourne.

Today Henry Packard Dunbar, known far and wide as "Hank," has become synonymous with the Brant Rock Fish Market. Hank bought it on 18 April 1960. He had previously worked at the market for Harry Phillips and Fred Staples. He is the first owner to operate the market year round. The lobsters are bought locally and stored in ocean water that is pumped directly into the fish tanks. At the present time, according to Hank, there is a serious problem with fish supply, probably due to overfishing. People drive for miles from all over the area to buy fresh fish at this famous and quaint village fish market and to talk to modern-day Brant Rock "character" Hank Dunbar.[30]

By 1900 George E. Tradd of Lowell ran a gift shop called the Silver Lake House on Middle Street (near the Brant Rock tower). A store called Tradd and Payne's sold linen and china, and auctions were held there in the summer. Arthur T. Tradd started operating the Rockwood Inn in 1906 at the corner of Ocean and South streets on the Brant Rock Esplanade. Shore

dinners were served. The Rockwood Inn, still operating in 1941, has been converted to condominiums. In the 1930s and 1940s Horton's Bakery was located in this area. Arthur Tradd later owned the Marshfield Inn at Route 3A and Ferry Street.[31]

Up at the Bluff in 1900, S. G. Capen's Store sold the latest goods and souvenirs popular with vacationers. His merchandise included groceries, tinware, cigars, tobacco, bread and pastries, ice cream, confectioneries, stationery, periodicals, bathing suits, boots, and fishing tackle "for sale or to let." A wooden walk ran between Capen's and the beach bluff in those days. The store became Briggs & Maxwell in 1907. Later it became Whitman and Wright, then Wright and Starrett's general store, but it was known far and wide as Bessie's for Bessie Wright. Bessie was a personality remembered by all who frequented the store during the thirties, forties, and fifties. On her mail scales she would carefully weigh in all the new babies when they arrived for the summer holidays. She was famous for her coot stew, made fresh from coot brought in by her uncle, Silas Wright, during coot season. Bessie died in 1963. On the day of her death the store was closed, a very unusual event. On the door was a sign which read, "Closed on account of Bessie's funeral." Later the store was referred to as Wright's. Today the Stella Maris house on the bluff occupies the site of Wright and Starrett's.[32]

The Ocean Bluff Post Office was housed at Capen's in 1900 and later at Wright and Starrett's. Bessie Wright and Gordon Starrett were postmasters. When this store was burned in the 1941 Ocean Bluff fire, a small barbershop building was moved from Marshfield and placed on the opposite side of Ocean Street on the site of the old Ocean Bluff Casino, where the present Ocean Bluff Packet Store stands. A new building was put up by Bessie Wright and Gordon Starrett about 1945 where the original building had been. Starrett continued as postmaster, succeeded by Jean Flagg. This post office was burned in 1978. The location of the post office then was moved to the Bristol Bakery building across from St. Ann's by the Sea, and Ernest Chandler served as postmaster. It became a substation of the central Marshfield post office and is presently located in the Ocean Bluff Packet (555 Ocean Street) block. As a substation it has no postmaster.

The Ocean Bluff Casino, owned by Briggs and Maxwell, was a popular place in its time. It offered movies, college ices (sundaes), dancing, and bowling. It even had two children's bowling alleys.

Ocean Bluff, about 1900. Come with us to the promenade at Ocean Bluff. We'll have an ice cream at Capen's Store and rent a boat to go fishing.
Photograph courtesy of Harris F. Penniman

COOT HUNTING
IN BRANT ROCK

For many years coot (scoter duck) hunting was popular in Brant Rock from September through November. Brad Blackman says that "in years gone by, they hunted them from beach dories. The hunters would go out in the dories, situate themselves in two rows forty yards apart in an east and west line, set their decoys, lay at anchor, and wait for the birds." They would fill the bottom of a 17-foot dory with straw to keep their feet warm. This became quite a sport, and arguments would take place over deciding who had shot what. Gunners without boats would hunt from the Rock and, if stranded by the incoming tide, would have to wait until it receded.

BRAD BLACKMAN'S
BRANT ROCK COOT STEW

2 coot - pluck, clean, leave skin on.

Prepare as a chicken, cut in pieces.

Stew for 2 to 3 hours with 3 or 4 onions covered with water.

Add 4 or 5 good-sized white potatoes and the same number of sweet potatoes, some carrots, turnips, parsnips, salt, and pepper. Thicken with flour.

Make dumplings for the top.

Some say put an old shoe in the pot and cook until tender, then throw out the coot. Others recommend baking the coot on a plank, then throwing out the coot and eating the plank.

Feeds six strong fishermen.

Coot hunter, after a successful day off Brant Rock

By 1900 a cluster of cottages at so-called Abington Village (on the west side of Ocean Street between Shawmut Avenue and St. Ann's) housed "tourists" from inland southeastern Massachusetts near and about the town of Abington, hence the name. There were summer cottages on every beach-front lot and on both sides of Ocean Street from Brant Rock village to beyond Abington Village. Building lots had been laid out by Bradley S. Bryant, the beach developer of this turn-of-the-century period. There was a grid of potential house lots for three blocks back from the beach with some houses already built on the parcels. North of Abington Village, including what is today 1st to 13th roads, was a layout for Webster Park, a Bradley Bryant development. To some old timers, this area at the north end of Ocean Bluff beach is considered to be a part of Fieldston. There once was a wide boardwalk which ran through the dunes at Webster Park, but it was destroyed in the 1898 storm. In 1907 John Foster of Hanson and Horace B. Maglathlin of Kingston owned and began to develop some of the land at Webster Park.[33]

In 1918 H. S. Kelsey started developing the area from 1st to 13th roads. He was very particular about who settled there. He gave preference to people of German descent, who could buy a lot for one dollar. Others paid $250 for a waterfront lot, $200 for a lot one row back, then $175, $150, and $100 each row back to Ocean Street. Those wishing to settle had to build a $1600 house. In 1929 Mr. Kelsey set aside ten waterfront house lots between 3rd and 5th roads for the neighborhood to use for picnics and parades. This was the origin of the Sunrise Beach Association, which was in existence, tax-free, for nearly forty years until 1967 when the property at Sunrise Beach was sold to George Michael. There are now three deserted and vandalized buildings on this beautiful piece of oceanside property.

Jeannette Hixon Avery described her typical beach cottage:

The cottage was a comfortable place. . . . There were five bedrooms upstairs, each with a set of spool furniture including bed, chest, commode with wash bowl and pitcher and the chamber pot in the cupboard below. Each room was painted a different color, pink, blue or yellow furniture. What

a price they would bring today! There was a table in the center of the living room with a hanging lamp over it with a red glass shade, with chains to pull it up or down. What I loved best was a lot of old Godey prints from the old fashion magazines which were kept in the drawer of the table. On the newel post in the hall sat a stuffed owl almost a foot high. Of course, there was no electricity. We used oil lamps. What a job it must have been to wash the chimneys! I remember my oldest sister putting the curling iron in the chimney and wetting her finger to test the heat. There was a big fieldstone fireplace and black stove in the kitchen. The brick chimney showed in the corner of the dining room and on a flat spot of it was a cowbell. That was a big bell with a wooden handle which Mother rang to fetch her brood for meals. I am sure that in good weather we were never in the house except for meals. We turned on the faucet for a bit till the funny taste of the old pipes was almost gone. That is one of my earliest memories, the taste of the drinking water at the beach.[34]

The population was largely a summer group at Brant Rock and Ocean Bluff with a total of 329 houses and four hotels in 1900. Only sixty-one fishermen and lobstermen living in twenty-two houses made the area their year-round home. The maximum combined summer population of Brant Rock, Ocean Bluff, and Green Harbor was estimated to be about twenty-seven hundred, compared to today's year-round population of around three thousand. In about this same 1900-period, street lamps were installed at Brant Rock with money raised by a local minstrel show. Deliveries to the cottage doors were made by the butcher, baker, vegetable man, and iceman. Helen Peterson remembers "ladies in long dresses strolling along the beach, shoppers going in and out of Tradd and Payne's store, horse-drawn barges carrying visitors to and from the railroad station and couples posing for photographs at 'Lover's Rock' on the beach near the Brant Rock."[35]

Bradley S. Bryant had a huge farm on Hewitt's Island which he had acquired from the Thomas Liversidge estate. It included all the area now bounded by Ashburton Avenue on the east, the river on the west, the Dyke Road on the south, and Chicatawbut Avenue on the north. It was all mowed by horse and team twice a season and the hay gathered into stacks in which

Contemplation at Ocean Bluff
Watercolor by Francis Mortimer Lamb, 1897, from collection of Lucy Stein Cushman

children loved to jump and play. A familiar landmark visible from up and down the beach was the wood-shingled water tower that stood on the Bryant farm. Behind the farm stretched fields of blueberries and wild blackberries, good for picking and making pies. Bryant also owned the Brant Rock Mineral Spring Pumping Station at what is now Hancock Street. It became the Brant Rock Water Company and supplied water to this island area so cut off from mainland Marshfield. Most of the Bryant farm area was developed after World War II and called Marshfield Acres.[36]

In 1905 a gentleman destined to make a special kind of history arrived at Brant Rock with a working crew to build a radio tower at Blackman's Point. Professor Reginald Aubrey Fessenden, an inventive genius, had worked with Thomas Edison and had himself discovered a system of wireless transmission. Fessenden eventually was credited with some five hundred patented inventions, including the oscillator, the Fathometer or sonic depth finder, the wireless compass, submarine detector, turbo-electric drive for battleships, and a loud-speaker system for musical instruments.[37]

In digging the excavation for the large nine-foot-high cement base for the radio tower, many Indian tools and artifacts were uncovered, indicating the extensive use of Blackman's Point by Native Americans as a lithic workshop. A 420-foot-high steel tower was erected and the world's first radio-voice broadcast was made from Blackman's Point, Brant Rock, on Christmas Eve, 1906. Fessenden made a speech. Handel's "Largo" was played on a phonograph, followed by a violin solo by Fessenden and a reading from the Bible. The broadcast was picked up in Machrihanish, Scotland, at a twin radio tower also constructed by Fessenden. The experimental radio station at Blackman's Point was considered the scientific marvel of its era.[38]

Fessenden continued his work over the years, but the company had financial problems. The equipment had to be sold and the radio patents were lost to Fessenden and acquired by RCA for $3 million. The station was closed in 1914 and dismantled, although Fessenden had left the company in 1911. He received many radio honors for his work and died in Bermuda in 1932.[39]

The tower was felled in 1915. Schoolchildren at Brant Rock School were dismissed for the event and felt the ground shake beneath their feet when the great tower came down. The laboratory was bought by nearby resident Cecil Taylor, who moved it to his home and converted it into a garage. Only the base of the tower remains today. A bronze plaque presented by the

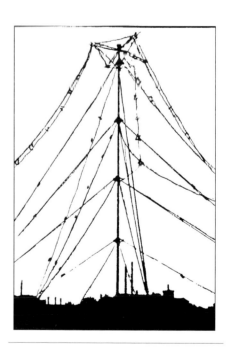

Fessenden Radio Tower
Pen and ink drawing by Anne Philbrick Hall, 1990

Massachusetts Broadcasters' Association and the Broadcast Pioneers was placed on the site in November 1966. For the past several years, Ed Perry of radio station WATD, Marshfield, has brought a mobile unit to Blackman's Point and broadcast live Christmas music on Christmas Eve to honor the first broadcasters.[40]

The early years of the twentieth century were the heyday of Brant Rock. Cottages continued to be built on every available lot. Sunday-school picnics, tennis and croquet, dances, band concerts, parades, fireworks, fishing and hunting parties were the order of the day. The two biggest celebrations of the summer were held on the Fourth of July and Labor Day. Jeannette Hixon Avery recalls that "Arthur Coolidge called it 'Illumination Day'(Labor Day). For the daytime parade we decorated everything: bicycles, doll carriages, and pony carts. There was even a make-shift band. We all marched. Then came the competitions: pie- and doughnut-eating contests, croquet and tennis matches. There were also potato and three-legged races." Arthur Coolidge was a professor at Northeastern University, an air raid warden in World War II, and a personality around Brant Rock. His large garden between Ocean Street and Ashburton Avenue was known as "Mr. McGregor's garden," and he was also a promoter of horseshoe games on the beach with his cheery greeting of "Pitch a few?"[41]

A cruise past Brant Rock on the *Priscilla Alden*, a side-wheel boat, made a grand outing from Boston or Plymouth. Later the New York excursion boat, owned by the Merchant and Minor Steamship Company, made its daily trip past Brant Rock at 7:15 p.m. People told the time by it and would sometimes jump into their cars and head for the Cape Cod Canal to watch the boat go through and wave to the passengers. Service was discontinued at the outbreak of World War II and the boat was used as a patrol boat during the war. The grand era of overnight cruises to New York ended forever.

By 1930 certain "modern conveniences" had come to Brant Rock. Town water was supplied to the area in the 1920s. The year 1927 saw the widening of Ocean Street in the village center, done under Chapter 249 of the Acts of 1927 by the Plymouth County Commissioners. The buildings on the west side of the so-called Esplanade were moved back toward the marsh. The landmark Brant Rock Comfort Station was built by Bradley Bryant in 1929, with a stipulation in the deed that it always be "used for public purposes." In 1931 the Green Harbor jetties, which had been built in 1899, were reconstructed and dredging of the river undertaken to keep the Narrows open for boats. By 1932 the sea wall along the ocean front at Brant Rock and Ocean Bluff was completed at a cost of $200,000, one-sixth of which was paid by the abutters, who each paid fifteen dollars per foot of their land. The rest of the expenses were carried one-half by the state, one-sixth by the county, and one-sixth by the town. The sea wall was built by men from the Works Progress Administration (WPA) who were paid thirty-five cents an hour. The structure replaced what had been a crude stone breakwater laid by hand about 1900. The waterfront owners built their own stairs to the beach at every other road through Ocean Bluff, with owners of houses behind the waterfront contributing ten dollars per household towards the expense.[42]

Stores, restaurants, and businesses flooded this summer beach resort. Sandy's Restaurant, owned by Arthur and Lucille Sandstrum, opened in 1928. At one time it was run by Julie Sandstrum. It continued serving its famous food at the corner of the Esplanade and Dyke Road until 1960 when Francis ("Bud") and Jane Mannix bought the restaurant and Sandstrum properties extending to what is now the road to the town pier. The restaurant was torn down and replaced with Bud's Beef and Fish Restaurant. The Mannix family also ran Bud's Country Store, which had a coffee bar, and rented and sold boats, bikes, and scuba-diving equipment. Today Leonard Schofield runs the Country Kitchen on Sandy's site. Other Schofield businesses in this area are the L & M Hardware & Sporting Goods Store, Harborside Video, and the L & M Sheet Metal.

Eli's store stood just south of the Ocean House from the 1930s to the 1950s. It was a department store known locally as the "linen store." It sold bathing suits, bathing caps and bathing shoes, summer clothing, beach towels, and satin souvenir pillows, which were all hung outside on the porch. The Eli family came from New York. The store burned in the late 1960s.

Alfred F. ("Fawn") Worthington ran a gas station in the old stable building on the east side of the Esplanade by the 1930s. The gas pumps were located nearly in the street. Many remember Fawn sitting by the doorway smoking his pipe. After he died in 1958, the gas station was run by Harry Tingley. It is now a furniture store.

In the 1930s a First National Store was located on the west side of the Esplanade where the Brant Rock Liquor Store is today. Groceries were plucked down from the shelves by a long-handled tong and the order was totaled by hand on a brown paper bag.

Haddad's Ocean Cafe has been operating for more than fifty years, since 1937. It stands on the site of what was George Tradd's and Lena Payne's cottage. The south side is a restaurant, famous for its delicious veal cutlets and spaghetti, fish, and fish chowder, and the north side is a bar. Haddad's is a popular place and draws people from far and wide to enjoy home cooking and friendly conversation. Many Marshfield residents make it a habit to go there weekly for a night out dining with fellow townspeople and friends. Today the restaurant is managed by Madeleine, George, Mitchell, and Charles (Chuckie) Haddad.[43]

The Haddads and the Najams have been in Brant Rock since 1918 and have owned and operated a number of businesses, including a barbershop, bar and restaurant, grocery store, and clam stand. Louis Haddad came to this country from Lebanon in 1917. With him came Philomena and Tammy

Brant Rock Esplanade before it was widened in 1927

Najam. Other members of the two interrelated families of Lebanon followed. Jimmy Haddad married Philomena Najam, and Louis Haddad married Saada Najam. A younger brother, Charlie Najam, and another sister, Hajie, came over in 1922. At first the two families lived together in Boston, where they ran a barbershop.

The Haddads were introduced to Brant Rock by Arthur Tradd, who brought them down to help in his various businesses. Soon the Najams and Haddads moved to Brant Rock. Louis Haddad started a barbershop and purchased the present Ocean Cafe building in 1928, opening it as a bar. The Haddads and Najams started the restaurant, still a family business, in 1937. The Najams bought property on South Street and on the waterfront and built houses on Fourth Road and Plymouth Avenue. In the 1940s Charlie and Olga Najam opened Charlie's Famous Fried Clam Snack Bar, a Brant Rock landmark. Hard hit by the severe winter storm of 1978, Charlie's survived to continue its popular seaside service of delectable fried clams and seafood. It has been owned and operated by Hazel Ruel since the 1970s and is now run by Paul Ruel. The Najams and Haddads are large and closely knit families that have made a significant contribution to the village of Brant Rock. Ties with Lebanon are still maintained and some members of the families regularly visit the mother country.[44]

Fife's Grocery and Meat Market was operated during the 1930s and 1940s next to the Ocean Cafe where the ice-cream shop is today. Opened during the summers only, the market delivered groceries throughout the area. At another time the building was called Whitman Market and run by Bob Cross.

In the 1940s the Beacon Novelty Shop, run by Mrs. Clifford Gassett, was located just south of today's Arthur and Pat's Restaurant. Among other things, Mrs. Gassett ran a lending library. She had moved the business from Green Harbor where it had been located next to the bridge on Beach Street.

The small restaurant now known as Arthur and Pat's, at the southwest corner of the Esplanade, was for years called Mommie's. It was bought in 1945 by Harry and Helen Tingley. Harry had previously been at the old IGA store at Fieldston. The soda fountain was originally on the left-hand side of the restaurant. The Tingleys sold tonics and ice cream, meats, milk, and eggs, the *Boston Sunday Globe*, and the *Brockton Enterprise*. All the food was home-cooked and the doughnut machine, in full view at the front of the restaurant, was a magnet for Sunday morning breakfasters. In 1972 Mommie's was sold to Rita Jenkins, who continued to run it as Mommie's until 1975 when she sold it to Arthur and Olga D'Allessandro. They continued Mommie's until 1978 when the name was changed to Arthur and Pat's. Today the restaurant offers home baking and serves "lumberjack portions." It is a place of character with old photographs on the wall, a ship's bell rung for patrons' birthdays, and a whistle blown to seat people "when the traffic gets heavy."

By 1945 Phillip's Lobster Claw restaurant was located across from Peterson's store. This rather elegant restaurant brought an air of genteel dining to Brant Rock and was especially enjoyed by the summer visitors.

The Breakers was at one time owned and operated by Russell and Biff Henderson, then by the McCarten family. It was sold in 1986 to Kang Yu. The site where Venus II is today was bought in 1927 by Arthur Tradd. He built the Ocean Breeze Bar and Grille, which later had a number of owners. The Venus II is a bar and cafe known especially for its pizza. It has been owned by Nick Drosopoulos since the mid-1970s.[45]

Summer fun

The waves at the beach were more than matched by the waves of music from the brass band at Brant Rock in the early 1900s, creating a harmonious summer day.
Photograph courtesy of Harris F. Penniman

By 1952 the Brant Rock Supermarket on Dyke Road at Plymouth Avenue had been built by Arthur Macker, an enterprising contractor. The Verrocchis were the first proprietors, then "Chick" Cheetem. The supermarket is now operated by the Donald Devines.

On Ocean Street, across from Hancock Street, was a small "oasis" known as Fairbanks Park, which was paved over when the sea wall was repaired in the 1950s. It had flower beds of portulaca, several wooden benches, and carefully clipped grass. From the park a wooden staircase descended to the beach. The park was cared for by a local man, Bill Ware, known to all as "B-Ware."

In the 1940s band concerts were given in Brant Rock. Two lumber trucks, parked in front of Peterson's store, provided the platform for a red uniformed band from Brockton and the National Award winning VFW Band of Bridgewater. The latter was resplendent in gold and blue uniforms and sported as its trumpet soloist Betty Magoun (Bates).

Joan Scolponeti, chairman of Marshfield's 350th Celebration Committee, remembers the concert on the night of 12 August 1945, V-J Day:

This remains a vivid memory for those of us in the Brant Rock Theatre watching A Thousand and One Nights. *The din outside the movie rose above the sound track and the bowling alley. Mr. Banzi turned off the movie and appeared on the stage to announce that the war was over. We poured out of the theatre to the square where blaring horns and joyous shouts greeted us. A concert was hastily put together on the lumber trucks and patriotic music filled the August night. Flags appeared everywhere, strangers hugged, kissed, and danced together. Everyone sang and, best of all, every light was on.*

At Ocean Bluff a stone Catholic church, St. Ann's by the Sea, was built in 1923 as "nearly one hundred houses have been erected there and nearly seventy percent of the people are Catholic." The influx of Irish Catholic families from Boston and communities south of Boston occurred in the 1920s. This group has made a lasting impact on the beach areas of Brant Rock and Ocean Bluff. Today many have made permanent homes out of the summer cottages which their families first occupied sixty or more years ago.

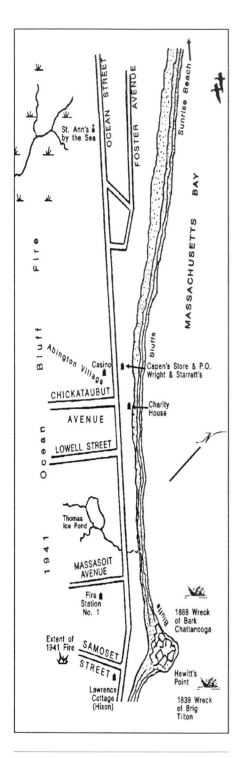

Ocean Bluff Village

St. Ann's by the Sea was originally a mission of St. Joseph's Parish in Kingston. The church was later destroyed by the Ocean Bluff fire in 1941. Masses were held in the ballroom of Fieldston-on-the-Atlantic in the summer and at the Ocean Bluff fire station in the winter until after the Second World War. In 1946 an army chapel, now used as the parish hall, was brought from Framingham as a temporary church until the present structure was built in 1957. The Reverend Patrick J. Gilmore is today's pastor.

Archambault's Bristol Bakery, famous for its fresh bread, bran muffins, and crusty doughnuts, was across from St. Ann's by the Sea church. The Ocean Bluff rooming house was just south of St. Ann's. Harry Edel's Casino, originally owned by Briggs & Maxwell, with bowling allies built by Charlie Brown, was located where the Ocean Bluff Packet is today. Winship's drugstore stood at the corner of Chickatawbut Avenue and Ocean Street. Many remember the famous Labor Day five-cent banana split sale at Winship's, first business rebuilt after the fire, and one of the last places in Marshfield to still have soda fountains. The Shore Haven Hotel stood across the street. One could slide down the sand bluffs to the beach below, the dunes in front were so steep. Hence the name Ocean Bluff, a term used since 1884 to designate this high, sandy dune area. Some remember picking the pink morning glories that grew between the rocks at the top of the sea wall here. The fire station stood on Massasoit Avenue where it stands today.

When the sun rose over the ocean off Brant Rock on the windy spring Monday of 21 April 1941, all the neat little cottages, the church, the stores, and public buildings on the crest of the sand dunes caught the glint of the sunshine on what was to be their last morning at Ocean Bluff. Before nightfall this long stretch of windswept beach lying between Fieldston and Samoset Street had become a scene of total destruction.

At precisely 1:40 p.m. a fire broke out at the corner of Ocean Street and Plymouth Avenue at Fieldston. It swept through the high, dry grass with winds exceeding thirty miles per hour. Such high winds, coupled with extreme dryness caused by a rainless spring, set in motion an explosive fire that shot flames one hundred feet high. Smoke could be seen from as far away as Provincetown and Nantucket. The Ocean Bluff conflagration raced before the west wind, leaping the blocks, firing the houses simultaneously, and exploding all the buildings in its relentless path southeasterly toward Brant Rock village. All attempts to stop it failed. Firemen and equipment came from all over the South Shore. Volunteers fought untiringly. Backfires proved useless. From the top of Rexhame Hill it appeared an unbelievable inferno capable of burning the sea itself. It seemed to threaten the existence of the earth, like Fourth of July fireworks gone crazy. One witness said that the liquor and beer in the Casino and package store exploded. Windows in the houses would cloud up with smoke, change color, then blow up as though a bomb had hit them, sending debris up to six hundred yards away. It burned for four hours. Finally at sundown the wind died and the fire was brought under control at 5:30 p.m., just before dynamite charges were set to go off in an attempt to create a backfire. These had been placed from Samoset Street to Brant Rock Chapel in front of the houses lining Ocean Street. The last house burned was at the corner of Samoset and Ocean streets.

The devastation was total: two hotels, the post office, the Casino, the church, twelve stores, 446 houses and cottages, and 96 garages. Burned hoses and fire engines littered the streets, but by a miracle, the summer residents having not yet arrived at their homes, not a life was lost. Thirty residents were left homeless. Over two million gallons of water were used

Smoke rolled before the west wind on the disastrous day of 21 April 1941 at Ocean Bluff. By nightfall a fire had destroyed over five hundred buildings. The fire changed the face of this summer playground forever.

on the fire and the last fireman left at 9:00 p.m. the following evening. The Ocean Bluff fire station on Massasoit Avenue, however, survived the fire.

A rehabilitation committee was created to reconstruct the Ocean Bluff area. A legislative act allowed the town to take over enough land to "lay out streets and a row of suitable lots on each side of said streets." It was rezoned into three residential districts with three lot sizes — five-thousand, ten-thousand, and twenty-thousand square feet — with a zone for business. Plymouth Avenue was laid out to open up the area for development and as a firebreak for protection of the great dyke meadow. People from the recently suspended WPA program were put to work constructing roads and clearing up the fire area at Ocean Bluff. Due to the outbreak of World War II in December 1941, the reconstruction of Ocean Bluff was slow until 1946.[46]

In 1941 the town voted to build the jetty out to Brant Rock itself and to build a jetty from Hewitt's Point. Two shorter jetties were built about 1947 from the foot of Webster Avenue and from the Coast Guard Station site.[47]

The story of World War II at Brant Rock is perhaps best told in the words of John ("Chuck") Taylor, a native of the village:

In the weeks following the Pearl Harbor attack [7 December 1941], the U.S. Army dug trenches and machine-gun emplacements at Blackman's Point and positioned two 75-mm cannon in an apparent attempt to defend us from German attacks. My friends and I had the honor of assisting with the pick and shovel work and inspecting the armament. Work also started on the Brant Rock tower and the adjacent barracks, although no one would tell us the exact mission of the tower. Apparently a series of similar towers was erected along the entire coast line as antisubmarine listening and spotting posts as well as observation points for coast artillery batteries. Gasoline was in very short supply during World War II and strictly rationed. I can recall walking the five miles to school after missing the school bus and being passed by as few as three automobiles in that distance[48]

About 1942 the 70-foot-high Brant Rock tower was erected by the United States government for defense purposes: specifically, for sighting enemy submarines during World War II. It stands where the old Brant Rock

House Hotel stood, adjacent to the Rock. It is eight stories high with a basement level also. It has walls that are fourteen feet square made of reinforced concrete twelve inches thick. After the war, John McCraig of Duxbury bought the tower from the government as surplus property. McCraig sold it to Joseph Barbuti of Waltham, an electrician, who brought town water and sewer to the tower and made it into living quarters. It is now owned by Don Cappelletti of Centerville, who recently painted it and improved the interior. The tower is still a landmark on land and sea.[49]

During the war, Coast Guardsmen were stationed day and night at the stairways along the beach wall all the way to Fieldston. Blackout regulations demanded that curtains be drawn over all the windows of the houses. No one was allowed to carry mirrors, cameras, binoculars, flashlights, towels, or radios down the steps to the beach. Troops from Camp Edwards (now Otis Air Force Base) periodically carried out maneuvers on the sea walls and on the Esplanade. They set up machine guns and lay along the walls with guns trained out to sea.

The late 1960s and early 1970s saw the decline of the Brant Rock area. A series of fires burned what had been Eli's linen store, Estes Candy Kitchen, and the Peterson building which, when it burned, still housed the Brant Rock Theatre and bowling alleys. With the coming of Route 3 to the Marshfield-Pembroke border and the resulting ease of commuting to Boston, the summer cottages at the beach areas were winterized. Today Brant Rock and Ocean Bluff have largely a year-round population. Beach property values have soared in the 1980s.[50]

Interest in forming a group to preserve this famous seashore turn-of-the-century resort began in the 1930s. The Daniel Webster Improvement Association was organized with Joseph Warren Keene as president. Keene was a retired vaudeville entertainer on the old B.F. Keith circuit, as well as a magician who had trained under Harry Houdini. His wife, Grace White Keene, was a direct descendant of Peregrine White. Today an active group, the Brant Rock Association is dedicated to preserving Brant Rock and discouraging detrimental development. There are one hundred members under the effective leadership of Esther Reed, president of the association.

The Marshfield Conservation Commission has acquired a number of parcels of land in the Brant Rock area. These include 20 acres of salt marsh

Surf at Brant Rock

at West Brook meadow, 6 acres of brushland at Saginaw Avenue, and 5.5 scattered acres of salt marsh.

The Marshfield Recreation Commission conducts programs at two playgrounds in Brant Rock, the Peter Igo Park on the site of the old Brant Rock dump and the Tower Avenue Park on the site of the old water tower.

The master plan for the improvement of the Green Harbor tidal basin area was introduced at the 1956 Marshfield Town Meeting and a town pier and bulkhead built by 1958 with state and town appropriations. By 1959 safety fences and benches were added and the parking lot completed.[51]

Plans for an updated sewerage system to replace an earlier system constructed in Brant Rock in the 1950s and a waste-water treatment facility were begun in 1978 by Marshfield town-meeting action. The plant and system were operating by 1980.

Town Pier Road, leading past the plant to the town pier, was completed in 1985 and the Harbor Park and new parking lot in 1989. Located at the town pier is the Seaflower, a restaurant operated by Sylvia Gentile.

Chuck Taylor says of the Brant Rock fishermen:

The senior citizens of Brant Rock, all too few in number, might agree with me that the old-time fishermen I recall from my youth were world class characters and it's a pity that more of their antics haven't been recorded for posterity. Some of these dear people include my grandfather [Alton Henry Taylor] (known as "Old Allie" to some), "Johnny" Paulding, Charlie "Pete" (Peterson), "Goody" Tyler, George Stetson, Wyman Jones, "Nate" Hatch, Bob and Charlie Newton, "Cliff" and Joe Vallier, "Smoky" Harlow, "Fred" Staples, Sr., "Jack" Shanley, Dana Blackman, Cecil Taylor (my dad), Henry & Albert Phillips of the fish market, Ellet Publicover, and others [Russell O. Chandler, "Chickie" Tolman] of whom I have only a dim recollection. For reasons of self-preservation I dare not repeat some of the more interesting tales concerning these gentlemen, but they were many and legendary. Today's fishermen are equally independent and hard working but generally too sophisticated and urbane to be compared with the real characters I remember from the 1930s.

Today fishing and lobstering continue at Brant Rock as they have for three hundred fifty years. The harborside bustles with pleasure boating all

summer. It is the center for the blue-fin tuna fleet with tuna fishing areas just off shore. The boats ply their way in and out of the Green Harbor River on their daily trips to fish for cod, bass, flounder, and tuna, and to pull their lobster traps from the waters off Brant Rock. Sadly, the number of fish caught has diminished and the clam flats, so rich with succulent soft-shell clams in the 1940s, are now contaminated and have had to be closed.

The old-time lobstermen of Brant Rock would be surprised to know that there is today a Massachusetts Lobstermen's Association with an executive director, William A. Adler of Marshfield. The association represents twelve hundred fishermen and is concerned with conservation, boating and seafood safety, and development. William Adler says, "Lobstermen are farmers of the sea. They always return to the sea the seeds for tomorrow."[52]

Perhaps the fishing industry is the most continuous thread in the area's history. Fishing provided essential food for the early settlers, shore dinners for the age of the grand hotels, and still is a livelihood for some residents.

In the winter when all else is quiet along the old Spectacle Islands at Brant Rock and Ocean Bluff, it is still possible to stand on the beach and be aware only of the sound of the waves, the crying of the gulls, the wind through the beach grasses, and perhaps the sound of a lobster boat "comin' in to the Brant" with its daily catch. The tide still rolls in and out twice a day. Winter storms still ravage the shore line and the summer beach still pulses with the heat. These things remain, untouched by the passage of time or by the activities of humankind.

Taylor Marina

The Taylor Marina property came into the Taylor family when my great-grandfather Captain William Henry Taylor purchased most of what is now Taylor Marine toward the end of the last century. Great-grandfather Taylor was a sailing master during and after the clipper-ship era. He sailed as first mate on the famous clipper *Red Jacket*, which still holds the record sailing time (for conventional sailing ships) from New York to England. At one point he was able to acquire his own ship, but he lost her in the Baltic Sea on her maiden voyage. He nevertheless was able to acquire and retain a considerable estate, including the location of Taylor Lumber Company (Ocean Street) as well as Taylor Marine.

My grandfather [Alton Henry Taylor] ran what was probably a typical old-fashioned Yankee boatyard. Gramp was a talented boat builder, carpenter, mechanic, and "jack of all trades." My remembrances of the place from childhood include visions of the salty fishermen with their old-fashioned boats and skiffs, as well as the scattering of mouldering hulks, nautical "junk," flotsam and jetsam lying abandoned around the property — and Gramp's laying hens, ducks, and innumerable cats.

My dad, A. Cecil Taylor, was a successful, hard-working lobsterman and a decent man by any standard. One cross he bore admirably for many years entailed keeping the peace between Gramp's second wife and my mother. Because of this situation, I believe, Dad never wanted to expand or develop the boatyard into a modern facility. Mother, on the other hand, often spoke of the potential of the boatyard property and encouraged my brother and me to do something with the place, should we ever have the opportunity.

Gramp's boatyard was the only one in this area for many years, but the relatively small fleet of fishing vessels and pleasure craft was not a great source of income in his day. He had a gasoline tank and pump installed around 1930. In my youth the fishermen routinely left their five-gallon gas cans at the pump every afternoon, and Gramp would fill them for pickup the next morning. The cans were left unattended overnight and, as far as I know, no cans were ever stolen. This was at a time when Marshfield had only one or two full-time policemen.

As a reflection of my grandfather's independent attitude and the tight money situation in the 1930s, I recall one fisherman asking how much he owed on a repair job. Gramp replied, "I'll take two dollars if you have it, otherwise forget it!" On other occasions he appeared to take more pleasure from "telling off" someone he perceived as a "stuffed shirt" than in making money. Despite his occasional gruffness he was kind to me and helpful in keeping my old lobsterboat running.

Lobsters could usually be sold for a half-way decent price in the 1930s, but fish and clams were a different story. I sometimes tried to peddle a few fish or a bucket of clams to pay for the matinee at the Brant Rock Theatre or for candy bars.

The fishermen, with few exceptions, maintained their skiffs and bait barrels on Gramp's beach during the fishing season. A common sight (and excuse for salty language) was that of dragging skiffs to the water at low tide. The town pier has eliminated this problem, although the salty language remains firmly entrenched to this day.

The bait barrels attendant to the lobster industry were much in evidence years ago. At one time they were kept next to the gasoline pump at the end of Central Street (in front of the present restaurant location). The flies, odor, and general disarray associated with the bait barrels was so objectionable that a baithouse was eventually constructed at the far end of the boatyard. This baithouse was intended to be refrigerated, but the funds were never available for a freezer unit, even though the need was evident. Occasionally the stench was so bad that local summer residents would complain to the Board of Health. Board Chairman Herbert Ryder was a friend of my dad, however, and he routinely gave us ample time to wash things down before making an inspection. Then Herb would comment that the "place looks pretty good to me." Probably the insulated section of the baithouse was intended to be cooled by blocks of ice, but seldom was.

After my father's death in 1967, my brother Captain William M. Taylor and I took steps to organize Taylor Marine Corporation and develop the old boatyard into the present marina facility.

There was considerable heartache and controversy connected with getting the business started. Charlie Brown, harbormaster during this time, expressed some reservations about our plans. I was particularly frustrated by Charlie's foot-dragging and asked him what he would do with our property if he happened to own it. After some delay he responded, "By the Jesus, I believe I'd do the same damned thing that you're doing." Other town officials wrote to the U. S. Army Corps of Engineers (a licensing authority for waterfront developments) to the effect that our plans were not in the public interest. However, our plans were subsequently approved by the federal and state authorities.

We were dismayed at finding development costs exceeded our expectations. Fortunately for us, we found that we had underestimated the market for marina slips, and we have maintained 100 percent occupancy from our first season. Starting with about forty slips in 1968, we expanded the marina to its present size (about 140 slips) within about ten years. During the past ten years we have added a retaining wall, rebuilt the marina buildings, improved the floats and docks, and maintained an effort to improve the appearance of the property. I am pleased with what we have accomplished, and I'm certain my dad and grandfather would be amazed if not pleased if they were to see the many changes.

— John (Chuck) Taylor

Storm of 1978

Waves that pulverized pavement and bounced higher than rooftops pounded Brant Rock homes, roads and landscape during the Blizzard of '78. Not since the Storm of 1898 had the elements unleashed such fury.

Each of the two high tides during the blizzard contributed its own brand of destruction. The evening high tide on 6 February 1978 brought excessive flooding and gale winds, and snow inland had already caused loss of electrical power.

By 10 p.m., bone-chilled residents were being evacuated by means of whatever high-riding vehicles the town could send down: fire engines, dump trucks, front-end loaders, even the cherry picker. Caught unaware by the unpredicted power of the storm, most householders were forced to abandon their own vehicles to the flooding, right where they were parked in their own driveways.

The earthen dike, which for years served as flood protection from the Green Harbor side, breached in two places. Once the water got in, there was no way out. It was met at the low spots by torrents of saltwater from the ocean side. Brant Rock Esplanade became a black basin of treacherous currents and debris that Monday night.

The Tuesday morning high tide did the worst structural damage. Just above the juncture of Ocean and Island streets, giant waves broke on the landside of the concrete seawall, smashing the asphalt pavement into pieces, then hurtling them along between houses to the lowlands, sorting and dropping them by weight as the current subsided.

Green Harbor residents, watching through binoculars, reported waves crashing and bouncing 40 feet up and over the rooftops.

At the bend in the seawall just south of the Rock, the entire front and side walls of an oceanside living room were demolished and swept away, leaving the second-story bedroom hanging unsupported, looking down at an awkward angle to where the beach had been.

The house next to it was pushed, relatively unharmed, off its foundation.

Storm damage near Charlie's Clam Stand in Brant Rock, 1978
Photograph by Craig Murray

The one-room cottage next to it was upended in one piece and left lying on its side, roof facing the street, the plumbing torn from the ground.

The "high road" leading to Blackman's Point was gobbled like a sandwich by the hungry waves — first the embankment, then the white rail fence and sidewalk, soon huge bites out of the road itself.

To the north of the Rock, where the seawall bends again, beach stones, carried in the raging torrent, crashed against shingles and windows, relentlessly pressuring porch posts and roofs until they gave. In one area, near the old Coast Guard station, the weight of water and stones shoved houses four inches off their foundations. One house succumbed entirely.

Wooden storm doors were easy prey. At one oceanfront house, the combined elements tore away the porch and storm door, sent a torrent of stones and water smashing through the frame and windows of a french door to a height of 40 inches, then hurtled them on through the living room and kitchen, exiting through the back door. Pieces of household furniture were later found floating in the Esplanade.

Where the land grade starts upward near Brant Rock Union Chapel, the spacious lawn became a repository for the beach stones, dropped by the swirling currents as their strength subsided. U.S. Army earthmovers cleared away tons of them, a foot deep, later in the week.

The evacuation of residents by fire, police and Department of Public Works crews was described as heroic. The snow never got a chance to land in Brant Rock due to salt spray and howling, gale-force winds, but the deep, treacherous flood currents and debris created life-threatening situations.

A fire truck piled high with evacuees nearly tipped over as it maneuvered through the underwater piles of stones in the Esplanade. A DPW dump truck, loaded with women and children, stalled dead in the deep water; the road grader came up behind the truck, still loaded with its precious cargo, and pushed it all the way to the evacuation center.

A mother and her one-month-old baby came out on the open seat beside the driver of a front-end loader, leaving behind her husband and their 7-year-old. She arrived distraught at the evacuation shelter. The first trip by the front-end loader had carried teenagers "in" the loader, barely above the swirling waters. The driver of the cherry picker returned time and again, until all four of the adults and the infant who had sought refuge from a flooded first story in a second-story apartment were safe.

It was a week until electricity was restored to Brant Rock. The National Guard stood watch through the February nights, guarding empty homes against looting. The manager of Brant Rock Supermarket took even IOUs to keep food and milk on tables. Then, Saturday at 5 p.m. utility crews, haggard from the double shifts, finished stringing new wire and safety-checking meters. People returned to their homes, and the rebuilding began.

— Faith Jean, *Brockton Enterprise*

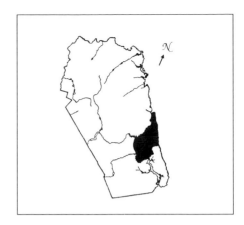

Rexhame Village

REXHAME is literally the King's hamlet, or village. Historian Marcia Thomas called it the "Eden" of Marshfield. Rexhame was early used as a name for the town, interchangeable with Marshfield. Although the first settlers were not kings, there were among them those who might be considered the royalty of the Plymouth Colony, namely, members of the prominent Winslow family.

Two brothers of Plymouth Governor Edward Winslow were each granted one hundred acres of land in the spectacularly beautiful coastal area at the seaward end of Marshfield Neck Road (Route 139 as it runs east from downtown Marshfield to Winslow Street today). It was an area cut off from mainland Marshfield by a tidal creek flowing under what is now Ocean Street near the Pilgrim Trail apartments. There once were great stands of cedars, white oaks, walnuts, and chestnuts at Rexhame Hill and along the low-lying land between the south side of the hill and the Green Harbor River. The height of land at Rexhame Hill commands a breath-taking view east over the sea, south over the Spectacle Islands (Brant Rock and Ocean Bluff), southwest over the far reaches of the Green Harbor River valley, west into the sunset up the South River valley, and north along the stretch of the Rexhame-Humarock barrier beach and the old mouth of the North/South rivers to Scituate.

The settlers of the entire Rexhame area, including the hill and the Neck Road, could be counted on the fingers of one hand. The first was Joseph Beadle, a carpenter and furniture maker of Duxbury. He married Rachel Deane in 1636 and moved to Marshfield, then called Rexhame, between 1640 and 1643, to settle on his 110-acre grant. He served the town in many capacities, among which was that of the builder of many of the first bridges over the rivers and streams of Marshfield. This seems a practical occupation for one who lived surrounded by water. Beadle was one of five prominent Marshfield furniture makers, the four others being his Marshfield Neck neighbors Kenelm and Jonathan Winslow, and Joseph and Anthony Waterman. This coastal area attracted craftsmen who saw the advantage of the coastal trade to market their products and who soon became involved in the growing shipbuilding industry. Furniture attributed to these Marshfield artisans is to be found in a number of prominent American furniture collections today. Beadle died in 1672. He was one of Marshfield's first public benefactors. Having no children of his own, he divided his estate between

In a field that rose gradually toward the old pastures where horse briers grew and thickets of sumach, and where the stunted savins and pitch pines all bent to the west because of the east wind, I saw two figures, one tall and almost swaying over from its slender height; the other that of a girl wearing a broad hat, and who swung a tin pail as she walked.

— Maria Louise Pool[1]

Seventeenth-century joined chest
of red oak and white pine, from
collection of the Historic Winslow
House Association. This chest,
which was handed down in the
Little family, was probably made
by one of the five Marshfield
furniture makers.

his wife and stepdaughter, his servant Jacob Bumpus, the Reverend Samuel Arnold of Marshfield's First Church, and the town's poor.[2]

The exact location of Joseph Beadle's house on Rexhame Hill is not known. His property was sold by his stepdaughter Martha Powell, wife of Ralph Powell, to Isaac Little in 1687, and then to John Kent. He built a house (today's 21 Holmes Road) at the top of the hill in 1709. In 1753 John Kent died, and his heirs sold their shares in his estate to Anthony Thomas. He died in 1781, and in 1787 the farm became the property of his son Major Briggs Thomas, fifth in descent from Green Harbor settler John Thomas. Briggs Thomas acquired additional land, a parcel of which was known for many years as the "fatting pasture." His homestead farm contained 180 acres at the time of his death in 1833.[3]

Briggs Thomas brought a court case against the inhabitants of Marshfield over his rights to pasture his cattle on the Rexhame beach. An 1829 state statute, accepted by the town, stated that "all neat cattle, horses and sheep were prohibited from going at large on Marshfield beach" and that anyone having legal title to the beach would be paid by the town for loss of beach grazing rights. The state statute took commonwealth title to the beach "for protection of navigation and of the beaches." There had been, prior to this date, a "right of commonage on that part of the beach which lies north of Hewitt's Island, for all such neat cattle, horses and sheep as are levant and couchant upon the farm." Briggs Thomas cited a 1685 ordinance which gave common rights of pasturage forever along the seashore to those who lived adjacent to the beach. Thomas had never fenced his land from the beach, but had allowed his cattle to roam at will the entire length of the beach from Hewitt's Island to South River. He argued that for "time out of mind there had been no fence between his farm and the beach," and that therefore he had a right to continue such pasturage. Thomas lost this plea of ownership of the beach, but made a strong argument for his beach pasturage rights.[4]

Waterman Thomas, only son of Briggs Thomas, was born at the farm in 1784 and succeeded to the estate in 1833. He married Sarah Deering

Thomas, granddaughter of Marshfield's famous Revolutionary Tory, Nathaniel Ray Thomas. Their daughter Sarah Ann Thomas married Elijah Ames and bought her brother John's interest in the Rexhame farm. In 1872 Sarah Ames divided the easterly part of the farm into house lots. A *Plan of Lots at Rexham* [sic] *Terrace* showed eighty-seven lots. Ray Thomas Ames, son of Sarah and Elijah, inherited the farm in 1899. In 1916 John Dana Thomas, great-grandson of Waterman Thomas, bought the property from Ray Ames, who continued to hold a mortgage. John Dana formed the Rexhame Farm Trust and sold off eight lots of land. In 1932 when Ray Ames died, his widow, Amy Ewell Ames, inherited the mortgage that her husband held on the property. In 1939 she foreclosed on the mortgage and bought the farm for fifteen thousand dollars. In 1941 she sold it to the Rexhame-Marshfield Trust, which divided and sold the remainder of the old Beadle/Kent land. In recent years the old Kent homestead was owned by Claire and Jaanus Roht. He is the current president of the Marshfield Historical Society. The house is owned now by John and Barrie Gleason.[5]

The so-called Kent place became an extensive farm over the years with cleared and cultivated fields and pastures in every direction. It was the only house on the hill until 1875 when Sarah Thomas Ames (Mrs. Elijah Ames) laid out part of Rexhame in seashore lots. Elijah Ames built the first cottage at so-called Rexhame Terrace from the timber of a vessel wrecked on the beach. It is the last house on the left toward the beach on Ames Avenue. Horace Baker bought a lot on Winslow Street and built a cottage in 1875. Four years later this house was occupied by the Sherrill family, who later bought the old Kenelm Winslow house in 1906.[6]

The next settler at Marshfield Neck was Josiah Winslow, youngest brother of Pilgrim Edward Winslow. Josiah was born at Droitwich, England, in 1605. He arrived on Plymouth's shore aboard the *White Angel* in 1631 with Plymouth Colony financier Isaac Allerton. Winslow had been summoned to serve the colony as an accountant, a position he was never able to fulfill successfully. He was probably in Marshfield by 1637 when he

John Kent house, built in 1709 on the Joseph Beadle grant at Rexhame. By 1768 the property had passed into the hands of the Thomas family who owned the farm until 1941.
Photograph courtesy of Katya Coon

married Margaret Bourne, daughter of Thomas Bourne who settled on Marshfield Neck in that same year. Josiah received a grant of one hundred acres at the foot of Rexhame Hill in 1637 and subsequently was given additional land by his father-in-law, Thomas Bourne. His two brothers-in-law, Robert Waterman and John Bradford, both of whom married daughters of Thomas Bourne, settled nearby. Intermarriage of settler families in Marshfield created intricate networks of kinship ties which persist down to the present time. These ties have been of great economic benefit in establishing and maintaining business connections between the families over the years.[7]

Josiah Winslow built his house and barns on the low-lying level land between the hill and the Green Harbor River (end of Old Colony Lane). He had easy access to the river for transportation, but his home and fields were threatened by excessively high tides. Josiah served the town as a selectman, as a deputy to the Plymouth Colony Court, and as Town Clerk continuously for nearly thirty years, from 1646 to his death in 1674. Among other duties, Josiah helped the Reverend Samuel Arnold move from Yarmouth to the Marshfield church in 1657, driving the new minister's cattle all the way up the dirt cart paths from the Cape.[8]

Josiah and Margaret Bourne Winslow had six children. Their only son, Jonathan Winslow, married Ruth Sargent of Barnstable and had a son, John, born in 1664, who succeeded to the ancestral home. Fearing the high flood tides, however, John soon left and the homestead was bought by William Ford. Five generations of the Ford family continued to live there. In spite of John Winslow's fears, the land has never been seriously flooded. After the dyke was built in 1872, there was no more threat of high water in this upper part of the Green Harbor River valley.[9]

Josiah's brother Kenelm Winslow was the next settler to arrive on the Marshfield Neck. Born in 1599 at Droitwich, England, Kenelm had followed his brothers Edward, Gilbert, and John to New England, arriving in 1630 on the second *Mayflower* (not the original). He was a freeman of Plymouth by 1632 and married Ellen Newton Adams, widow of John Adams, in Plymouth in 1634. In 1641 Kenelm Winslow moved to his 100-acre Marshfield grant (1636) at Rexhame Hill. He built for himself a house (123 Winslow Street) in a prime spot, nestled on the southwest shoulder of the hill. This early house was later enlarged into the elegant home which stands there today. It is a magnificent square colonial building with a huge central chimney, six fireplaces, the traditional center doorway framed with two windows on each side, and five windows across the second story. A third-story garret once housed the family spinning equipment, while the servant or slave quarters were located in the rear part of the second floor. The house faces due south and commands a sweeping view of the Green Harbor River, the ocean off Ocean Bluff and Brant Rock, and the South River valley to the west. Kenelm Winslow created a far-reaching farm here, clearing the fields for tillage and pasturing his cattle on the fertile land and on the grass at the foot of Rexhame Hill. He laid out an extensive English park around his home.[10]

Kenelm and Ellen Adams Winslow had four children, all of whom grew up at the house on Rexhame Hill. Two sons moved away. A daughter, Ellen, married Samuel Baker of Marshfield. Nathaniel, born in 1639, married Faith Miller of Yarmouth and succeeded to the Kenelm Winslow homestead.[11]

Kenelm and his brother Josiah were among the first representatives to the Plymouth Colony Court. They both were elected at a town meeting on

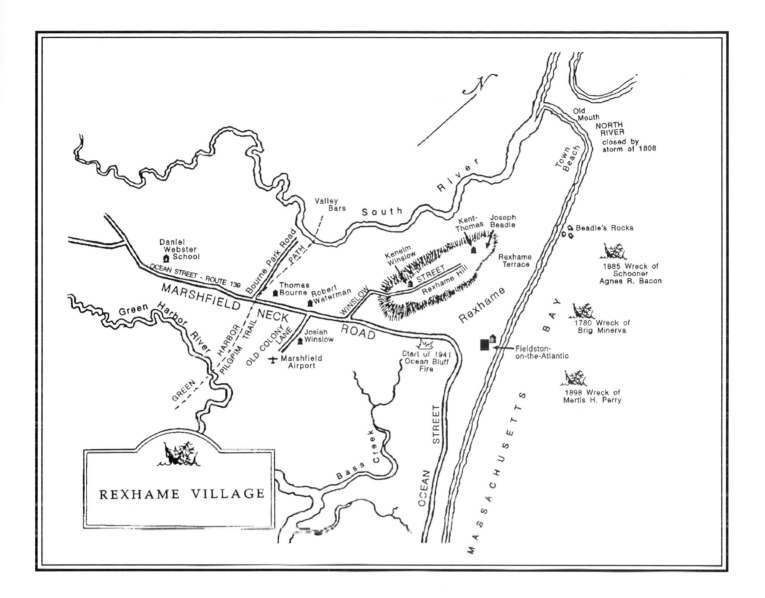

9 October 1643. Kenelm was also a selectman and served on many committees and juries. He was one of the subscribers to a publicly supported school established by the Town of Marshfield in 1645. In spite of his public service, records show that Kenelm was frequently brought to court for various acts of misconduct. In 1640 he was fined for neglecting his position as surveyor of highways, and at another time he was put under bonds and imprisoned for saying of the Marshfield church that "they were all liars." He was, by trade, a furniture maker or "joyner" and examples of his craft exist to this day. Among other items, he made coffins for the Plymouth Colony. He died while visiting in Salem and was buried there in 1672.[12]

The house passed to Kenelm's son Nathaniel Winslow, who married Faith Miller in 1664 and had seven children between 1665 and 1681. One of their five sons, Captain Nathaniel Winslow, born in 1667, shipped timber out of Careswell Creek, Green Harbor, to Boston in the sloop *Seaflower*. Nathaniel followed the family tradition of serving in the Plymouth Colony Court. A son, Kenelm, born in 1675, succeeded to the Rexhame homestead. He married Abigail Waterman, daughter of a neighboring Marshfield Neck

The coast of Marshfield from Rexhame to Brant Rock, showing Beadle's Rocks (upper left).
Prior to the great storm of 26 and 27 November 1898, the old mouth of the North and South rivers was located at the north end of Rexhame beach (off lower left corner).
Photograph by Gerhard O. Walter, 4 July 1982

family. Their son, another Kenelm, inherited the Winslow home and married Abigail Bourne of Barnstable, no relation to the Marshfield Bournes. The house passed, in time, to their son Kenelm, who moved to Kennebec County, Maine, where he established a long line of Winslows still found today in Lincoln and Waldo counties, Maine. Thus five generations of the Kenelm Winslow family lived at the old Rexhame Winslow homestead, just as the descendants of his brother Edward lived at the Green Harbor Winslow estate at Careswell for the same number of generations.[13]

The Kenelm Winslow house passed through in-laws to Captain Asa Waterman in 1783 and thence to Captain Curtis Goodsell in 1864. Sarah Sherrill bought the Winslow place from Edward Ames in 1906 and it passed to Carrie E. Sherrill in 1920 and to her brother, Edgar B. Sherrill. In 1939 Episcopal Bishop Frederic C. Lawrence and his wife, Katherine, bought the house which had been held for four years by the Rockland Trust Company. At that time there were about twenty-three acres of land in the estate. Lawrence sold the place to Richard J. Ossolinski who in turn sold to Stephen Whoriskey in 1988. The old Kenelm Winslow estate is now divided into small house lots with new homes. Streets on the property are appropriately named

Sherrill Road and Eden Road. The original house has been considerably altered, although covenants drawn up by the Marshfield Historical Commission and the planning board have attempted to set standards of historic preservation.[14]

The fourth settler on Marshfield Neck was Thomas Bourne, thought to be one of the Scituate "Men of Kent." He was the "eldest of the Marshfield settlers and a patriarch on its Eden." He and his wife, Elizabeth, built a house (1308 Ocean Street) on the Neck Road about 1637 when both were nearly fifty years old. The house was designated as a garrison where settlers gathered for protection against an Indian attack. Bourne served as a deputy for the town at the Plymouth Colony Court, was a rater or assessor in 1643, and was one of the subscribers to the public school fund in 1645. Two of his daughters married two of his neighbors, Josiah Winslow and Robert Waterman, thus adding to the growing neighborhood family network. Elizabeth Bourne died in 1660 and Thomas in 1664.[15]

Thomas Bourne's son John inherited the homestead. John Bourne's marriage to Alice Bebeech (Bisbee) in 1645 was the second marriage to be recorded in the Marshfield town records. He served as selectman from 1667 to 1683 and died in 1684. His 1686 probate indicates that he had a large farm with six oxen, ten cows, one horse, two calves, twelve pigs, fourteen sheep, two lambs, and one bull. He is listed as having one Indian servant. His estate passed to his son Thomas, and five succeeding generations of Bournes lived at the homestead, including John Bourne, the patriot. He fought in the Revolution at the battle of Bunker Hill and lived to be present at the 1825 dedication of the Bunker Hill monument at which future fellow-townsman Daniel Webster gave the principal speech. By 1838 another Bourne house was built on the north side of Ocean Street.[16]

Fifth and last of the original settlers on Marshfield Neck at Rexhame was Robert Waterman, who married Elizabeth Bourne in 1638 and settled north of Josiah Winslow and east of his father-in-law, Thomas Bourne. His house was located opposite today's Old Colony Lane, but is no longer standing. He served the town as a deputy to the Plymouth Colony Court. He had four sons who, when he died in 1652, were put under the guardianship of his neighbors Josiah Winslow and Anthony Snow. His son Joseph, born in 1639 or 1640, inherited the home and, not unexpectedly, married Sarah

Summer at the beach

The schooner Agnes R. Bacon, *wrecked near Beadle's Rocks on 10 February 1885 in a violent winter storm. All were rescued by breeches buoy. Oxcarts and horse-drawn wagons were used to salvage goods from the ship.*
Photograph courtesy of Harris F. Penniman

Snow, daughter of his guardian. Perhaps the isolation of the Neck Road contributed to the closeness and mutual support of the families there. Marriages between the families of the Neck continued for many generations. The farm remained in the Waterman family for six generations and was sold eventually to Captain Otis Baker, whose widow, Mary, died there in 1900 at the age of 102.[17]

These first comers to Rexhame arrived either by foot up the Green's Harbor Path from Plymouth, or by boat up the Green Harbor River from Plymouth Bay. Taking the Green's Harbor Path north from the Winslow Burying Ground, the travelers would continue over the Green Harbor River valley, crossing the tidal estuary either by small boat or, later, on a corduroy road made of laid logs. The path crosses the Neck just east of the present Gerard farm and follows the course of today's Bourne Park Road. It continued over the South River at a narrow crossing, known as the Valley Bars, passed through what is today Kent Park, following along the foot of Snake Hill to a ferry crossing of the North River near the present Humarock Bridge.[18]

We can picture our Rexhame families — the Beadles, the two Winslows, the Bournes, and Watermans — arriving at Marshfield Neck and dispersing to their homesteads spread widely from the lowlands of the river valley to the top of Rexhame Hill. Soon their farms and their families became interconnected and interdependent. They attended religious meetings and town meetings at the Marshfield First Church and took their grain to be milled at Ford's Mill (present Veterans' Memorial Park site), but kept a sense of their own special community at Rexhame. For over two hundred years there were only the five farms of the five original settler families at Rexhame. The fields were cleared and cultivated as time went by. There was extensive pasturage for sheep and cattle. Watches were set up to protect the livestock on this vulnerable shore area during both the Revolution and the War of 1812. There were barns and outbuildings on all the farms, as well as servants and farm hands. And all about on every side was the blue sparkling water of either the ocean or the rivers. Little wonder that the families stayed on these farms for so many generations and that, even today, the descendants of these original Marshfield Neck settlers are many among us.

This fragile oceanside setting has been the scene of many violent northeast storms over the years, and shipwrecks were not uncommon off the shore. In 1780 the brig *Minerva* was wrecked at Rexhame. In a violent winter storm on 10 February 1885 the 129-foot schooner *Agnes R. Bacon* came ashore near Beadle's Rocks. It was midnight with hurricane-force winds. Captain Stanley at the Fourth Cliff lifesaving station headed down the beach with equipment and men to aid in the rescue, crossing the old mouth of the North/South rivers at Rexhame to reach Beadle's Rocks. A breeches buoy was shot out to the floundering schooner and all were rescued, with Captain Haley the last to leave the wreck. The *Mertis H. Perry*, a schooner owned by Captain Francis H. Perry of Brewster, grounded two hundred yards off Rexhame beach in the great storm of 26 and 27 November 1898. This was the storm that broke through a new mouth for the North/South rivers, closing the old one at Rexhame beach. The *Mertis H. Perry* sank with a cargo of fifteen thousand pounds of fish. Of a crew of

The schooner Mertis H. Perry *grounded two hundred yards off Rexhame beach in the great winter storm of 26 and 27 November 1898. Nine of the crew were saved and five lost in the turbulent waters.*
Photograph courtesy of Harris F. Penniman

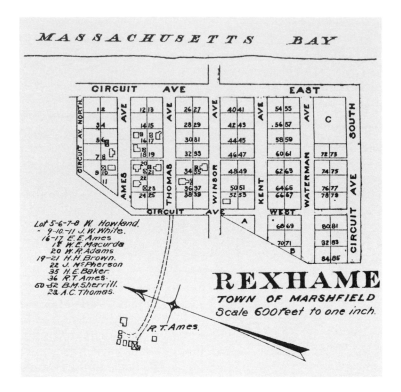

fourteen, nine were saved and five died in the frigid waters. Captain Perry jumped off the ship in a suicide attempt. He was washed ashore and found refuge at the Ames farm. Parts of the ship were washed up on the beach eighty years later in the great blizzard of 6 February 1978.[19]

Houses at Rexhame Terrace began to be built in 1875. Elijah Ames built the first cottage, followed by Horace Baker. In 1880 Dr. Azel Ames built a cottage, and Willard Kent in 1885 built a house that was later moved. Seven more houses were built in the next ten or twelve years. Sarah Ames would not sell a lot to anyone unless she knew and approved of the buyer, so there developed a closely knit, friendly neighborhood with Sarah as the "mother of them all." Sunday evening services were held at various houses, and everyone went to the Ames place to celebrate Thanksgiving. Some people today remember playing as children around the "Sheep Rocks" at the top of the hill near the old Winslow House. There were bonfires on the beach and evening parties at the Rexhame Terrace homes. In all, twenty-three houses were built between 1875 and 1915. There was, at one time, a Rexhame Country Club with the ninth hole where Atlantic Street is today. John Clancy began developing in the area of the old golf club in 1938.[20]

Later, other people came to live at Rexhame Terrace. Among these have been the Coon, Davidson, Hathaway, Hutchinson, Marston, McCurda, Peabody, Smith, and White families. During the summers of the late 1940s, a day camp for the children of Rexhame Terrace was conducted by Cynthia Hagar (Krusell) and Barbara Damon (Prouty).[21]

People living on Rexhame Hill in the 1930s remember the wild blueberries, grapes, and apple trees that grew in the fields. Twin pear trees were all that remained of what was once a large orchard. Still to be seen were the magnificent walnut and chestnut trees described by the first comers to Rexhame in the 1640s. Though motor cars had come, the old

watering trough was still standing at the intersection of Winslow and Ocean streets. Winslow Street was still a dirt road beyond Ford Street.

The arrival of Joseph P. Spang at Rexhame in 1925 brought considerable changes to this special place by the sea with its high dunes and stretches of beautiful, sandy beach. Spang acquired all the land on the southeast shoulder of Rexhame Hill from Winslow Street to the ocean at Fieldston and on the hill as far as Mayflower Lane. At the ocean's edge, he built the famous Fieldston-on-the-Atlantic entertainment complex in 1925. Ball fields and parking lots filled the area from today's BP station to Fieldston. A man-made pond with little bridges and islands of green grass was alive with families of white ducks. Spang had a farmhouse on the hill, barn and chicken houses on Winslow Street, and a summer home at 15 Alden Road. Spang sold his considerable holdings at Rexhame after World War II.

Later, John Clancy operated the Rexicana and the Salty Horizon Restaurant on this property. The Rexicana burned to the ground in 1978.

By the 1930s the Neck Road had acquired two farms, the large Capen farm and the Wildwood Dairy Farm. Frank I. and Annie L. Capen started a number of enterprises along Ocean Street in the late 1920s. They ran a variety store in 1926 and F. Herbert Capen sold milk. Samuel G. and Hattie L. Capen operated the Old Reliable Real Estate Agency at Brant Rock, Ocean Bluff, and Sunrise Beach. In 1930 Annie Capen had a tearoom. The Capen farm extended on both sides of Ocean Street from just east of where Gerard Farm is today (1331 Ocean Street) to Winslow Street. There were fields of strawberries, potatoes, corn, and string beans. The Capen Farm Stand offered "vegetables picked fresh hourly" and "farm-grown fruits." Young people of the time remember picking strawberries for the Capens.[22]

The Wildwood Dairy Farm, run by Albert A. Dennis, was another landmark for Rexhame in the 1930s. It was located where Gerard Farm is today. Dennis delivered milk and dairy products to the doorsteps of the Rexhame community. Later the Gerard family bought the Dennis house and enlarged it. Today Gerard Farm is a popular place to buy holiday turkeys, homemade pies, bread, frozen dinners, and delicatessen items. Open year-round, it has became a source of delicious food for miles around. The farm is now operated by Arnon T. and Constance Gerard who bought it in 1961 from Raymond V. and Clara H. Gerard.

Fieldston-on-the-Atlantic

Fieldston-on-the-Atlantic was built in 1925 by Joseph P. Spang as a large entertainment complex located by the ocean. The Spang property ran from the intersection of Winslow and Ocean streets east along Ocean Street to the ocean, then north as far as Mayflower Lane, west to Winslow Street and back to Ocean Street. Part of the Spang complex consisted of a small farmhouse, a large barn, and three chicken houses located on Winslow Street across from the Kenelm Winslow house. On Rexhame Hill on Mayflower Lane was the summer home of the Spangs. On the oceanfront, they owned summer houses that they rented.

In the summer of 1927 my brother J. Russell Henderson began working for Mr. Spang at Fieldston-on-the-Atlantic. Russell also worked for Mr. Spang in Boston at his Cube Steak Machine Company, Mr. Spang being the inventor of the cube steak machine. He befriended this hard-working boy and guaranteed Russell year-round work, my father six months' work, and two teen-aged sisters and a brother summer work at Fieldston-on-the-Atlantic. In 1932, the family left Hanover and became caretakers of the Spang farm and properites. Fieldston-on-the-Atlantic became a big part of our daily life, and we all loved it.

The Fieldston complex consisted of a large main building by the ocean and the Bavarian Village, built by Leo Bencordo and Russell. The waitresses wore authentic German outfits and served beer in a pitcher for fifty cents. One hundred and twenty 50-gallon barrels of beer were sold each weekend.

Fieldston-on-the-Atlantic was famous for its salt-water swimming pool. A shower sprayed continuously in the center of the shallow area used by children. At the deep end were diving boards. There were two lifeguards. There were locker rooms — fifty cents for a locker room, twenty-five cents returned when the key was given back!

Overlooking the pool was an open bar. A soda fountain was along the side of the building. There was a cashier, either my sister Ethel or Velma. Tickets were purchased from the cashier for everything you wanted to do or to eat.

Behind the soda fountain was a building with eight bowling alleys. Bowling was fifteen cents a string, two for a quarter. My brother Wilfred ("Biff") and other pinboys were paid four cents a string.

Upstairs was a restaurant managed by Mr. Starkweather and catered by the Seiler family, who became famous for their clam chowder. Also upstairs was a beautiful ballroom which had a stage, a fieldstone fireplace, and a balcony overlooking the swimming pool and the Atlantic Ocean. The ceiling of the ballroom was lattice work (built by Russell and my father), and in the center was a spectacular revolving crystal ball whose reflected lights danced around the room. There was dancing six nights a week. Four nights were taxi dancing — ten cents a dance, three for a quarter. All the big bands of the era played at Fieldston-on-the-Atlantic: Tommy Dorsey, Jimmy Dorsey, Harry James, Gene Krupa, Kay Kyser, Benny Goodman, Vaughn Monroe, Duke Ellington, Count Basie, Tony Pastor, Guy Lombardo. The Ink Spots and Mills Brothers performed. Fats Waller set the record with two thousand people in attendance. No one danced that night. Everyone just stood, watched, and listened.

Fieldston-on-the-Atlantic had a magnificent beach. On the corner before the main building was a Howard Johnson stand surrounded by a park that included a man-made waterway with swan boats and two arched bridges crossed the waterway. There was a miniature golf course and baseball fields. Across the street was a boarding house for the summer help managed by Florence Jordan.

Fieldston-on-the-Atlantic was the place to go in the middle twenties, thirties, and early forties. Twenty-five to thirty busloads of people arrived every day of the week for daylong outings.

In 1932 my brother Biff asked Mr. Spang's permission to have the Marshfield High School prom at Fieldston-on-the-Atlantic, which Mr. Spang granted. The proms were held at Fieldston-on-the-Atlantic annually and became one of the social highlights of the year.

Mr. Spang ran Fieldston-on-the-Atlantic from 1925 to 1941. During World War II, the Bavarian Village was closed due to strong anti-German sentiments. In 1942 the Howard Johnson stand was converted into a small cordage factory to aid in the war effort.

In 1945, after the war, Mr. Spang sold all his Marshfield properties. Mr. Rochford bought Fieldston-on-the-Atlantic. Later, it was sold to Mr. Capiferri, then to Mr. Clancy. The Bavarian Village and the Howard Johnson stand were never reopened. Fieldston-on-the-Atlantic's name was changed to the Rexicana.

The excitement of the beautiful complex disappeared. Today, all its building are gone except the houses and barn. It brings sadness to us who remember Fieldston-on-the-Atlantic.

— Joanne Henderson Josselyn

In the 1930s, three hundred years after the settlement at Rexhame, there were the five original farms, an additional Ford house (91 Old Colony Lane today), the twenty-three cottages at Rexhame Terrace, the two Joseph P. Spang places on the shoulder of Rexhame Hill, the Capen farm, the Wildwood Dairy Farm, a few houses on the north side of Ocean Street between Winslow Street and Fieldston, a Howard Johnson stand, and Fieldston-on-the-Atlantic.

The Howard Johnson Garden Restaurant, where once one could buy a complete dinner for fifty cents, was owned by Joseph Spang in 1941. It had replaced an older Dutchland Farm Stand which had been built around 1927. Later, the Beacon Restaurant was to occupy the same site, followed by a miniature golf course and today, by a group of houses on stilts.

In the 1940s Joseph Spang also owned a gas station at Fieldston, later bought by Harold Bourne. At the corner of Old Colony Lane and Ocean Street there was a Drive-In-Theatre in the 1950s, bowling alleys built by Peter Rinaudo in 1964, and later a Chinese restaurant, all no longer there. In 1952 the Town Beach at Rexhame opened, drawing streams of summer traffic along Winslow Street to swim and sunbathe at the new Marshfield public beach. Gone were the cattle on the beach, along with the 1826 concern with beach erosion. A lifeguard program established for protection of Marshfield beaches in 1956 was, however, concerned with safety.

In the 1960s everything changed in Rexhame, as it did all over Marshfield. The Southeast Expressway was extended to the town's border, making Marshfield an easy commute from Boston. The population began to soar as people bought land and built new houses, or winterized their summer places at the beach. Rexhame Hill sprouted new streets and new houses until today, thirty years later, there is almost no open space left. In the midst of all the growth, one house, however, disappeared from Rexhame, the old home of original settler Josiah Winslow (end of Old Colony Lane). The property was owned by Peter Rinaudo at the time. A shed on the property was moved to the grounds of the 1699 Winslow House in 1974 and converted into a blacksmith shop. The Josiah Winslow house was razed in 1975.

Along the edges of commercially zoned Ocean Street, small businesses were opened, modest apartment complexes built, and some house developments started. Bourne Park Road was begun in 1960, Gratto Road in 1966, Marshview Drive in 1967, Woodbine Road in 1968, and Liberty Road in 1971. Houses were soon built along these roads and some are still being erected today.

Leo Gagnon's bakery (1185 Ocean) became a meeting place for the community in 1958. Leo and his wife, Blanche, were warm and welcoming hosts. The business grew from a small doughnut shop to a large enterprise. Today it is owned by Leo's son Robert Gagnon and his wife, Sheila. They took over the operation of the shop in 1968 and today their two sons, Scott and Robert, Jr., work in the family business. Sheila Gagnon was the first woman selectman in the town and was co-chairman, with Dan Welch, of the parade committee for the 350th celebration. The Gagnons have given generously to the community.

The building was considerably enlarged in 1988 to include a liquor and a grocery store. A branch bakery and coffee shop, started in 1974, is located at the corner of Stratton Avenue and Ocean Street. It is a popular place for a downtown morning coffee break, or for purchasing doughnuts, birthday cake, pastries, and candy.

Nessralla's Farm Stand (1190 Ocean) opened in 1977. This farm, along with the Gerard farm, have taken the places of the earlier Capen and Wildwood farms on the Neck Road. Nessralla's 5.4 acres was partially built up with apartments in 1971 by Anthony Auditor. These buildings were removed in 1973 because of a violation of the rules of the zoning board. Nessralla's is now operated by Nacklie and Naja Nessralla who live nearby on Winslow Street.

Marshfield Elks Lodge 2494 acquired a building just east of Gerard Farm in 1973, when this chapter of the fraternal organization was first chartered. The deer may be gone from the Neck Road, but the Elks have come! There are five hundred members today, led by Exulted Ruler John Nolan, Jr. The organization supports scholarships, senior citizen programs, POWs, and the Brockton Veterans' Administration Hospital.

The rapid increase of population in the town brought pressures on the school system which, having abandoned the old district schools in the 1940s and 1950s and centralized the educational system, was now faced with dispersing the schools again to better serve the growing number of elementary children in each area. The Daniel Webster Elementary School opened on 20 December 1965 with Leo Dauwer as principal. The new school accommodated grades one through five. Kindergarten was not included in Marshfield schools until 1973, when it was state mandated.

In the same year, the town purchased the Marshfield Airport from Plymouth Copters for about $30,000. The Marshfield Airport Commission took over the management of this 150-acre municipal airport with three buildings. The airport was originally started in 1948 by Joseph Ford, a former navy pilot. The district was rezoned to accommodate this use. Improvements have been made over the years, including a paved runway, parallel taxiway, perimeter fencing, runway resurfacing, parking ramp, and a nondirectional beacon. At present the airport is leased and operated by Shoreline Aviation, owned by Keith Douglass and Edward Novak, Jr. It is a thriving operation with a multitude of activities. George Harlow, chairman of the Airport Commission, reports that "the flying school has nearly two hundred students. There are approximately seventy aircraft based at the airport, many of which are used in business. The airport offers, in addition to flight training, aircraft maintenance and repair, hangar storage, aircraft rental, charter for point-to-point transportation, and sight-seeing flights."

What would the early foot-travelers along the adjacent course of the Green's Harbor Path have thought of these great winged birds soaring and alighting from this large, cleared fertile field at the very doorstep of their old estates! They would, however, recognize the huge old barn that sits on the airport property and which once belonged to Samuel Franklin Hatch. He stored his salt hay in that barn and kept his horse there during salt-haying season.

Only a few scattered wet lots along Bass Creek meadow at Rexhame have been saved by the Marshfield Conservation Commission. This is a small but valiant attempt to preserve some "common land" in an area once open farmland and common pasturage for cattle.

As the 1832 Briggs Thomas complaint against the Town of Marshfield states:

The beach was a place of common resort for fishermen, fowlers and haymakers coming from all parts of Marshfield and the adjacent towns and other places, who time out of mind had been used to turn out their horses on the beach for depasturing, fishermen one or two days at a time throughout the fishing season, haymakers in the haying season and fowlers at all times of year. . . . Horses were turned out on the beach at Brant Rock and often fed on the whole beach northerly therefrom.[23]

Today, although the beach at Rexhame still knows the gathering of the swallows in September, the howling northeast winds of winter, the returning flocks of flashing shore birds in spring, and the gentle breezes of a summer day, perhaps the only landmark that settler Joseph Beadle would recognize would be the group of rocks just off the beach, appropriately named Beadle's Rocks.

Solitude

Pilgrims at prayer

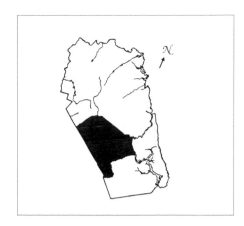

Marshfield Village

Pointed cedars stand
Their green spires reaching
  skyward
Like devout Pilgrims
      — Cynthia Hagar Krusell[1]

Marshfield is the village downtown. At times it has been referred to as South Marshfield. It lies on the plain with its head resting against Zion's Hill, its feet propped against the north bank of the Green Harbor River, one side pressed by Duxbury, the other bounded by Rexhame. The entire area is belted around the waist by the marsh-trimmed ribbon of the South River and guarded by Ward's Hill (Pudding Hill). Its heart is Town Hall, its soul the white-steepled First Congregational Church on the old Training Green, and its main artery, Route 139/Ocean Street.

Today downtown Marshfield draws residents from the scattered Marshfield villages to shop and bank, eat and talk, pay taxes at Town Hall, confer with realtors over land and homes, pick up mail at the central post office, visit the elderly at Tea Rock Gardens and Winslow Village, or simply to contemplate the past in the quiet of Cedar Grove Cemetery under an ancient gnarled cedar tree. In an earlier time, Marshfield people came downtown to grind their grain at the mill, to worship and attend town meetings at the meetinghouse, to gather at the local ordinary for food and sociability, to barter their goods, or to turn in their quota of blackbirds or wolves for a bounty from the selectmen.

A "baker's dozen" of families settled downtown Marshfield, attracted by the flat, fertile farmland, the easy access to waterways, and the potential water power of the South River. They came at different times, sometimes left for brief intervals, and often were listed as being in the town before actually receiving or purchasing land here. After the town was founded in 1640, a board of proprietors, comprised of the already settled freemen, was responsible for granting land within the town. Together these settlers brought all the skills necessary for establishing and maintaining a town in Plymouth Colony. There was the minister, the miller, the blacksmith, the shoemaker, the farmer, the innkeeper, the surveyor of roads, the businessman, the politician, the benefactor, and the land speculator. Marshfield even had a religious dissenter, Arthur Howland, to create controversy.

The principal settlers in downtown Marshfield were Timothy Williamson, Arthur Howland, John Walker, Thomas Chillingworth, John Foster, Samuel Sprague, William Ford, Samuel Baker, Robert Carver, John Dingley, Arthur Lowe, the Reverend Edward Bulkley, and Anthony Snow.

Ancient gnarled cedar tree that stands near the banks of the South River in the Cedar Grove Cemetery. Pen and ink drawing by Anne Philbrick Hall, 1990.

These families, once settled, became a closely knit group, intermarrying again and again from generation to generation. Seventeenth-century marriages in the town were civil ceremonies, and seldom did a marriage occur with a family outside of this inner circle, even with those families in the nearby villages.

Male settlers of the town were the freemen, or voting members of the community, the deputies to the Plymouth Court, the supporters of the public school, raters (forerunners of the assessors), jurors, constables, highway surveyors, moderators, and selectmen. The women were the daughters, wives, and mothers; the homemakers and teachers; spiritual caretakers; spinners, candle dippers, and harvest gatherers. They bore the children, cared for the ill and aged, and laid out the dead. The family provided for the sick, the poor, the aged, and the homeless — all the social services provided by government today. Each family was involved in self-sufficient farming, in addition to whatever other occupations it might pursue.

The centers of life were the church and the mill. The Marshfield Congregational Church, second church to break away from the "mother church" at Plymouth, was originally located at what is now Winslow Cemetery. Tradition states that the second location of the meetinghouse was near the intersection of Parsonage and Webster streets. It is believed that the present site of the church on the Training Green was not used until 1706. The present First Congregational Church building dates to 1838.

The majority of the first-comers to Marshfield were Separatists, being that faction of the English Puritans which favored complete separation from the Anglican Church, rather than purifying and remaining within oppressive mainstream Anglicanism. It was a liberal, tolerant group, which perhaps explains why dissident Quakers were permitted to live in their midst, although under some protest.

The Congregational Church was the only church in Marshfield for the first one hundred years. Many who settled in the town walked to the church.

Some of today's street are named for the families who used them as ways to the meetinghouse, such as Eames Way, Sherman's Path, and Rogers' Way. Current minister of the First Congregational Church is the Reverend Robert H. Jackson.

The other center of activity was the gristmill, first located on the South River at the site of the present Veterans' Memorial Park, created in 1948. Here William Ford and Josiah Winslow built the mill in 1656. Over the years there have been many milling and manufacturing activities at this site. The idea for a park originated with the Servicemen's Auxiliary Association and the park was developed by a group of trustees. Today it is a popular place for weddings and celebrations.

The chairman of the present Board of Trustees of Soldiers' Memorials is John ("Buddy") Nangle, Jr. Buddy has served in this position since 1951. He has also been part-time veterans' agent for thirty-one years and has been active on many town committees over his forty years of public service. Among other civic activities, Buddy founded the Marshfield Community Christmas, a goodwill program that distributes food and gifts to the townspeople.

The settler in the center of present-day downtown Marshfield was Timothy Williamson. He assured himself of a certain immortality when, on 20 May 1663 (or 1665), he conveyed to the town a Common or Training Green for the militia, the ground for the meetinghouse, and land for an animal pound. These pieces of land remain much the same today, though the Training Green is smaller, the pound has disappeared, and the cattle are no more. Williamson's ordinary for "lodging and victualling," for which he was licensed as an innkeeper by the Plymouth Colony Court in 1673, may still exist as a part of the Marshfield Office Supply Company and Marshfield Travel Advisors building, located just west of the church at Ocean and Moraine streets.[2]

Timothy Williamson's home, which stood near the ordinary, is lost to time. Williamson was twenty-six when he came to dwell on the south bank

Water wheel at Veterans' Memorial Park. This has been the site of many milling and manufacturing operations since 1656, when William Ford and Josiah Winslow erected the town's first gristmill.

of the South River in 1642. His grant included the area from the Willow Street Bridge (built in 1646 and first named Otter Bridge) to Snow Road, Tea Rock Hill, the Common or Training Green, and the church site. The town gave Williamson additional land on the north side of the South River in exchange for the parcel he gave for the Common and the church. He was listed as a freeman in 1643. He married Mary Howland, daughter of Arthur Howland, who lived across the river on what is now South River Street. They had eight children. Williamson served on jury duty, was surveyor of highways, and frequently acted as constable. He died on 6 August 1676 while serving the colony in the Indian War, known as King Philip's War. His son Nathan Williamson, who married neighbor Mary Sprague, succeeded to the homestead.[3]

It is interesting to note that Timothy Williamson was appointed keeper of the first town pound, built in 1659. The original pound was an enclosure constructed of wood and made "horse high, bull strong and pig tight." In the long tradition of Marshfield town animal keeper is today's animal-control officer, Norma Bullock Haskins. She has been honored recently by two statewide agencies as the "Animal Control Officer of the Year." With three thousand dogs, an indeterminate number of cats and horses, squirrels, raccoons, opposums, skunks, seals, and whales to tend, Norma has a formidable task. Although there is no town pound at the present time, an animal shelter is planned for Clay Pit Road.

After Timothy Williamson's death, the ordinary was kept by his widow, Mary Howland Williamson, who was appointed innkeeper by the colony court. This was the only acceptable occupation for a woman in this period. In 1679 Mary married Robert Stanford and he was granted the inn license. Part of the present building was erected by Proctor Bourne about 1709.

The old ordinary served as a store and a post office for many years. In 1812 the post office at South Marshfield was the only one in the town. Mail was conveyed just twice a week. Postage was ten cents to Boston, twenty-five cents elsewhere. In 1833 C. M. Harlow was the postmaster at this location, followed by George Martin Baker in 1855. From time to time the post office was located on Main Street at Old Plain Street, where in 1894 the postmaster was Luther P. Hatch (58 Main Street). By 1898, however, the Barstow family was running a general store and a post office in the old

The old ordinary building as it appeared about 1900. The original building has been enlarged and used for many purposes over the years. Today it is occupied by the Marshfield Office Supply Company and Marshfield Travel Advisors.
Photograph courtesy of Lois Hubbard Chandler

ordinary building, still owned by the Baker family. Martin Baker, son of George Martin Baker, remodeled the building, making the first floor into three stores. In 1901 the Barstow store was advertising itself as "Servants to a High Class Summer Trade." Augustus Barstow was succeeded as postmaster by his son Alliston Barstow in 1926, and then by Paul Callahan.[4]

In 1957 the location of the post office was changed. It occupied two different buildings on Snow Road until it was moved to its present site at 111 Snow Road in 1976. Recent postmasters include Peg Last, Frank Sullivan, James Hawley, and at present, Edward Fonseca. The Marshfield Post Office was the focal point of the first event of the town's 350th celebration. A cachet with 350th commemorative cancellation, and featuring Daniel Webster, was issued in honor of the event.

Part of Timothy Williamson's seventeenth-century ordinary was used as Ralph Newdick's hardware store in the early twentieth century, followed by Toabe's Hardware until 1940. In 1948 Oscar and Lillian LaForest of Plymouth bought the property from Edith Sprague, who had acquired it from Martin Baker in 1936. In the 1940s and 1950s the military draft board was located upstairs on the west end of the building. Lillian sold the property to Leonard John and Olga LaForest in 1955. They began operating a business which included the sale of patent medicines and stationery, as well as running a breakfast and lunch counter with a soda fountain. In 1957 when the post office, which had occupied the middle section, was moved, the LaForests took over the entire building and ran a gift shop in addition to their other enterprises. Today the structure is the home of Marshfield Office Supply Company (2000 Ocean Street) and Marshfield Travel Advisors (2008 Ocean Street).

Timothy Williamson's original land holdings in Marshfield were the site of some of the first actions of the American Revolution. At midnight on 19 December 1773 the local patriots, in protest of the British tax on tea and inspired by the Boston Tea Party, broke into the ordinary, then owned by John Bourne, and seized the tea stored there. Dragging it by oxcart to the top of a nearby hill, later called Tea Rock Hill, they set the tea ablaze, thus kindling patriot fervor against the hated Tory residents of the town. The drama unfolded at the church next door, where the Tories drew up a set of Resolves supporting the British colonial government at Boston, only to be

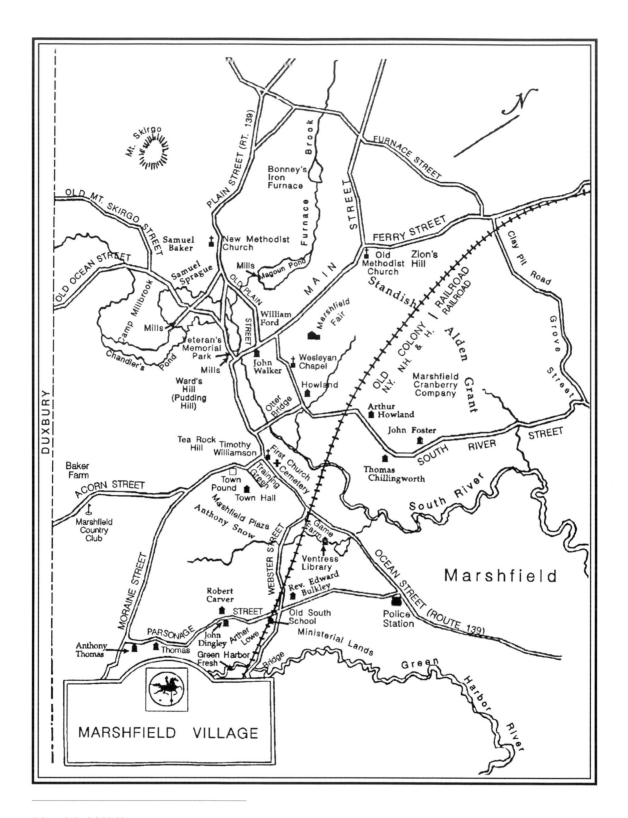

Marshfield Village

Marshfield: 1640-1990

countered by a list of patriot protests against Tory activities. The Marshfield Tories, led by Nathaniel Ray Thomas and Isaac Winslow, called for troops to protect them. General Thomas Gage sent Captain Nesbitt Balfour with 114 men of the King's Own 4th Regiment by boat to defend the king's rights. The British soldiers arrived at South River the afternoon of 23 January 1775 and marched past the old ordinary and the Training Green on their way to take up residence at the Thomas place on Webster Street. Children attending the little school near the Training Green at that time never forgot seeing the British marching in formation past the school. Isaac Thomas, a schoolboy of ten, wrote of the sight of the British in their red coats and "the brightness of their bayonets as they glittered in that midday sun."[5]

The Marshfield chapter of the Daughters of the American Revolution appropriately chose the name Tea Rock for their organization. This chapter is no longer in existence.

A house built in 1909 on Tea Rock Hill later became the home of Rosella S. Ames, the first chairman of the Marshfield Historical Commission, established in 1965. Part of the Tea Rock is included in the foundation of the house (851 Moraine Street). Rosella was active in the town for many years as a Girl Scout leader and devoted member of the First Congregational Church. She led bird walks for the Massachusetts Audubon Society, and her deep love of nature is fondly remembered by many Marshfield people.

The land on which Timothy Williamson originally settled became the location of some of Marshfield's early schools. A publicly funded school was established in 1645, being one of the earliest in America. For a while the small number of schoolchildren met sporadically in the homes of some of the leading residents, usually the ministers, who served as the early schoolmasters. The first reference in the town records of a public school building is one in South Marshfield in 1700. An early location of this school was between Webster Street and the Training Green. The so-called "old" South School (1822 to 1857) stood at the southwest corner of Parsonage and Webster streets. The building was later moved across the street and is now a part of Chandler's Gas Company (760 Webster Street). It is said that the old slate blackboards are still under the inside sheathing of the gas company building.[7]

In 1857 a new building (present Hancock Paint Company) was built on Ocean Street across from Willow Street. It was called the South Grammar School and was the principal grammar school in the town for many years. The faded-yellow stucco building on Hatch Street, which had served as a high school, became the South School in 1940 when a new high school was built (later called the Grace E. Ryder School). The Hatch Street school has been, for some time, referred to as "the Alamo," a name given it by Richard Martinez, long-time history teacher in the Marshfield school system. Since it was often used for overflow school needs, he felt that it might be thought of as the "last stand."[8]

The present South River School opened in 1951. John F. Tobin became principal in 1952. By 1954 this elementary school, the only one in the town, was so crowded that double sessions were held with grades one, two, and three maintaining a regular school day, while grades four, five, and six were split to alternate morning and afternoon sessions. This practice was discontinued in 1955 when an addition was put on the school.

In 1884 Seth Ventress left a legacy to the town "for a public library and other town purposes," and the Ventress building on South River Street was built and dedicated in 1895. It has been variously used as a library, a town hall, a school, and as quarters for the police department which at one time

Surely 'twas a rustic school-room
All unplastered there it stood,
Broad and deep its ancient
    hearthstone
Where they rolled the logs of wood;
Coarse the furniture within it,
Diamond lattices for light,
Cross-legged table for the master
Where he did the copies write.

— Isaac Thomas[6]

First Congregational Church, built in 1838. This is the fourth church building on this site, the first one having been built here in 1706.
Photograph by Dennis H. Oakman

had a lockup in the basement. It serves now as the school administration building. In 1940 the Ventress Memorial Library was moved from the old Ventress building to the old South School building on Ocean Street across from Willow Street, where it remained until it was moved to its present site at Marshfield Plaza East in 1984. A huge effort by the Marshfield community made possible the funding of this new library, remodeled from the former First National Store building. Richard Rapacz was chairman of the Ventress Memorial Library Building Committee. General chairman of the development fund was the late Katherine Wolff and honorable chairman was Donald C. Hagar.

The Hancock Paint Company (2033 Ocean) now occupies the building vacated by the Ventress Memorial Library on Ocean Street. Mention should be made here of the long and devoted service of Josephine Baker as librarian of the Ventress from 1908 to 1946. Later Sylvia Keene, Edna Pratt, Helen Andrews, Anne T. Hickey, and Eleanor Barstow served in this capacity. Present library director is Dennis R. Corcoran. The services of the library have been greatly expanded in the last five years. The circulation for 1989 was 190,650 items. Fifty years ago, at the time of Marshfield's Tercentenary, the circulation was 24,210 books and magazines.

George M. Greenamyer's sculpture, *Webster, the Farmer of Marshfield*, sponsored by the Massachusetts Arts Lottery Council, was dedicated on the new library grounds in 1986. It is made of forged metal and stands seven feet high. George has lived in Marshfield since 1970 and has been an art professor at the Massachusetts College of Art. He is known nationally and internationally for his steel sculptures.

The seat of Marshfield government has come home to dwell across the Training Green from the First Congregational Church where many of the town meetings were held until 1838. From 1838 to 1895 town affairs and town meetings were conducted in a town hall which stood on the east side of Route 3A/Main Street, just north of today's Carolina Hill Respite Center (728 Main Street, at one time the town home for indigent people). From 1895 to 1971 the Seth Ventress building on South River Street served as the town hall. In 1971 town offices were moved into the "new" town hall, located on 2.5 acres of land given by Thomas E. Curtis. Town business has become vastly more complicated than in the days of Timothy Williamson when the biggest decisions were where to lay out roads, how to care for the poor, where to impound the cattle, what bounty to set on crows and wolves, what people

Marshfield Town Hall, built in 1971, overlooks the old Training Green.

Town Hall weathervane depicting Peregrine White astride his black horse. The weathervane was designed by Anne Philbrick Hall in 1971.

Pen and ink drawing by Anne Philbrick Hall, 1990

might be allowed to live in the town, who should tend a ferry, and who would serve the town as representative to the court at Plymouth.

Timothy Williamson's land is still central to the activities of Marshfield. We are indebted to this early Marshfield benefactor, who saw the necessity for an open space in the middle of downtown and a place to set the church. Arthur Howland, who came to dwell across the South River from Timothy Williamson, was of a different character. He was a Quaker and defied the church and the townspeople of Marshfield for many years. He and his son Arthur Howland, Jr., refused to attend either religious or town meetings and rebelled against the authorities. Ironically, Quaker Arthur Howland's daughter Mary married Timothy Williamson, staunch supporter and benefactor of Marshfield's First Congregational Church.

Arthur Howland, Sr., brother of John Howland who came on the *Mayflower*, arrived in Duxbury in 1640, married the widow Margaret Read and was listed as a freeman of Marshfield in 1641/42. He was not deeded land in Marshfield, however, until 1647. He acquired one-half of a 300-acre parcel of land granted to Pilgrims Myles Standish and John Alden in 1638 and conveyed to Edmund Freeman in 1645, then to Arthur Howland, Sr., in 1647. The first place that Arthur Howland, Sr., lived on his acreage was on the north side of South River Street near today's Marshfield Cranberry Company. The house at 295 South River Street is on the site of the old Howland place. This area was on the edge of the dividing line between Arthur Howland's land and that of his neighbor Thomas Chillingworth. Chillingworth acquired the other half of the Standish-Alden grant from Edmund Freeman in 1648.[9]

Arthur Howland ran into trouble immediately with the church authorities, who in 1651 admonished him for refusing to attend church and who continued, unsuccessfully, to try to stop the Quaker meetings that Howland was conducting in his home. They threatened to take his cattle away. He was put on trial at John Alden's house in Duxbury, fined, arrested, and released "because his estate would not bear further fines, and he was too old and infirm to be whipped." He died in 1675 and willed his property to his son Arthur Howland, Jr., who continued his Quaker defiance of authority. Arthur, Jr., courted Elizabeth Prence, daughter of Plymouth Governor Thomas Prence. A Plymouth Colony Court order tried to prevent this marriage between a dissident Quaker and the Plymouth governor's daughter, but to no avail. Arthur and Elizabeth were married in 1668. They continued to be harassed by the Marshfield church, which excommunicated them from the community, took their possessions, invoked the Devil against them, and finally put them briefly in jail on 4 April 1684. Following their release, they returned to Marshfield and apparently were left alone by the church authorities thereafter.[10]

A Howland house, probably built in the mid-seventeenth century, still stands today at 127 South River Street. Perhaps Arthur Howland, Jr., and Elizabeth built and lived in this house. It was located conveniently just off the path to Scituate, which ran over the Willow Street bridge and continued along the course of South River Street to the ferry crossing of the North River at White's Ferry. Another early northerly route ran through the north part of Howland's property at Ferry Street. The house remained in the Howland family until 1736 when John and William Howland sold the property to Gershom Thomas, grandson of John Thomas, Green Harbor settler and protégé of Edward Winslow.[11]

The Thomas family continued to live in the Howland house for 183 years. They farmed the land on the north bank of the South River around their home and where the Marshfield fairgrounds are today. Zenas Thomas, son of Gershom, was a founder of the First Baptist Church at Standish (Route 139/Plain at School Street). His granddaughter Maryan Thomas inherited the family home from her father, Isaac Thomas, in 1859. She was unmarried and living on the farm at the time. Her illegitimate son Lucius Thomas, born in 1837, became heir to the place at Maryan's death in 1895. When Lucius Thomas, tackmaker, died unmarried in 1911, he left the home to Lydia Turner Chandler. She, in turn, sold it to Sarah L. Sherrill in 1919 and it remained in the Sherrill family until 1946. Recent owners were William and Maureen Ruff, who ran a ballet school there in the 1970s and early 1980s. Today the house is owned by Brock and Pauline Reeve.[12]

At one time a cobbler's shop stood across the street from the old Howland house. Thomas Baker and his son Joshua made fine quality boots and shoes. Joshua started in the business in 1857 at age eleven and was still working as a cobbler eighty-six years later at the time of his death in 1932.

Arthur Howland deeded a house and land in May 1663 to John Walker, his stepson-in-law. This old home site lies between Route 3A/Main Street and the South River School. The Walkers are one of the thirteen settler families of downtown Marshfield. They were Quakers, like the Howlands, and lived in the homestead for many generations, marrying into neighboring families. It was Asa Walker of the sixth generation who sold the land to Luther P. Hatch in 1879.[13]

The area at the intersection of Main and Old Plain streets was the center of commercial Marshfield around the turn of the century. Luther Hatch built the large mansard-roof store (52 Main Street) about 1879. This was at first called the Marshfield Company Store, run by Johnnie Merrill. Josephine Strange Ellis wrote of the Marshfield Company Store, "It was kind of a social event, where you met your friends either at the grocery counter lining one side of the store, or the dry goods counter." Later an Atlantic and Pacific (A & P) grocery store occupied this building in the 1930s and 1940s. It was first run by Ralph Houghton, then by his sons Irvin and Francis Houghton. Reed's Ark, a treasure chest of antiques, books, and

The Marshfield Company Store as it appeared about 1910. This general store was built about 1879 by Luther Hatch. The building has been restored as a store and office building.
Photograph courtesy of Marshfield Historical Society

collectibles, was located here from 1952 to 1977. The building is now used for offices and stores.[14]

In addition to Luther Hatch's store, there was Henry Croceley's store across the street, Franklin W. Hatch's livery stable at the corner of Main and South River streets, and a hotel run by David Brown and later by Lizzie Flavell whose husband, John H. Flavell, ran the "Boston Express" service. The hotel, known as Flavell's Hotel, was operated in the house (58 Main Street) which from 1972 to 1988 was the home of the *Marshfield Mariner*. It is interesting to note that the "free voice of the press" came to dwell on the land where the town authorities had tried in vain to repress the voice of Quaker Arthur Howland some three hundred years before. The *Marshfield Mariner* moved its location to Enterprise Drive in 1988.[15]

There was David Brown's blacksmith shop (29 Main Street) on the west side of Main Street near the site of what in more recent years has been Hubbard's Cupboard. Dunham's sawmill, owned by the Flavells in this period, stood on the South River at the site of the first gristmill (Veterans' Memorial Park), and a wheelwright shop owned by Charles Tilden Hatch was located on the banks of the river. It was Charles Tilden Hatch who in 1855 purchased the Concord coach now owned by the town and ran the coach route to Hingham for many years.[16]

Lizzie Flavell was very active in Marshfield from about 1900 until her death in 1917. She was born in 1860, the daughter of Charles and Sarah Williamson and direct descendant of our Timothy Williamson. She married John H. Flavell in 1882 and had three children, one of whom, Marion L., married Lloyd Frisbee. The family still lives in the neighborhood. Lizzie Flavell served on the school committee from 1902 to 1917 and was a trustee of the Ventress Library. At the time of her death she owned many properties, including those at 52 and 58 Main Street. Lloyd Frisbee and his son Richard continued in the family transportation business for fifty-three years, running school buses until 1978.[17]

The first Marshfield telephone office was upstairs in the Luther Hatch/Reed's Ark Building (52 Main Street) in 1910. The chief operator was Jessie Sinnott. About ten years later the telephone office moved to a building at 165 Main Street at what is now the north entrance of the Grace E. Ryder Senior Center. Operators in these early years included Doris Boylston, Ethel Simmons, Grace Held, Gladys Langille, Rachel Damon, Thelma Boylston, and Ina Atwood. Nighttime operators were Bart Pinkham, Charles Sinnott, and Frank Mallory. In 1957 the dial system came to Marshfield and at about this time, the present telephone company building was erected on Main Street. Many residents still remember the kindly telephone voice of operator Doris Boylston, granddaughter of Charles Tilden Hatch, the Concord coach owner. Her cheery voice and knowledge of Marshfield people were a delight. Doris would tell you where a fire was located, whether school was to be held, where your grandmother was to be found, or when someone might be expected home. She could even engineer a three-way telephone conference with your friends.

Today we find in this area Hubbard's Cupboard, owned from 1952 to 1959 by Glenn and Evelyn Hubbard, then by Alfred Khoury, then Paul Doyle, and now Mark Shanahan; the South River Motel, built in 1978; an apartment house, which replaced an earlier bakery and a number of restaurants; the Eagle's Nest bridal shop and antique shop, owned by Hilde Lindsay, at 40 Main Street; the Switterbee Shop, run by Lyn Vaisey; and the Lord Randall Bookshop with Gail Wills, proprietor. The bookshop, which deals in used and rare books and prints, is located in the barn end of a house

that was owned by George Herbert Chandler. He ran a funeral parlor in the house from 1885 to 1915. Across the street is the Bagnell Auto Supply, located where the Keene brothers, the Sinnotts, and Lincoln Davis had a series of garages. Another landmark garage for many years was a Chevrolet Agency, later a service station run by Bernie Ayre, at the corner of Ocean and Main streets, now the Texaco station.

On the north end of the Arthur Howland land stands a high hill, early called Tolman's Hill, but renamed Zion's Hill after a Methodist Church was built there in 1825. Located at Ferry Street at the intersection of the loop of Old Main Street, this church was founded by forty-one people, including the Tolman, Williamson, and Chandler families. A second building was erected in 1857 and razed on 18 January 1938. The last services held at the Zion's Hill Methodist Church were in 1917, when there began to be a shortage of ministers during World War I. A parsonage built for the Methodist minister still stands at the end of Hummy Lane.

An organizational meeting was held in 1965 to reactivate the Methodist Society. The members purchased the old Naham Packard house, built in 1824 at the corner of Cross and Plain streets, and held services there until the present United Methodist Church was built at 185 Plain Street about two years later. Land for the present building was given by Josephine Strange Ellis, whose parents bought the Packard house and property in the

The old center of commercial Marshfield, about 1900. To the left is the old mill building where Veterans' Memorial Park is today. Next to the mill building stands David Brown's blacksmith shop. The windmill in the center was used to pump water from the South River.

Looking south from Zion's Hill near the intersection of Ferry and Old Main streets, about 1890. In the distance can be seen Pudding Hill.

early 1900s. The Methodist Church Hall was dedicated to the memory of Josephine's husband, Benjamin W. Ellis. Present pastor of the Methodist Church is the Reverend Birchfield Aymer.

An article in a New England Methodist Historical Society publication tells that "in 1823, in Marshfield, arrived thirteen packet sloops, [and] two schooners, to swell the already burgeoning attendance [at the camp meeting] to ten thousand. It took twenty-five tents to house the crowd and forty-seven ministers from six denominations" to hold their religious services. This meeting, which probably took place in so-called Ray's Woods between Webster and Careswell streets, predated the famous Methodist camp meetings at Oak Bluffs, Martha's Vineyard.[18]

At the southeast corner of Main and Furnace streets stands the Kingdom Hall of Jehovah's Witnesses (255 Furnace). This building was started in 1976 and finished by the congregation in 1977. The purpose of the Kingdom Hall is for the worship of Jehovah and the study of the Bible. It is the focal point where the church members meet before dispersing to carry the Bible message to the community.

The Daniel Webster Masonic Lodge was built in 1973 (412 Furnace). Rexhame Chapter 103, Order of the Eastern Star, is related to the Masonic fraternity but is not a part of that organization. Members must be related to a Master Mason. Eastern Star undertakes a variety of benevolences and contributes to several world-wide charities. Rexhame Chapter was founded in 1907 and held early meetings in Ventress Hall. After 1954 members met in the GAR Hall, Marshfield Hills. Since 1974 Eastern Star has met at the new Daniel Webster Masonic Lodge building. Present officers are Danine and Seymour Hall, and Sheryl and Richard Taylor.

In 1927 Main Street/Route 3A was rebuilt and widened. The Marshfield Inn, at the intersection of Ferry and Main streets, was built in the 1930s by George Tradd and Lena Payne. The restaurant has changed proprietors many times. In the 1960s it was called the Pilgrim Trail Coach. In recent

years Joseph and Helen Berrini operated the Casa Berrini. Later the restaurant became the Faregrounds, owned by William Last, and is now called the Common Man.

The largest parcel of Howland's land is today the Marshfield fairgrounds. The Marshfield Fair was established in 1862 by the South Marshfield Farmers' Club under President John T. Dingley. Later it was called the Fairgrounds Association, then incorporated as the Marshfield Agricultural and Horticultural Society in 1867. The inspiration for a competitive agricultural fair came originally from Daniel Webster, who encouraged the local farmers to turn out high-quality produce and cattle. Land for the fairgrounds was purchased in that same year from the Wesleyan Meeting House. The first president was George Martin Baker. In the early years cattle shows, collations, and speeches were held on the Marshfield Training Green. Porter Wright, who was still overseer of the Webster Farm some fifteen years after Webster's death, exhibited livestock.

The exhibition hall was built by John Baker in 1872. Damaged by the storm of 1898, it was replaced by the present hall. When the Duxbury and Cohasset Railroad was extended to Marshfield in 1870, the tracks ran along the east side of the fairgrounds and through the old Arthur Howland land. There was a special stop made during the fair week at the fairgrounds. The

Grandstand at the Marshfield Fair
Acrylic on paper by Carolyn Harvey, 1988
Courtesy of David Fehr

AUTO
Racing
MARSHFIELD
FAIR
SAT. AUG. 28, 1926
The Biggest and Best
Event Ever Put On
$1,000 FOR THE WINNERS
FORD TOURING CAR OR ROADSTER CONTEST
Get Your Entry Blank Early

grandstand was erected in 1900. The famous financier Thomas Lawson, who was fair president from 1905 to 1910, designed the half-mile race track.

The Marshfield Fair is today one of the only remaining agricultural fairs in Massachusetts. Livestock and poultry are exhibited and judged. The 4H Club participates with entries and competition. An organization which supports the efforts of the fair is the Webster Grange, organized in 1891. Open to all family members over the age of fourteen, its purpose is to promote farming practices and support the state agricultural committee. The Women's Board of the Marshfield Fair organizes exhibits and judges handiwork, home furnishings, arts and crafts, home economics, canned goods, flowers, fruits, and vegetables. Pari-mutuel horse racing and amusement rides are popular features today.

Presidents of the Marshfield Fair since the 1940 Tercentenary period have included Ernest Sparrell, Charles Langille, Frank L. Sinnott, Edward Dwyer, Eben Briggs, Frank Melville Sinnott, and Russell Chandler, who has held the office since 1981. One of Chandler's first associations with the fair was in the late 1930s when he drove his white sound truck, with its loud-speaker, around the town and the fairgrounds to announce events.

In 1858 a Wesleyan Chapel stood on a part of what is today the Marshfield fairgrounds at the edge of South River Street across from the present Central Fire Station (old Station No. 3). In the 1930s and 1940s an A. R. Parker's Ice Cream Stand was located on the corner of South River and Main streets. Later it was owned by Fred ("Hash") and Kay Studley and called Studley's Restaurant. For a while it was operated by the MacDonald family. Today the Marshfield Agricultural and Horticultural Society has an office on this property.

Of all the buildings and activities that have come to be on the Howland land, perhaps the schools would interest our Quaker settler the most. First there came the Seth Ventress building in 1895, soon to provide space for the town's high school as well as the town's first library. It is hard to imagine that these two institutions which we take for granted today are barely one hundred years old. In 1923 came the first shuffle of schools and libraries. The high school moved to a new building, "the Alamo," behind the Seth Ventress building on Hatch Street. In 1940 everything moved: the high school to a new building (later called the Grace E. Ryder School) on New Street at Main Street, the library to the old South School at Willow and Ocean streets, and the South School to the Alamo. The grammar school children picked up their books and belongings and marched across the old Willow Street bridge to their new quarters at the Alamo on Hatch Street. The present South River School was built in 1950, and the Alamo continued to be used for overflow students. The old Seth Ventress building, which was used, among other purposes, as town hall from 1895, became the school administration building in 1971. The Grace E. Ryder School was named and opened as an elementary school in 1968. Discontinued as a school in 1981, it has been converted to housing for the elderly, some of whom will be familiar with the building from their high school days.

The Central Fire Station on South River Street was constructed in 1957. Long-time chief of the department was Morton Leonard. The little old Station No. 3 can still be seen behind the 1957 station. Fire Chief Frederick P. Gibson retired in 1990. The present chief is Roy McNamee, who has been a member of the department for almost twenty years.

Another one of the baker's dozen of Marshfield settlers was Thomas Chillingworth, who came as a shoemaker to Marshfield about 1645. He purchased 150 acres of land in 1648. This land was the other half of the

Standish-Alden grant that Edmund Freeman sold to Arthur Howland in 1647. This parcel extended northwest as far as Zion's Hill, and northeast near the Peregrine White place on South River Street. The land that Chillingworth bought was to be paid for in "money, corn and cattle" within three years. The large square colonial house at 380 South River Street, across the street from the cranberry bogs, stands on the site of the original Chillingworth house.[19]

The cranberry bogs, which represent one of Marshfield's continuing industries, have been there since about 1903 when Charles H. Rand started the bogs. In 1913 George Herbert Chandler founded the Marshfield Cranberry Company. He was a many-talented man who was not only a cranberry culturist and the inventor of a special cranberry scoop (1931), but also an undertaker. In the 1940s when Russell Chandler, grandson of George Herbert, ran the bogs, the berries were taken to be screened in the basement of the agricultural building at the fairgrounds.

Presently the bogs are being reclaimed by George Chandler's great-grandson Carleton Chandler and his wife, Barbara Henderson Chandler, who live at 371 South River Street. Their twenty-eight acres of cranberry bogs produce three varieties of cranberries: Early Black, Howes, and Stevens. These varieties produce a larger berry so production is double and triple that of older cranberry varieties. These cranberries are sold to marketers in Massachusetts.

Thomas Chillingworth was in Lynn in 1637 and came to Marshfield by way of Sandwich, as did Daniel Webster nearly two hundred years later. Chillingworth lived in Marshfield only seven years, during which time he served as deputy to the General Court at Plymouth and was one of the subscribers to the public school in 1645. He was "a prominent freeman and large landowner, but physically infirm." He died in 1652. His widow, Joane, married Thomas Doggett, the North River ferryman, as her second husband

Marshfield Fire Department

Until 1867 firefighting was the responsibility of every citizen. In 1867 a loosely organized fire department was established. After the railroad came to Marshfield, the railroad company reimbursed the town for fires ignited by sparks from passing trains.

In 1912 three companies — Hook and Ladder Company No. 1 (Brant Rock), No. 2 (Marshfield Hills), and No. 3 (Marshfield) — were organized under a Board of Engineers. Each company had twenty-five call firefighters. The Board of Engineers consisted of a chief engineer and a captain and a fireman from each company.

The first fire chief was Charles W. Bartlett, followed by Morton Leonard, Frank Simmons, Darrell Smith, Edgar Simmons, Louis Cipullo, and Frederick P. Gibson.

In 1926 the first motorized chemical truck was purchased. In 1929 the town established a water department, making water available for firefighting. In 1934 a fire net was purchased, and in 1936 the first combination pumper, hose wagon, and ladder truck was acquired.

The 1941 Ocean Bluff fire was the largest conflagration in the town's history. As a result zoning laws regarding density of settlement and building codes were changed. Between 1949 and 1956, many administrative, firefighter safety, and communication improvements were made. The fire department began keeping logs, and 357 hydrants were installed. By 1963 the town had twelve pieces of apparatus, and by 1967 there were eleven permanent and sixty call firemen. By 1972 all three stations were

manned twenty-four hours a day, seven days per week. A Fire Alarm Console to receive alarms was installed in 1975 and a "Jaws of Life" purchased in 1978.

In 1990 the Marshfield Fire Department reduced its staff, due to budget restrictions. There are now eight to ten firefighters covering the town's 28-square-mile area and six volunteer call firemen.

The stations in Brant Rock and Marshfield Hills each have one pumper in full-time service. Station No. 3 in Marshfield has one pumper, one aerial ladder, a Fire Alarm Console, and the townwide fire alarm system.

The Marshfield Fire Department is reportedly the third busiest fire department in Plymouth County. There were nearly two thousand emergency calls in 1989.

and died over thirty years later in 1684. Chillingworth's property was sold by his heirs in 1666 to his two sons-in-law, John Foster, a blacksmith of Plymouth who married Mary Chillingworth, and Samuel Sprague who arrived from Hingham in 1665 and married Sarah Chillingworth. Foster and Sprague were also of the baker's dozen of Marshfield downtown settlers.[20]

Deacon John Foster served the town as a selectman and was on the jury that laid out the highways in 1692. Samuel Sprague came to Marshfield with Anthony Eames in 1650. He served as secretary of Plymouth Colony from 1686 to 1692. He died in 1710 and his son James Sprague inherited the homestead, which he sold to his brother Nathan Sprague. James Sprague bought part of the Baker property on Mt. Skirgo. The Sprague family has been associated over the years with property in the Old Plain Street, Plain Street, and Old Ocean Street areas around the network of streams and brooks that flow into the South River.[21]

William Ford (1604-1676) arrived in Marshfield sometime before 1652, when he was listed as a freeman, a surveyor, and a constable. It was he who surveyed the Training Green which Timothy Williamson gave to the town in 1663. Ford first appeared in Duxbury in 1643 and was a miller there before coming to Marshfield.[22]

The William Ford grant of land lay along the north bank of the South River, west of Howland's land. It included some of what is today Old Plain Street, Parson's Pond, the valley of Furnace Brook (early called Puddle Wharf Brook), perhaps as far north as Furnace Street and west on Plain Street, possibly as far as Forest Street. It was a place of rivers and brooks, of rapids and waterfalls. The water system of the South River and its major tributary, the Furnace Brook, provided the power for what became a multitude of mills and manufacturing operations. In 1653 permission was given by the Town of Marshfield to William Ford of Duxbury and Josiah Winslow of Marshfield to build a "sufficient mill to grind the corn for the town" near the house of Arthur Howland. Fifty acres on the north side of the South River were granted to Ford and Winslow for this purpose. The first gristmill was built in 1654 at the site of the present Veterans' Memorial Park. The next year Ford was granted an additional two acres next to the mill for a dwelling house. In 1657 Josiah Winslow sold his one-half interest in the mill to Ford.[23]

William Ford and his wife, Hannah, had four children: William, who married Sarah Dingley; Michael, who married Abigail Snow; Margaret, who married Zachariah Soule; and Millicent, who married John Carver. All these were downtown Marshfield families except Zachariah Soule, probably of North Duxbury. Thus the kinship network of Marshfield village families was woven.[24]

The Ford family continued to run gristmills and sawmills at the original South River site. In 1810 the Marshfield Cotton and Woolen Manufacturing Company acquired land and began manufacturing at the Ford mill site and also at Baker's Pond (Chandler's Pond today on Pudding Hill Lane). The company founders and proprietors were from several surrounding towns and included Azel Ames, Samuel Baker, and Chandler Sampson of Marshfield, and Ezra Weston, the famous shipbuilder of Duxbury. Jonathan Stetson of Bridgewater was appointed agent for the company which continued to operate until the late 1830s. By 1851 the factory was owned by another cotton manufacturing company, known as the Duxbury Manufacturing Company.[25]

The old mill building that stood where Veterans' Memorial Park is today. Variously used as Dunham's sawmill, a paint shop, a storehouse, and in its last years, as Stanley Baker's wet wash, the building was torn down before the park was created in 1948.
Photograph courtesy of Lois Hubbard Chandler

The supply of imported cotton cloth was cut off by President Jefferson's Embargo Act of 1807 and then by the War of 1812. The manufacture of cotton cloth, satinet, and woolen goods involved weaving, spooling, drawing, and cording, all activities done by women employees. Mill employees were paid $1.17 per day in 1810. Factory boarding houses to accommodate the women workers were built at the mill sites. Two of these houses still stand on the north side of Ocean Street near the old Ford mill site (2154 and 2148 Ocean Street). At one time the fields around the mill were spread with cotton sheeting to dry and bleach in the sun. Thomas Foster White took the cotton cloth to Boston and brought back raw cotton in 100-pound bales.[26]

By the late 1850s Henry C. Dunham was operating a sawmill where the cotton factory had been. It was still a sawmill in 1900 and over the next few years was used variously as a boxboard mill, a paint shop, storehouse, and icehouse. By the 1930s Stanley Baker ran a wet wash, or laundry, in the mill. Those who knew the site in the 1940s when the then falling-down mill buildings were there, were pleased when the Veterans' Memorial Park was created in 1948. This is a busy intersection today, made safer by the installation of traffic lights in 1973, thanks to the efforts of Evelyn Cecil who, as a reporter with the *South Shore News*, advocated the need for them over many years.[27]

Marshfield has had its share of inventive geniuses, but perhaps none so well known as Jesse Reed who, in 1807, invented a nail-making machine that revolutionized the building industry. He was living in Kingston at the time, but moved to Marshfield in 1819, when he bought rights in Ford's gristmill and land along the Furnace Brook. He bought the Elisha Ford homestead (42 Old Plain Street), later known as the Squire Ford house, that is presently owned by radio personality Jerry Williams. Squire Ford (John Ford, Jr.), grandson of Elisha Ford, was a land surveyor. He drew the 1838 map of Marshfield as well as other 1830-period maps of surrounding towns. Another descendant of Elisha Ford is Lucy Ford Callahan, daughter of surveyor William Ford. She and her husband, Paul Callahan, live in another old Ford house (310 Furnace Street) near Puddle Wharf Brook.[28]

Jesse Reed built a new house for himself (95 Main Street) in 1839, it being one of the first houses built with machine-made nails. He constructed an elaborate nail-manufacturing complex on the Furnace Brook water system. He erected a factory and a forge, put in a water wheel, and built a canal system. Later the factory burned. Other nail and tack factories sprang up on many of the millponds in Marshfield during this period. Jesse Reed eventually had numerous inventions and thirty patents to his credit.[29]

By 1838 the Bonney family was running an iron furnace, which continued to operate on Furnace Brook for some thirty years. This was an area rich in bog iron deposits that produced a crude type of iron. John Magoun had a boxboard mill on Magoun's Pond on this same water system. Here in this wet area, rich with springs, where once there were nail factories, iron foundries, boxboard mills and sawmills, today we have town wells and pump houses located between Main, Furnace, and Forest streets. Along with other problems created by Marshfield's burgeoning population, these wells that once produced such unusually pure spring water, some of the best to be found anywhere, have become polluted and, from time to time, condemned and closed. In 1986 four town wells were closed because of contamination; two of them were reopened in 1987. A study was undertaken by the water department to find the source of the contamination. Three of the wells are currently closed because of chemical contamination. An aquifer protection bylaw, as passed at the April 1990 Town Meeting, restricts development in areas where groundwater feeds into town wells.[30]

Over the early years of the twentieth century, there was a person who came to dominate and influence the educational, political, and social life of Marshfield in a memorable way. Grace Earle Ryder was born in 1884, daughter of David Brown and Carrie E. Ford. David Brown had a blacksmith shop on Main Street where Hubbard's Cupboard is located today. Grace married Herbert Ryder. The Ryders lived on Sandy Hill Drive and operated a poultry farm known as Sandy Hill Farm. Grace taught in the Marshfield school system from 1917 to 1954. She influenced many generations of schoolchildren, who as adults today remember her strict discipline, her high standards of achievement, her abilities as an athletic coach, her leadership in music activities, and her patriotism. She was proud of all her students

---

Marshfield Council on Aging

Marshfield was one of the first communities in Massachusetts to institute a Council on Aging, as provided by an act of the General Court of Massachusetts in 1956. In 1957 Grace E. Ryder, who was at the forefront in having a council established, was named chairman of the first council, whose members were appointed by the Board of Selectmen. During its early years the Council on Aging occupied a room in the American Legion Building. A place was provided for seniors to meet and socialize and a consignment shop opened where seniors could bring handmade articles to be sold.

From this beginning the Council on Aging expanded its services and activities for the senior population of Marshfield. In 1984 the first Drop-In Center was opened in the newly renovated Ventress Memorial Library, and in 1985 the town voted to establish the full-time position of a director for the Council on Aging. As well as providing a broad spectrum of social activities, the Drop-In Center is the focal point for many service programs in 1990. A hot lunch is served here weekdays, and meals are home-delivered to those needing them. An outreach program provides friendly visitors and telephone contact with homebound and isolated seniors and offers assistance in accessing the services they may need. Daily shuttle-bus service provides transportation for shopping and medical appointments. Additional transportation, provided by volunteers, is available when needed. The Council on Aging also handles the distribution of surplus foods to people of all ages and, in cooperation with the AARP, assists the elderly in preparing tax returns. Counseling relating to problems with medical insurance coverage and benefits, as well as other information, is made available to the approximately twenty-three hundred senior citizens living in Marshfield in 1990.

Today's Council on Aging (nine members, chaired by Barbara Graham) continues to develop policies and programs to assist Marshfield's elder population. These policies and programs are carried out under the direction of Barbara Farnsworth, the first and current director, who works with local, state, and federal agencies to enhance the health and life style of an increasing senior population.

— Barbara Graham, *Chairman*

and truly proud of her "boys" doing duty on the military fronts during World War II, but most of all, she was proud of Marshfield. She was chairman of the Tercentenary celebrations for the town in 1940, served many terms on the board of the Marshfield Fair, was secretary of the First Congregational Church for years, and was a continuing voice in town affairs and active on many town committees until her death in 1967.

One of Grace Ryder's greatest interests during the last part of her life was the Marshfield Council on Aging, which she was largely responsible for establishing and on which she worked for many years with similarly dedicated Rose McGee. The school built in 1940 on Main Street across from the Marshfield fairgrounds was officially named the Grace E. Ryder School in 1967. Its recent conversion into a home for the elderly seems appropriate, considering Grace Ryder's efforts on their behalf. Renovation of the building was, like Tea Rock Gardens, a project of the Marshfield Housing Authority. Renovation was started in 1988, and the Elderly Congregate Housing Complex, now called the Grace E. Ryder Senior Center, was dedicated in January 1990. Rose McGee served on the Marshfield Housing Authority for nineteen years, in addition to her many other community activities. Two days after the new Housing Complex was dedicated, she resigned her seat on the Housing Authority, stating that her major goal had, at last, been achieved.[31]

Housing developments started along Plain Street in the 1960s as elsewhere in the town, due to the population increase caused by the coming of the new Route 3 to our doorstep. Flaggler Drive and Helena Road were built in 1965, Parson's Walk in 1970, and Ladyslipper Lane in 1976. The most recent large-scale housing has been the Mariner Hill complex, built on the east slope of Pudding Hill in 1987-88. This is a multiple-use facility, the first of its kind allowed by the Zoning Board of Appeals under a comprehensive permit.

Along Ocean Street between the lights at Route 3A and the First Congregational Church are a number of businesses. Friendly's Ice Cream Shop arrived in the early 1970s, while Johnson's Drive-In restaurant has been there for a longer time. The Taylor Lumber Company was at first, fittingly, a sawmill in this one-time area of mills. It was located back from the street in the 1940s; the present building is located nearer the road. Other businesses include the Clifton H. Marsh Insurance Company (2036 Ocean Street), established in 1851 by John M. Baker, one of the oldest continuing businesses in town. Fred W. Roberts Insurance Company (2030 Ocean Street) was started about 1963.

With the advent of the automobile came the garages and gas stations along Ocean Street. For some years one of the garages was operated by John Ford, direct descendant of settler William Ford. There was a Ford real-estate business, and the William G. Ford Insurance Agency operated from 1908 to 1973. Many descendants of the Ford family have continued to live on the old Ford grant. In their tradition of remaining on family land, the Fords are typical of Marshfield's stable founding families.

The next one of our baker's dozen of Marshfield founders is Samuel Baker himself. He acquired the land at Mount Skirgo, or Mount Scargoe, as it is referred to in early deeds. It is thought to be an Irish name and used in early deed references. What connection any of the first comers to Marshfield had with a Mount Skirgo, Ireland, has not been discovered, but the name has never been lost to time.

Baker originally received thirty acres from the town on 7 November 1659. He acquired additional land from John Adams and from James Pitney.

Chandler's Pond, Pudding Hill Lane. The Baker family had a gristmill on this pond before 1706. A variety of other milling operations continued to be carried on here until 1936.

Later he sold a 30-acre piece of this land to Resolved White in 1672. Samuel's son Kenelm Baker got sixty additional acres in 1706. Kenelm married Sarah Bradford, daughter of William Bradford, Jr., in 1687. The Baker holdings stretched from Mount Skirgo to Moraine Street, including what is today Old Ocean Street, Pudding Hill Lane, part of Tea Rock Lane, Baker's Lane, and Acorn Street. Baker married Ellen Winslow, daughter of Kenelm Winslow of Rexhame Hill. Baker descendants still live on some of Samuel Baker's original land.[32]

By 1706 the Bakers had a gristmill operating on the South River at Baker's Pond and two gristmills by 1771. In 1810 the Marshfield Cotton and Woolen Manufacturing Company began operating a cotton mill here in a new building on the site of an old gristmill. It was called the Upper Mill, to be distinguished from the Lower Mill at the site where the Veterans' Memorial Park is located today. The company owned a large acreage and several buildings.[33]

There was a factory, a blacksmith shop run by Leavitt Delano at the corner of Old Ocean Street and Pudding Hill Lane, a dye house on Cross Street, a gristmill, a store, and boarding houses. There was even a factory school, located on Old Ocean Street at the foot of Pudding Hill. This short-lived district school closed in 1851. The cotton mill closed in 1835, and by 1847 Elijah Ames ran a woodworking shop which made coffins, barrels, trunks, and boxes. This shop burned in 1857. Later, Gilbert West used the water rights for a grist and sawmill until the 1920s. At one time Simeon Bartlett (Bart) Chandler manufactured lobster pots here. He also made shoe racks, did sawing, planing, carriage building, and blacksmithing. The Chandler mill burned on 29 January 1936.[34]

After the era of the mills at Baker's/Chandler's Pond, the site was used for many years, starting in 1938, by Camp Millbrook, a camp for boys. It was owned and operated by David and Lillian Volk. Some of the buildings from the old Marshfield State Game Farm, which once stood at the site of the present Ventress Memorial Library, were moved for use at Camp Millbrook. In 1970 the camp was bought by Norman Frank. From 1960 to

1985 the camp was used, after the regular camp season ended in August, for a basketball clinic by the Boston Celtics. Such notable coaches and managers as "Red" Auerbach, Bill Russell, K.C. Jones, and Tommy Heinson were instructors at the camp. It is no longer in operation.

This place that once attracted so much milling now seems to attract the world of sports and music, drama and art. Some members of the world-famous Aerosmith Rock Group currently reside in the area. Jay O'Callahan, who lives on Old Mount Skirgo Street, is an internationally known story-teller. He started his unusual career by telling stories to children at the Marshfield YWCA and the Clift Rodgers Library. The National Fine Arts Committee engaged him to perform at the 1980 Winter Olympics. He has appeared on National Public Radio network in the "Spider's Web" and TV's "Mr. Roger's Neighborhood." Jay is today connected with many theatres and colleges across the country and his performances have taken him all over the world. *Time* magazine calls him "a genius among story-tellers."

Anne Philbrick Hall, a member of the Marshfield Historical Commission who lives on Pudding Hill Lane, is a noted animal sculptor. She is perhaps best known for her bronze of an English setter in the small sculpture garden at Brookgreen Gardens, South Carolina, and for her large bronze of a sitting husky dog in the Ell Student Union Building at North-eastern University, Boston.

Today Pudding Hill Lane has a number of houses on it, one being the home of Elizabeth Bradford, direct descendant of Governor William Bradford of the Plymouth Colony. A teacher for many years in the Marshfield school system where she did original work with dyslexic children, Miss Bradford has in recent years become known for her bell-ringing groups. She also has been active in the Marshfield Historical Society. Elizabeth's mother, Edith F. Bradford, bought a 43-acre parcel of land from Augustus B. Seeley in 1920. Seeley's mother was related to Barnum of the Barnum & Bailey Circus, another connection of Pudding Hill Lane with the famous.

The Ellis family cranberry business is located on Samuel Baker's old domain. Cranberry production is one of Marshfield's little recognized industries but continues in many parts of the town. The Ellis cranberry bogs are in the area bordered by Ocean, Cross, and Old Ocean streets. The land was once used for orchards by sea captain David P. Strange. When the Strange family moved to Marshfield from Stoneham in the early part of the century, they loaded their cattle on the train at Stoneham and traveled via Framingham to the railroad station at Marshfield, where they unloaded the cattle. Then animals, children, and parents proceeded by foot up Ocean Street to the family farm at Cross Street. David Strange's daughter Josephine and her husband, Benjamin W. Ellis, built the cranberry bogs about 1938. Four and one-half acres of bogs produced two hundred barrels of cranberries annually in the 1940s and 1950s. Today the bogs are owned by the Ellises' son David and his wife, Lucy, and their daughter Kathlyn. The business is known as the Old Mount Skirgo Cranberry Corporation. The bogs are located behind the Ellis home (a Baker/Sprague house) at 134 Old Ocean Street.

Perhaps the most historically significant farm on the old Samuel Baker grant is that of direct descendant Howard Baker. Howard has raised peaches for many years, and people come for miles to buy the fresh, succulent native fruit. Howard's wife, Daphne Baker, was for many years interested in providing housing for the elderly. A member of the First Congregational Church, she was active in the efforts of that church to sponsor the Winslow Village Complex.

Marshfield Country Club, about 1925

Another notable person, Frank Cavanaugh, lived on Acorn Street from 1930 to 1933. He was a nationally known football coach and a hero of World War I, during which he earned the name of the "Iron Major." He served as football coach to several major colleges including Holy Cross and Dartmouth, but was best remembered for his outstanding coaching at Boston College. Frank Cavanaugh died in Marshfield in 1933.[35]

After starting out in a small way with five cans stuck in the ground at the Thomas farm at Ocean Bluff in 1919, the Marshfield Country Club was founded on 28 May 1922 by Dr. James J. Duddy, William Rapp Cook, and others. Duddy, a dentist and orthodontist, was chairman of the Marshfield Board of Health in the 1920s and was responsible for instituting a dental clinic in the high school.

The country club land, purchased in 1921, included the Peregrine White, Marcellus Hatch, and Walker farms. Later, the Winsor and Baker farms, adjacent to the original land, were purchased. More land acquired in 1928 and 1929 brought the total to 125 acres. A second nine holes were added to the golf course in 1930, and since that time the course has appeared much as it is today.

There were ninety-five men and six women in the club's original membership. Activities included clambakes under a tent in August and dances on the old piazza. Today there are four hundred fifty members, eighty percent of whom are men. The course qualifies as a site for the Massachusetts State Amateur, the U.S. Open, and U.S. Amateur Championships. The club still offers a James J. Duddy cup in honor of one of the founders. About one-half of the original building burned in 1976. The present elegant club headquarters opened in May 1978. Dinners are served and the facility is available for meetings. Today's president is Ken Joy. Golf professional is Jim Dee.

Two early Marshfield settlers, Robert Carver and John Dingley, established farms still recognizably in existence on Parsonage Street to this day. Interestingly, Parsonage Street, unlike any other in Marshfield, still dips and curves along the old course that cattle and horses trod over the many years since the 1640s. Farms and open spaces remain in this area tucked in behind the busy shopping and downtown section of the town.

Robert Carver received a 20-acre grant from the Plymouth Colony Court in 1638. This land, located on Webster Street, was exchanged for a place on Parsonage Street in 1643. Robert Carver, brother of *Mayflower* passenger and first governor of Plymouth Colony John Carver, was listed as juryman for Marshfield in 1643, and was a freeman of the town by 1648. Among other activities associated with staking out a farm and homestead, Carver killed three wolves in 1654 and delivered them to the selectmen for bounty. His son John Carver married Millicent Ford and they had ten children, many descendants of whom have continued to live in Marshfield down to the present. William Carver of the third generation married Elizabeth Foster, thus uniting the Foster, Ford, and Carver families in another of Marshfield's kinship networks. Edwin White of White Brothers' Milk Company had cattle on the 70-acre farm in the 1940s. A part of the old Carver homestead is said to be incorporated in the present house which stands at 290 Parsonage Street. It is owned by Craig and Polly Washa, who appropriately graze sheep on the old land.[36]

John Dingley, a blacksmith, arrived in Marshfield in 1643 and was listed as a freeman in 1644. Born in 1608 in Cropthorne, Worcestershire, England, Dingley grew up not far from the home of Edward Winslow at Droitwich. He settled on one-half of a parcel of land originally granted to

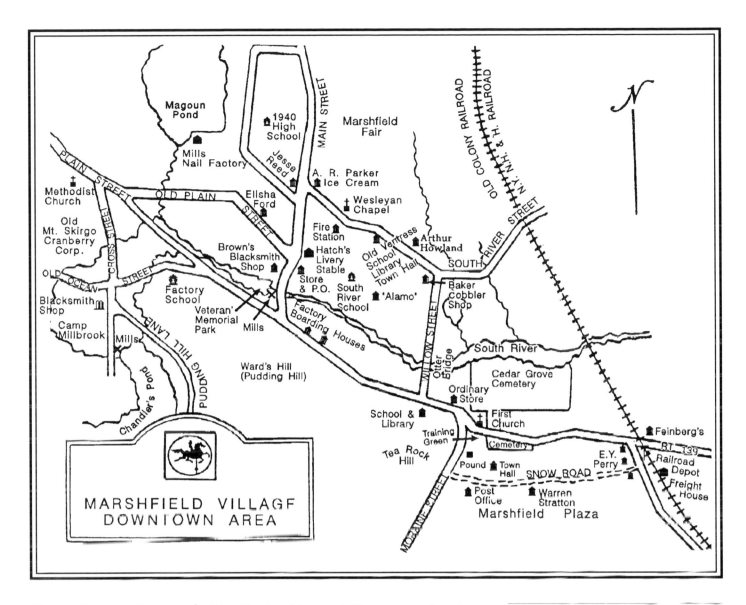

Downtown area of Marshfield Village

Thomas Prence, who never built or lived on his grant. This acreage lay along Parsonage Street and Webster Street, north of the Green Harbor Fresh. Dingley brought with him, as his servant and blacksmith apprentice, Arthur Lowe. Both the Lowe and Dingley families remained in the town for many generations and have descendants here today.[37]

John Dingley's children married into the nearby Ford and Keene families. Dingley was deacon of the Marshfield First Congregational Church for twenty-five years. He contributed one barrel of beef in 1659 towards the building of a parsonage, near the intersection of today's Webster and Parsonage streets, for the Reverend Edward Bulkley. This building no longer exists. John Dingley served the town as constable, grand juror, and highway surveyor. He died in 1689.[38]

Nathaniel Hawthorne's story *The Scarlet Letter* is said to be based on an incident in the life of Deacon Dingley. It is believed that Hawthorne visited a relative who lived in the Dingley house. The house is well preserved to this day with its enormous eight-foot fireplace and rich, wide pine paneling. Present occupants of the house (275 Parsonage Street) are Robert and Judy McCracken, who maintain a small farm on the old fields. Bob McCracken has contributed much to the historical interests of the town, serving as chairman of the Marshfield Historical Commission for the past eighteen years.

Last of the first settlers on Parsonage Street was Edward Bulkley, who was ordained as minister of the Marshfield First Congregational Church in 1642. He remained here until 1656, attending the first Marshfield town meeting on 27 September 1643. He also served as a rater, or assessor, and was a subscriber to the public schools in 1645. He built a house which was later purchased by the town as a parsonage. Money was raised for purchasing the house through the contribution of barrels of beef by townspeople in the 1657 period. The Housing for Independent Living, built in 1982, is located on the site of Edward Bulkley's house (780 Webster Street and 40 Parsonage Street).[39]

Two other historically important houses stand on Parsonage Street. These are the patriot Colonel Anthony Thomas's house, now belonging to Gerald McCluskey (497 Parsonage Street), and another Thomas house, belonging to John and Natalie Corse (449 Parsonage). One is a full square colonial house, the other an eighteenth-century half-house. Both these Thomas families were descendants of Green Harbor settler John Thomas.

On Moraine Street, the old road to Duxbury, the Garretson cranberry bogs near the Duxbury line cover a large acreage today. These bogs were started by Ephraim H. Walker about 1894 on land which once belonged to Solomon Hewitt and Sarah Waterman Hewitt. The old Cape Cod-style house (230 Moraine Street) that the Hewitts built in 1710 still stands. It is owned by James and Barbara Chase.[40]

The last of our baker's dozen of Marshfield downtown settlers was Anthony Snow, for whom Snow Road is named. He received one-half of the Thomas Prence grant in 1649. The other one-half was acquired by John Dingley. The parcel included a part of Cedar Grove Cemetery that Snow gave to the town and the swamp (Snow's Swamp) where much of the shopping and parking areas are today. It also included land along Ocean Street easterly as far as the Bourne grant (near Bourne Park Avenue). In

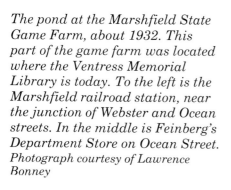

The pond at the Marshfield State Game Farm, about 1932. This part of the game farm was located where the Ventress Memorial Library is today. To the left is the Marshfield railroad station, near the junction of Webster and Ocean streets. In the middle is Feinberg's Department Store on Ocean Street. Photograph courtesy of Lawrence Bonney

this flat land between the rivers were meadows and streams, wetlands, and swamps. Anthony Snow, a feltmaker by trade, farmed and fished here, served as a constable and a deputy to the court, contributed a barrel of beef toward the purchase of Bulkley's parsonage, and served as one of the town's first selectmen, chosen 5 April 1667. He could not possibly have imagined either the place or the complexity of today's selectmen's meetings and duties. Anthony Snow married Abigail Warren, daughter of Pilgrim Richard Warren, and the descendants of this family are many among us today.[41]

Of the many buildings, activities, and people which have come to Anthony Snow's downtown Marshfield property over the years, perhaps the one that would have the greatest meaning to Snow would be the Marshfield game farm. It was started in the 1890s in the area south of Ocean Street where the Ventress Memorial Library is today. By 1915 Lysander (Sandy) Sherman was the game culturist at what was then referred to as the Marshfield Reservation, a state farm where ducks and geese were bred and raised as a part of a program to propagate wildfowl. Known as the Marshfield Bird Farm from about 1916 to 1920, it was officially called the Marshfield State Game Farm by the time it closed in 1965. There were twenty-five acres given over to the raising of game birds, including pheasants and quail. A vast area of pens, sheds, cages, brooders, and shelters for the birds was under the direction of a state game bird culturist, first Sandy Sherman, then Lawrence Bonney from 1947 to 1965. Many of the buildings were built by WPA labor. In its later years there were six people working full time for Larry Bonney and additional seasonal labor, making a total of fifteen workers. A brook, tidal from the South River, runs through the property and is visible today at Webster Street near the Dairy Queen and at Parsonage Street near the police station.

The small business buildings across the street from what was Feinberg's Department Store were once the garages and sheds of the game farm. Sandy and Ada Sherman ran the Golden Pheasant tea room in one of these buildings in the 1930s and 1940s, just east of what was later Chandler's Marshfield Television and Radio Company. Chandler's was a landmark in downtown Marshfield for forty years. Russell Chandler started

The Golden Pheasant tea room and Hot Dog Kennels in 1932. The tea room was operated by Sandy Sherman, the game culturist at the Marshfield State Game Farm, and his wife, Ada Sherman. Today there are a number of small shops in these buildings that once belonged to the game farm.
Photograph courtesy of Lawrence Bonney

his radio business in a building on the farm of his father, Arthur H. Chandler, on Ocean Street (now Southport). After serving in World War II, Russell married Lois Hubbard. On 19 November 1948 he opened his television and radio business at 1871 Ocean Street. He enlarged the building and, in 1984, sold the business to his son Carleton Chandler who owned it until 1988.

Cable TV came to Marshfield in June 1983 with the arrival of Greater Media, replaced in 1986 by the Adelphia Cable Company. The office is located next to the Ventress Memorial Library at Marshfield Plaza East.

The present location of the Pilgrim Trail Apartments (1801 Ocean Street), built in 1975, was also once part of the game farm. Many Indian arrowheads and artifacts were unearthed here at the time the apartments were built. This narrow piece of land at the edge of the creek which ran between the Green Harbor and South rivers was a perfect location for a Native American camp site. The pond, or wet marshy place, behind and beside the apartments is referred to as Island Creek Pond in the early deeds.

Continuing east along Ocean Street and on the other side of the creek is MacDonald's Funeral Home, opened in 1959. It was started by J. Robert MacDonald and today three of his sons, Robert E., Steven P., and Mark W., are in the business. The late Richard J. MacDonald was associated with his father and brothers for several years. At first it was difficult for the MacDonalds to attract customers in the community, since the Protestants already had familiar funeral homes with which they did business, while the Catholic families made use of services of a Boston funeral home. Today the business is a "staunch part of the community."[42]

The new police station on Ocean Street was built in 1958 and the adjoining highway barn in 1960. Today the Marshfield Police Department has one captain, three lieutenants, five sergeants, and thirty-five officers under Chief of Police William P. Sullivan (since 1984), a threefold increase in staff since 1940. Voluntary auxiliary police assist the department when additional manpower is needed. The department has ten cruisers, including both marked and unmarked vehicles, and one motorcycle. Fifty years ago the department had only three cruisers and a chief's car. Community services include traffic/accident analysis, crime prevention, school safety, and parking enforcement. The department also conducts investigative services, has a detective unit, and responds to juvenile needs in the community. The total incidents received and logged by the police department in 1989 was 14,135. Police chiefs since 1940 have been William H. Pratt, Marshall Burpee, Clifford Vallier, Joseph H. Whelan, Frank M.(Mel) Sinnott, Robert E. Frugoli, John A. Roderick, and Charles R. Chaplin.[43]

Off Ocean Street near the police station are Carr Road and Woodland Circle, built in the early 1960s, and Homeland Drive, built in 1972. Further east on Ocean Street is Macker Terrace, built in the mid-1950s.

The first major housing development in Marshfield was Southport, started in 1960 on the north side of Ocean Street across from the present police station. This includes Anderson Drive, Pierce Road, Chandler Drive, Harlow Road, Frisbee Road, and Gates Road. Clyde Gates sold a small portion of land to the developer in 1971, hence the name of Gates Road.

This flat, fertile piece of land bracketed by the rivers has had an interesting history, little known by those who live at Southport today. Arthur H. Chandler, son of George H. Chandler who had operated the Marshfield Cranberry Company on South River Street, bought the Harlow Farm on Ocean Street in 1937. The farm had been owned first by Gideon and Olive Thomas Harlow, then by their son John Alden Harlow. It might

be noted that a daughter, Olive Harlow, married Thomas Blackman and settled at Brant Rock. There was a cranberry bog on the Harlow Farm as early as 1907. The cape-style Harlow house was moved in early 1960 to 112 Parsonage Street and is today owned by Daniel and Susan Walsh. When Chandler owned the property, there were 120 acres of land with a few buildings, 13 acres of cranberry bogs, 2 acres of cultivated blueberry bushes, strawberries, peas, and corn. Water from the South River was used to supply the bogs. Russell and Howard Chandler, sons of Arthur Chandler, worked on the bogs and delivered the cranberries to Ocean Spray Cranberry Company in Hanson. A Chandler farm stand was located on Ocean Street.

Chandler sold the farm in 1960 to developers Ward and Johnson of Abington. They built prefabricated homes on the old Harlow/Chandler farm. Houses sold for from $7,000 to $11,000, and 199 houses were built on half-acre lots, the last lot being built on in 1989. It was the first major large-scale housing in Marshfield, drastically changing the needs of the area for schools and services. Yet this was but a preview of what was to come!

Next to Southport stands Winslow Village (1520 Ocean Street), one of two housing projects for the elderly in downtown Marshfield, the other being Tea Rock Gardens at Moraine Street. Winslow Village, built in 1972, was sponsored by the First Congregational Church under the enthusiastic dedication of Grace E. Ryder and Daphne Baker. It was funded by federal Housing and Urban Development money. It has sixty-four units in four buildings, and thirty-two additional living units are being added. The old gambrel-roof house which stood on the property was moved across Ocean Street opposite Anderson Drive in 1989. Tea Rock Gardens was completed in 1973, and it has the same number of apartments as Winslow Village. It would be difficult for our first downtown settlers to comprehend a society so complex and populated that there is a need for public housing to care for the elderly outside of their family homes.

In discussing the enormous changes that have occurred in the center of downtown Marshfield in the last fifty years, two old established businesses deserve special mention: B. M. Feinberg's Department Store and Toabe's Hardware.

Benjamin M. Feinberg, born in Lithuania, arrived in Marshfield by train from Boston in 1885. He started peddling his wares from a backpack, traveling on foot. The merchandise that he sold included sewing items, fabric, clothing, shoes, pots, and pans. Later he went door-to-door with a horse and wagon through Marshfield, Duxbury, Plympton, and Halifax. He moved permanently to Marshfield in 1901 with his wife and five children and began running a business from the front of his house, which stood just east of Feinberg's Department Store (now site of McDonald's Restaurant). The old Feinberg house, built in 1868 and originally belonging to Luther Thomas, was moved to 727 Webster Street in 1962. Benjamin built and opened the store (1880 Ocean Street) in 1912 as a full department store carrying furniture, appliances, and clothes. His sons Joseph, Moritz, and Bernard continued to run the business. Joseph died in 1949. Moritz and Bernard managed the store through the 1960s, when a third generation of Feinbergs took over. In time the second floor was used for the shoe department, women's department, and furniture section. Benjamin continued active in the store until his death in the 1950s. Bob and Alan Feinberg, sons of Bernard and the most recent proprietors, worked in the store from the mid-1960s. Largely a clothing store, it was renovated and modernized by them. Sadly, on 13 February 1990 a sign appeared on the Feinberg building stating that this long-established store was going out of business. It is, indeed, the end of an era in Marshfield! Bob and Alan's mother, Beatrice Feinberg, was very active in the Marshfield Women's Club and served on the Republican Town Committee until her death in 1969.

The Feinberg building has seen other uses over the years. At first the Feinberg store occupied only the middle one-third of the building. The Marshfield Pharmacy, operated by E. L. Pinkham and later by Francis Wherrity, was in the west end, while in the east end, Arthur E. Dorr ran a grocery store that later became the First National Store. At one time a dry-cleaning business was located in the west end. The second floor was given over to apartments, while the third floor was storage.

The Toabe Hardware Company opened about 1938 in the old ordinary building near the Training Green. Owners were Abraham J. and Hilda Toabe. The business moved to its present location on Ocean Street in the 1940s. The building was, at that time, a house, which has been considerably enlarged over the years. Abraham Toabe was a volunteer fireman and Kiwanis member for many years. Hilda Toabe assisted in the store from the earliest days. Today the business is owned and operated by John and Janet Nectow Miller, third generation of the Toabe family. With the closing of Feinberg's, Toabe's Hardware is now the oldest retail business in Marshfield.

Between these two established and respected Marshfield businesses there once ran the tracks of the Old Colony Railroad Company (originally the Duxbury and Cohasset Railroad Company). The last company to operate this line was the New York, New Haven and Hartford Railroad Company. There were five depots in Marshfield. The central station was located where the parking lot at the southeast corner of Ocean Street and Webster Street is today.

The arrival of the first train at the Marshfield Railroad Station was memorably described by Charles P. Sinnott:

Late one afternoon in 1871 the sound of a locomotive whistle reached our ears, and we knew that the laying of rails was nearing our station. The next morning great crowds were out to witness the actual placing of the last

rails that were to connect our little station with the great city of Boston. You may be sure that my brothers and I were present among the interested spectators. I remember a great freight engine, the John Quincy Adams, was standing in a cut a short distance from the station. In front of it were several platform cars loaded with sleepers and rails. As the new track was placed, the great engine pushed the cars forward for the convenience of the workmen. We who stood upon the edge of the cut had an excellent view of the whole scene including the locomotive as it stood there panting as engines do when under steam ready for instant service. . . . Suddenly without the slightest warning the old engine let off steam with a terrific roar.[44]

When the track was completed, the railroad company offered all residents of Marshfield a free ride to Boston. The Marshfield railroad station was the center of activity for seventy years. Trains arrived at regular intervals and for many years were met by horse-drawn barges and carriages which transported the passengers to their homes, or to hotels and cottages at the beach areas. The tracks were removed in 1939. On June 24 of that year, old No. 655 passenger train rolled over the rusty rails into Marshfield on her last trip. She was going backward slowly from Duxbury to Boston. The town's population at that time was two thousand year-round and ten thousand summer residents. One hundred people gathered at the station to see the last train arrive. Someone had fashioned a horse trough into a coffin with an inscription on the top that read "1872-1939, Age 67 years — Only the Good Die Young." Bugler Robert Handy delivered a dirge and Norman Costello played the part of undertaker. This surely marked the end of a colorful and practical era in Marshfield transportation history and opened the way for today's maze of roads and superhighways that link the town to the world at large. There are many who wish the return of the train.[45]

A little south of the old railroad station stood an array of storage sheds and the freight house (later moved to Parsonage Street near the police station). It was in this area that Phillips Bates Grain and Coal Company was started in 1892. A large grain shed (now a furniture store) was built by Luther White. Fred Rand (father of today's Ellis Rand), who lived next door to the store, was manager of Phillips Bates for fifty years. The railroad

Marshfield Railroad Station, about 1890. Horse-drawn barges took people to the beach from the station, which was located at the southeast corner of Webster and Ocean street.

Last train through Marshfield, 24 June 1939. A farewell ceremony was staged with Robert Handy playing a funeral dirge on his bugle and Norman Costello acting as the undertaker.
Photograph courtesy of Ruth Baker Sinnott

delivered the coal and grain in freight cars to the unloading platform located at the track siding. The grain was scooped into the shed, then raised to the top of a tower by buckets and dumped into bins. Each bin held a boxcar full of grain. The coal arrived in hopper cars, forty to fifty tons to a car. Across Webster Street there was another shed for the storage of hay, which was especially saleable at the time of the Marshfield Fair. Later this building was used for a cordwood business where, at one time, wood sold for eight dollars a cord.

Three of the buildings and houses on the west side of Webster Street were built in the 1890s and owned by the E. Y. Perry estate. These include the present house of Charlotte Rand Handy, the office of dentist Dr. William Glynn, and the office of Anderson & Baker Insurance Agency. A fourth company house, which stood on the corner of Webster and Ocean Streets, was moved to a location opposite today's Daniel Webster School.

In 1940, after the departure of the railroad, Phillips Bates went out of business. The old overhead railroad pass on Webster Street was removed in 1951. The Rand-Handy Oil Company bought the buildings from Phillips

Bates Company, although Rand-Handy had started an oil business prior to the closing of Phillips Bates. The Rand-Handy company was founded by Fred and Ellis Rand and Louis Handy. Today Kenneth Rand, son of Ellis and third generation of the family, owns and operates the business. The office is at 900 Webster Street. At 829 Webster Street is John Foster Lumber Company, established in 1889.

Along the south side of Ocean Street where Toabe's Hardware, the Colonial Pharmacy, and Papa Gino's are today, there were only two residential houses in 1930. A glance at the roof lines of the pharmacy and Toabe's still reveals the location of these residences.

On the north side of Ocean Street there was the Marcia Thomas house built in 1835, now Gallery 360 - Rutledge & Carlisle real estate (1914 Ocean Street), and Sandy Sherman's house where the Dr. Lawrence Vienneau building (1900 Ocean Street) is today. Stenbeck & Taylor surveying company (1932 Ocean Street) was founded in 1951 by the late James Taylor and Victor Stenbeck. Jim's son Brian Taylor carries on the land surveying and consulting business. He has recently established a wetlands resources department, specializing in environmental design and construction. Seaside Homes (1952 Ocean Street) was founded in 1985. This real estate business is owned by four women: Janet E. Lightfoot, Madeleine McDonald, Carole Virtue, and Nancy J. Lane. Seaside Homes has the distinction of being number one in volume of listings and sales for the last five years for the South Shore area.[46]

In 1930, behind the row of stores on Ocean Street where the parking areas are today, in the middle of an open field with a yard full of chickens, stood Dr. Warren W. Stratton's house. There were no commercial properties in the area of today's shopping center. By 1940 a row of stores, built by Francis Wherrity, had come to occupy the south side of Ocean Street. They were Francis Wherrity's Drug Store, a First National Store, and Frank N. Bencordo's barbershop around the corner on Webster Street. In 1950 came Archer's Marshfield Pharmacy, owned and operated by Robert and Marilyn Sinnott Archer, to replace Wherrity's. Archer's Marshfield Pharmacy was sold in 1980 to Ralph Harrison and is now called the Marshfield Colonial Pharmacy. A few more stores were built west along the south side of Ocean Street in the 1940s. These were Toabe's Hardware, Buttner's Clothing Store, and Duca's 5 & 10. Leonard Jordan's Family Pharmacy and Gratto's Mobil

Ocean Street shopping center, about 1940
Photograph courtesy of Lois Hubbard Chandler

Dr. Warren W. Stratton's house. It stood where the Marshfield Plaza parking areas are today.

gas station appeared in the 1950s. The gas station is now owned and operated by Arthur Ayre. Walter Petrocelli's carpet, vinyl flooring, and tile shop and Tots to Teens (1943 Ocean Street), owned and operated by Gloria Petrocelli, were both started in the early 1950s.

The American Legion Post No. 88 was located in the building next to the Mobil station. This veterans' organization was formed after World War I. George Earle is the present commander. The American Legion Auxiliary is the women's organization associated with the veterans' group. It was founded in France in 1918 after the First World War. The Marshfield chapter was formed in 1925. Both organizations are concerned with the welfare of veterans of all wars. Elizabeth Whitford and her sister, Margaret Brown, were active for years as presidents of the Auxiliary. Today's president is Josephine Keohane.

Great changes occurred in downtown Marshfield in 1963. Dr. Stratton's house had been razed by that time and the land near the intersection of today's Snow Road (built about 1971) and Stratton Avenue had been acquired by Tom Curtis. He built the Curtis Farms market in 1963 and the area now called Marshfield Plaza began to be developed. Curtis Farms was eventually replaced by Angelo's Supermarket in 1972. The Webster Room Restaurant, located in Angelo's, was a popular downtown eating and socializing spot for many years. Today's Mug and Muffin Shop, owned by Carol Meyer and Joyce Bostwick, occupies the old Webster Room restaurant site. In 1981 another major extension of the shopping area brought a new Angelo's and the beginning of the current landscape of small businesses to downtown Marshfield. Today's Purity Supreme market opened in 1986.

A recent store on Ocean Street is the popular Jackanson's, opened in 1981 by Jack Danahy, generous contributor to the community. Jackanson's sells newspapers, tobacco, magazines, candy, greeting cards, stationery, and school and office supplies.[47]

The Rockland Trust Company branch office came to Marshfield in 1948 when it took over the accounts of the old Marshfield Savings Bank. Previous to this date, the Rockland Trust had operated a mobile banking service from a chauffeur-driven car that came from Rockland once a week. The bank was at first located at 1923 Ocean Street where Leo's Bakery is today, and was moved in 1962 to its present site on Town Parking Way next to Toabe's Hardware. The Plymouth Five Cents Savings Bank was established in 1962, and the Lincoln Trust Company in 1968.

Thanks to the town Beautification Committee, established in 1973, the shopping area now has rows of cherry trees and gardens of daffodils. Islands of plantings break up the parking areas. Under the chairmanship of Ruth Weston in 1975, the citizens, businesses, and Kiwanis organization planted about one hundred cherry trees (the official Bicentennial tree) along Route 139. Ruth is finance chairman of the 350th Commemorative Trust.

Marshfield Plaza East, where the Ventress Memorial Library is located, began to be developed in 1968 by John Clancy. The First National Store that was located there closed in 1980. In 1983 the building was bought by the Town of Marshfield and remodeled into the current library.

As the population of the town has increased and demands for public services have changed, town government has proliferated. New committees and commissions have been established, and town boards have taken on additional responsibilities. From 1930 to 1950 the population doubled from 1,625 to 3,267. By 1960 it had doubled again to 6,748. By 1970 it had more than doubled again to 15,223. In 1980 it reached 20,916 and by 1988 the figure was 23,010.[48]

Very little land has been protected by conservation in the area of downtown Marshfield. There are a few small pieces along the Furnace Brook watershed, ten acres called the Taylor Fund Woodland between South River Street and Ferry Street, scattered acres of salt marsh in the South River valley, a small acreage called Fetlock Farm off Parsonage Street, and a piece at the South River junction between Plain and Old Plain streets. There are three larger acreages known as the John F. Veader, Sr., Memorial Forest, the Drake-Powell Memorial Forest, and the Rear Admiral Albert T. Sprague, Jr., Forest at Mount Skirgo. Perhaps we should consider ourselves fortunate that Timothy Williamson gave us land for the Training Green and for the church in 1663 and that Anthony Snow gave some of the land for the Cedar Grove Cemetery. The Training Green was partially restored to its former extent by the elimination of Centennial Street in 1976.

Marshfield has experienced a great metamorphosis since our baker's dozen of settlers arrived in Marshfield in the 1640s. But the river remains with its twice daily tides, Pudding Hill and Zion's Hill still stand watch over downtown Marshfield, town affairs continue, people come and people go, and the bell in the steeple of the First Congregational Church strikes the hour, a constant reminder of past, present, and a future yet to come.

*Primitive drawing of Centre
Marshfield, artist and date
unknown. Shown is the Tilden
and Willena Smith Ames farm at
the corner of Church and Ferry
streets. To the far right can be seen
the Benjamin Keene house where
the Centre Marshfield Post Office
was located.*
Drawing courtesy of Robert Davis

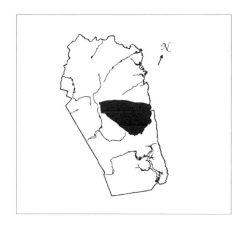

Centre Marshfield Village

Sentinels against the western skies
My hills proliferate with pines
Thrusting their steeple tops
heavenward.

— Cynthia Hagar Krusell

CENTRE MARSHFIELD is the village at the geographical center of Marshfield. It is at 70° 42′ W, 42° 7′ N. This is where the grandstand of the Marshfield hills begins. The center of Centre Marshfield (junction of Ferry, Grove, and Church streets) sits on a step between the rise of land at Snake Hill (Telegraph Hill) on the southeast, the great height of Carolina Hill on the northwest, and the crest of Holly Hill on the northeast.

Were it not for the encircling hills, Centre Marshfield would command a panorama of the curving course of the South River with its broad marshes and the sweep of bright blue sea beyond. Indeed, from Centre Marshfield's eastern flanks along Snake Hill and Sea Rivers and at the place where South River and Ferry streets meet, there is a Super Bowl view of Marshfield's seacoast arena.

The hills are both Centre Marshfield's glory and its undoing. Rich with sand and gravel, debris of glacial deposits thousands of years ago, the small drumlins and eskers of the area have produced more wealth than any other resource or industry that Marshfield has had to offer in three hundred fifty years. To this land between the hills and at the edge of the rivers came settlers in search of pasturage and tillage, timber, and fish. The broad mouth of the North/South rivers that, prior to 1898, was located opposite Snake Hill at Rexhame Beach, provided an entrance to the area and a passage to the world beyond.

Centre Marshfield might have been aptly named Whitetown for the Whites, who were the principal settler family here. They came early, liked what they found, and stayed. Their story is the history of Centre Marshfield. First came Peregrine White straight up from the farm of his stepfather, Governor Edward Winslow, at Green Harbor. He came, not because he received land here, but because he married Sarah Bassett about 1648. Sarah's father, William Bassett, had been granted one hundred acres of land at the foot of Snake Hill on the river's edge in 1640. Bassett, a master mason and blacksmith from Sandwich, Kent, England, had come on the ship *Fortune* in 1621 to Plymouth. Peregrine settled on his father-in-law's land near the "united inlet" of the North/South River.[1]

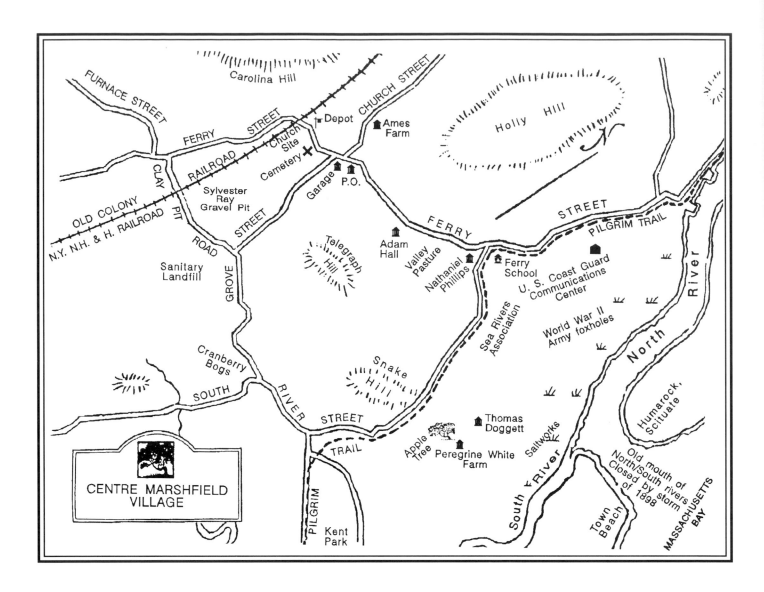

Centre Marshfield Village

In 1655 Peregrine was granted two hundred acres elsewhere in the colony, described as "along the path from Bridgewater to the Bay" by the Plymouth Colony Court, in honor of his being the first-born child of the Pilgrims. He sold this acreage, but from time to time received additional land in other parts of the colony from the court. During his years in Marshfield he purchased several pieces of land adjacent to his farm.[2]

Peregrine was born in 1620 on the *Mayflower* at Provincetown. He was the son of Susannah and William White. His childhood was spent in the household of his stepfather and mother, Edward Winslow and Susannah White Winslow. The family lived in Plymouth until they moved to the Winslow homestead, Careswell, at Green Harbor in 1636. At sixteen he served the colony in the Indian uprising known as the Pequot War. He continued in the military, becoming a lieutenant and then a captain in the militia. During his long life in Marshfield, he was a farmer and public-spirited citizen, serving the town as a surveyor and as a representative to the General Court. In 1700, at an advanced age, he became the town's schoolteacher. He must have been an independent Yankee since he saw no need to join the Marshfield church until he was seventy-eight years old. He died in 1704 at the age of eighty-three.[3]

Peregrine and Sarah Bassett White had six children. Some moved elsewhere, but a daughter, Mercy, married neighbor William Sherman in 1697 and settled nearby. Peregrine's son Daniel White, born in 1649, was deeded the homestead and land by his father in 1674, the year that Daniel married Hannah Hunt. He and Hannah had seven sons and continued to live in the homestead. The Whites became an established Marshfield family, with many descendants still living in the town today.[4]

It is said that Peregrine White daily visited his mother in the old house at Careswell. He rode to see her on a black horse and wore a coat with buttons the "size of a Spanish dollar." He doubtless traveled down the Green Harbor Path, crossing the South River at the Valley Bars, then taking the old corduroy road across the Green Harbor River valley to the site of the church and cemetery at Winslow Burying Ground, past the Thomas place (Webster's) and down the path to Careswell. A weathervane depicting a sprightly horse and rider, designed by Anne Philbrick Hall, graces the top of Marshfield Town Hall today and memorializes the story of this dutiful young man. Another Peregrine White legend concerns an apple tree on his farm which survived for two hundred years until 1848. It is said that there can still be found offshoots of this famous tree planted by the first-born of the Pilgrim settlers.[5]

A portion of the Peregrine White house stood for many years, and tradition has it that a small part of the old house is incorporated in the present house on Peregrine White Drive. Five succeeding generations of Whites continued to live in the old homestead. A grandson of Peregrine's, John White, inherited the farm from his father, Daniel. In 1700 John married next-door neighbor Susanna Sherman, daughter of Samuel Sherman and Sarah Doggett. Settlers William Sherman and Thomas Doggett had land adjacent to the Whites at Snake Hill. As in other villages of Marshfield, residents tended to marry close to home. In this neighborhood of shipbuilders and merchants, the kinship network thus established was of special economic significance, various family members being engaged in interrelated and interdependent businesses. Some cut timber, others built ships, others captained the ships to foreign ports and returned with goods for small local stores run by other family members. John and Susanna had seven children, some of whom married into the neighboring families of Sprague, Little, and Phillips. One son, Jesse, however, married far afield in

Peregrine White Weathervane
Marshfield Town Hall

Looking up at Telegraph Hill from the Peregrine White farm on the banks of the South River, about 1890
Photograph courtesy of Harris F. Penniman

Germany while on a merchant voyage. His wife was Catherina Charlotte Wilhelmina Sybellina Warner.[6]

John White distinguished himself by giving land at Centre Marshfield for a Baptist church, which was erected in 1745. This was destined never to be used as a Baptist church, but became Trinity Episcopal Church, the church of the Whites and Littles. The Baptists, a small and impecunious group, could not afford the high taxes demanded by the town officials, whereas the wealthier Episcopalians were able to support their church. Taxes were levied on any church that was not the established Congregational church. Prior to 1745, the Episcopalians of Centre Marshfield had attended an Episcopal church located in South Scituate (Norwell). The Marshfield families probably sailed up the North River to attend services. The Centre Marshfield church building was moved to Marshfield Hills village in 1838 and is a part of the North River Arts Society building (formerly the GAR hall). Neither the Baptists nor the Episcopalians stayed at the Centre. The Baptists moved to Standish (Plain and School streets), and the Episcopalians to Marshfield Hills. Only the cemetery remains today to remind us of the traveling church of Centre Marshfield.[7]

John White's brother, Cornelius White, was a shipbuilder. He lived in the cape-style house at today's 740 Ferry Street. He had possibly the first shipyard at White's Ferry near present Humarock Bridge. He began building vessels as early as 1705. He owned and operated the ferry boat at the North River crossing. He gave his son Benjamin a large acreage of "heavily timbered land" in Hanover, a horse, two cows, a yoke of oxen, and a gundalow (flat-bottomed boat). Benjamin "cut and carted his valuable ship-timber to

Marshfield Meadows
Oil on canvas by Martin Johnson Heade, 1878, from collection of the Currier Gallery of Art, Manchester, New Hampshire: Currier Purchase, 1962.13. Photograph courtesy of Frank Kelly

the North River, loaded it aboard his gundalow and freighted it down to his father's yard at the ferry."[8]

Over the years, the Whites were farmers and seafaring merchants. They acquired extensive properties, had servants, built and owned vessels, and were engaged in the lucrative coastal trade. Their merchant activities and connection with Anglicanism in the Episcopal church gave them particularly close ties with England. Most of the Whites sided with the mother country at the time of the American Revolution and became Tories. The Whites numbered more Loyalists among their members than any other single family in Marshfield. Their long association and family connections with the Winslows may also have been a factor in their Loyalist leanings. The patriots among them were usually younger sons with small farms and no political or economic connections with the British interests.[9]

Loyalist Abijah White of the fifth generation married Anna Little of nearby Littletown (Sea View) and inherited the homestead. Abijah was appointed by a Marshfield town gathering in January 1774 to convey to the General Court at Boston the controversial Loyalist "Resolves of the Town of Marshfield," affirming allegiance to King George III and denouncing the patriot action of the Boston Tea Party. Harassed by the hostile Marshfield patriots, White eventually sought refuge in Boston. After much suffering and torture, he died and was buried at King's Chapel Burying Ground. It is an indication of the divided sympathies of many Marshfield families during the revolutionary period that Abijah White's daughter married one of Marshfield's most famous patriots, Luther Little.

Centre Marshfield Village

*From a mural in the home of
Walter and Margery Frye,
depicting an early saltworks near
the old Peregrine White farm
Oil by Carl Blaha, 1935*

Abijah's granddaughter Sybil White was the last of the White family to live in the house. At the end of her life she lived in a house (506 Pleasant Street) overlooking Wales Pond in Marshfield Hills. Tradition says that the house was the old Sea View schoolhouse, moved to the pond location. Sybil died in 1875, leaving eight hundred dollars in a trust fund for "worthy and destitute spinsters in Marshfield." The White homestead off South River Street was sold to Peleg Ford, and later owners were Alonzo Ewell and then Dr. Ethan Allen Brown. At one time, there was a saltworks on the White property, owned by Samuel Brown and Daniel Phillips.

Abijah's cousin Gideon White, son of Cornelius, was living in Plymouth at the time of the American Revolution. He had married Joanna Howland of the *Mayflower* Howland family, and resided on North Street next door to Loyalist Edward Winslow of the Marshfield Winslows. Gideon fought with the British at the battle of Bunker Hill. Forced to leave Boston at the time of the British evacuation in 1776, he went to Halifax, Nova Scotia, where he conducted trade between the Maritimes and the West Indies. On a voyage along the New England coast, he was captured by the colonial forces off Barrington, Rhode Island, imprisoned in his own town of Plymouth, released, and banished. He left New York in 1783 with other Loyalist exiles and spent the remainder of his life in Shelburne, Nova Scotia. He named the area Port Roseway and tried, unsuccessfully, to make it a rival merchant center with Boston. He was engaged for many years in an extensive maritime trade with members of the Phillips family back at Centre Marshfield.[10]

Peregrine White's granddaughter, Joanna White, married Captain Nathaniel Phillips in 1734, thus uniting the two leading Centre Marshfield families. Daughter of Cornelius White, she brought money and land into the Phillips family. Long active in the lucrative coastal trade, Cornelius had accumulated considerable wealth. At the time of his death in 1755, he gave Joanna "all my Vally Lands which I bought of Thomas Doggett Jr & Ebenezer Doggett lying at the head or southwesterly of the Pond Pasture." In other deeds this land was called the "Valley Pasture," identified today by a new road and housing development started by Marshfield's present selectman Daniel McDonald in 1988. Nathaniel and Joanna Phillips built the elegant Georgian home at the junction of Ferry and South River streets (1299 South River Street) in 1740.[11]

The Nathaniel Phillips house, built about 1750. Located at the intersection of Ferry and South River streets, this house remained in the Phillips family until 1953.

Earlier generations of the Phillips family lived in the family homestead on the banks of the South River at the foot of Ferry Street hill. John Phillips, the first of the family to come to Marshfield, had received land in this beautiful location between the south slope of Holly Hill and the South River. Here was fertile farmland and a waterway running along the eastern border of the farm to the sea. Ironically, Phillips's second wife, Grace Holloway Phillips, and two of his sons were killed by severe lightning storms that struck Marshfield in 1654 and 1666. John married as his third wife, Faith Doty, widow of *Mayflower* passenger Edward Doty. Successive generations of the Phillips family married into the John Thomas family of Green Harbor and the Edward Stevens family of nearby Centre Marshfield.[12]

Nathaniel and Joanna White Phillips had five children, born between 1739 and 1751. The eldest son, John, was lost at sea in 1762 at age twenty-three. Sons Nathaniel and Daniel became prosperous merchants in the coastal trade with the West Indies and the Maritimes. They developed a family trading network with Nathaniel based at St. John's, Newfoundland; Daniel at the North River at Marshfield; and cousin Gideon White at Halifax, and later, at Shelburne, Nova Scotia. They traded in West Indies molasses, sugar, tea, and spices; New England farm produce and horses; and Maritime fish and timber. This trade was well established before the Revolution. Largely because of their involvement in this trade, the Phillips family remained loyal to England when the Revolution broke out in the colonies.

Nathaniel Phillips moved permanently to St. John's, Newfoundland, in March 1776, after being arrested and imprisoned in Plymouth for his Loyalist sympathies. He acquired a large amount of property and a considerable fortune in Newfoundland. When he died, unmarried, in December 1798, he left a large inheritance to his brother Daniel of Marshfield.

Some of the correspondence of Nathaniel Phillips from Newfoundland to his cousin Gideon White in Nova Scotia tells of his business activities and of his state of health and concern for friends and family at Marshfield and Plymouth. He did not return to Marshfield, although his letters indicate that he would have wanted to, had he been allowed.[13]

After Nathaniel's death, his brother Daniel made a trip to Newfoundland in 1799 to settle his estate. Although no specific amount of money is mentioned in the accounts that we have, it is assumed that Daniel received a considerable inheritance, since when he died twelve years later, he was a wealthy man for his time. His real estate included three large farms valued at $19,560 and personal property valued at $30,898. The family also owned a sloop, the *Sophia*, weighing thirty-five tons, built at the Brick-Kiln Shipyard in Pembroke in 1811. Captained by David Church of Marshfield, it was used as a packet to deliver goods from Boston to the North River. It was sold on 21 November 1816 for about three hundred dollars.

The Phillips house on South River Street is often referred to as the "ghost house." The story goes that when Daniel Phillips returned from Newfoundland with his inherited wealth, he was set upon and murdered by robbers as he stepped ashore on the banks of the South River. However, since Daniel did not die for another twelve years, in 1812, there seems little substantiation for this tale. Many subsequent residents of the house have claimed encounters with spirits, but the identity of the "ghost" remains a mystery. The house stayed in the Phillips family until 1953 when Ella Phillips Lindley died and her son John Marshall Lindley sold the property. Subsequent owners have been Dana and Marjorie Djerf, Kenneth and Cynthia Alman, John and Barbara Steele, and now Richard and Nicole Brennan.

Two other families — the Kents and the Keenes — have long been associated with the area. A son of the John Kent who settled Rexhame moved across the river and built his house on the peninsula of land that we now know as Kent Park. Five successive generations of Kents continued to live at this beautiful spot on the edge of the river at a place near the Valley Bars. The Kents served as selectmen of Marshfield and representatives to the General Court and were avid patriots at the time of the Revolution.

Their memory survives today in the name of the Kent Park neighborhood. Land in this area was acquired by the Great Northern Land Company about 1912. In the 1920s Warren Smabach laid out Kent Park with forty-foot wide roads and subdivided the area into fifteen hundred lots, each measuring twenty feet by one hundred feet. The lots were made small in order to accommodate gunning shacks and summer camps. Smabach promoted the sale of the lots by busing people to Marshfield from Boston and serving them chowder dinners. The old Kent house which stood on the property was used as a clubhouse for the Kent Park Association.

The Keene family's connection with Centre Marshfield started with Benjamin Keene, great-great-grandson of Josiah Keene who settled in Littletown (Sea View) in the seventeenth century. The Keenes were another shipbuilding family in this community of shipbuilders. They owned and operated a shipyard at the ferry (Humarock Bridge, Marshfield side). Active in merchant shipping, they were, like their neighbors the Whites and Littles, loyalist in their sympathies at the time of the Revolution.

Benjamin Keene is believed to have built the house at the center of Centre Marshfield by the triangular green at the junction of Church and Ferry streets (580 Ferry Street). The house dates to 1828, the year that Benjamin married Mrs. Nancy Sherman Joyce. Their son Benjamin F. H. Keene was postmaster of the Centre Marshfield Post Office, which was located in the house in 1894. Benjamin F. H. Keene died in 1915, and his daughter Florence Keene continued as postmistress until about 1925, when the Centre Marshfield Post Office was discontinued.

The Ferry School served the children of Centre Marshfield. Located across from the Phillips house at the intersection of South River and Ferry streets, the children walked from the various parts of Centre Marshfield to the one-room schoolhouse overlooking the South River. The school closed in 1917, there being too few children to continue. The students were transported to nearby district schools and the building (later razed) was moved to Ocean Street near where Friendly's Ice Cream Shop is today. Another building gone from Centre Marshfield!

The train came to Centre Marshfield in 1871, the year the tracks were extended through the town by the Duxbury and Cohasset Railroad Company. The depot was located north of Ferry Street where it makes the big curve into Centre Marshfield from the west. This soon became the center of arrivals and departures, taking the place of the wharfside on the river. The train served as the major means of transportation until the age of the automobile. The tracks were removed from Marshfield in 1939.

A new era for Centre Marshfield began in 1892 with the arrival of eight Methodist ministers. The Centre Marshfield church, both the building and the congregation, had been gone from the village for fifty-five years when a group of Methodist ministers discovered the area. They were in search, not of a church or of a congregation, but of a place of quietude away from the city to bring their families for the summer. The ministers came from near Boston and some from as far away as Summit, New Jersey, and New Orleans, Louisiana. Classmates at Boston University Theological School, they purchased three farms on the hillside directly across from the old mouth of the North/South rivers. The ministers were Edward M. Taylor, James H. Humphrey, Wilbur P. Thirkield, William I. Haven, Josiah Wear Dearborn, John Galbraith, William G. Richardson, and John W. Hamilton. Two of the farms they purchased were the Watson and Perry farms, and by 1896 they had acquired one hundred acres of land that had once belonged to Peregrine White. They began to build houses, coming down to Marshfield only in the summer. The area soon became known as Ministers' Hill.

In 1895 the ministers formed the Sea Rivers Association. A plot plan was drawn up and an equal acreage of land given to each member. About one hundred acres of marsh and common land were set aside, including an area of the beach at Rexhame. There were no restrictions about selling the land, but no one could have "ferris wheels or pigs." The Sea Rivers Club was organized in 1935 to maintain roads and oversee the area. Club members were property owners who were also members of the association.

With the threat of development pressing on Marshfield in 1964 and a request by the United States government to acquire the land at Sea Rivers for the erection of radio towers, the Sea Rivers Association began to rethink its organization and its land policies. Over five acres of beach at Rexhame

Two of the ministers' houses at Sea Rivers. On the left is the James H. Humphrey house with the Reverend John Galbraith standing on the doorstep. On the right is the Wilbur P. Thirkield house, originally the Paul White house, built about 1737.
Photograph courtesy of Doris Goodwin Ewart

were sold for fifteen thousand dollars in 1950 to the town to be opened as a town beach. In 1973 the association and the club were merged and became the Sea Rivers Trust. Membership in the trust is dependent on ownership of property, rather than descending from an original member. Largely the work of George Wood, the trust made a legal and binding association of the members, setting up preservation restrictions and retaining a core section of land under the trust. This, in effect, created an area of open space and restricted housing and is of great benefit to the historic preservation of the town of Marshfield.

Descendants of original Sea Rivers Association founders, still living at Sea Rivers, are Pearl Thirkield Wood and her daughter Betsy Budd, and Gladys Haven North. Doris Ewart, widow of the late Robert Galbraith Ewart, lives in the old Galbraith house at 180 Pilgrim Road. Bob Ewart was a member and chairman of the Advisory Board for ten years and an administrative assistant to the Board of Assessors for six years. Doris has worked for the school department and been a long-time member of the town Republican committee.

Memories recorded in 1941 by Louise Richardson, who summered as a child at Sea Rivers, tell of life at Centre Marshfield in the early years of the twentieth century:

There was the laconic Benjamin Keene who used to meet us at the Marshfield Centre railroad station with his old horse. One of our greatest joys was to ride with the trunks on his hay wagon. There was the placid Mrs. Keene who at her infrequent times in the post office would allow us to use the Marshfield stamp on our hands. . . . There were the picnics at the haunted house when we crept in with chocolate layer cakes and watermelon, and then scurried out because we thought we heard ghostly footsteps. We little thought then that this haunted house was to be the charming home of Mrs. Lindley. And there are the Sundays when we went to church (Methodist at Zion's Hill). It is not the sermon I remember, but the fun we had lining up in the vestibule for our drink of water from the old pail and the long-handled dipper. Gone is Zion's Hill [church]! But happy memories remain with us.

Benjamin Keene house, built about 1828. The Centre Marshfield Post Office was located here from before 1879 until 1925. The house still stands near the intersection of Ferry and Church streets.

During World War II the summer residents of Sea Rivers were not allowed to live in their homes. The United States Army occupied the meadow to defend the open beach areas along the coast. Army foxholes can still be found on the property. In all areas of Marshfield blackout measures were enforced. Black shades had to be drawn in windows and automobile head-lights had to be painted half black. Lights in the streets were not allowed and air raid wardens were on patrol.

The Marshfield Center Garage at Grove and Ferry streets has been a landmark in the village since the early part of the century. Built about 1923 by Charles Curtis, then owned and operated by Philip B. Oakman, the garage was acquired by Walter and Fred Oxner in 1926. It has been operated by the Oxner family ever since. Current owners are Thornton ("Sonnie") J. and his son Wayne Oxner. In the early years the garage offered trucking, heavy teaming, wood and lumber, estimates on road construction, and sand and gravel hauling. Fred Oxner once operated a machine shop at the garage. Today it is mainly an auto repair business. The Marshfield Center Garage was the first home of the town highway department in the 1920s. The department owned only one tractor and rented all other necessary equipment.

During the 1920s there was a tea shop in Centre Marshfield called the Lindens. It was in a separate little building which stood in front of the house now owned by Ethel and Paul Macomber (570 Ferry Street). The tearoom was built and opened by Mr. Curtis, followed by Temple Lynde and then David and Isabel Banner. It did business only in summer and served cold drinks, coffee, clam chowder, sandwiches, pies, and cakes.

An important family in the history of Centre Marshfield is that of Tilden and Willena Smith Ames. They lived at 44 Church Street and owned considerable land on both sides of the street, extending up the back side of Holly Hill and as far as the railroad track. Tilden Ames, a farmer, was ninth in descent from Anthony Eames/Ames who came to Marshfield Hills in the 1650s. Tilden and Willena's daughter Bessie Bell was born in 1907. She and her brother Robert T. Ames were well known for many years in Marshfield. Bessie kept two cows in the open meadow between Church Street and the railroad track, and had a white horse named Nancy. A three-story barn stood behind the house. Extensive cornfields stretched along the borders of Church and Ferry streets. The Ameses sold fresh corn in season. Bessie and her husband, the late Robert S. Davis, maintained a farm with pigs and chickens. Bessie is perhaps best remembered for her devotion to the Marshfield school-lunch programs and her nearly twenty years of working in the South River School cafeteria. Bob Ames was owner of the Marshfield Sand and Gravel Company. Current occupants of the house are fourth-generation Susan Davis O'Grady and her husband, Steven.

To this village of ministers and spirits came the United States Coast Guard to keep watch over the ships at sea. During World War II a Coast Guard communications station was established in 1943 in an elegant house built by Dr. Harold Hunt in 1901. Commanding a superb view of the South River and the sea, the station is now used by the Coast Guard for transmitting weather maps by radio facsimile, exchanging long-range communications with stations as far away as the Gulf of California and the Antarctic, and for participating in an international ice patrol, sending out bulletins twice a day from Marshfield.

At one period, fifty Coast Guardsmen lived at the station on South River Street. Dr. Hunt's large house on the property was used for the staff until 1976. The house has been sold recently. The Coast Guard communications station is housed now in a smaller facility at the foot of the hill. The station keeps track of shipping from the North Atlantic to the Caribbean and the southwestern coast of the United States twenty-four hours a day. The station is equipped with the most up-to-date communications equipment.

Neatly tucked into the side of the hill on Ferry Street, across from the Coast Guard property, stands a cape-style house. It was built in 1820 by Bela Lewis, Jr., who was a cordwainer, or leather craftsman who made shoes. It is now the home of the Hatherly Shop Antiques. Hazel Sjoberg, the gracious owner of this interesting antique business, has been running the Hatherly Shop for more than thirty years. She specializes in glass, china, and small pieces of silverware. Hazel was instrumental in organizing the first antique show and sale sponsored by the evening division of the Marshfield Women's Club in 1960. She and an enthusiastic neighbor, Cathy Whalen, who runs Calendula Antiques, exhibit and sell their wares at antique shows. Cathy is a Marshfield schoolteacher. She has long been involved in town historical activities and served on the 350th Commemorative Trust. Her husband, Lawrence Whalen, was chairman and member of the Advisory Board in the 1970s.

This village of merchants and shipbuilders, Loyalists, and Methodists became a lucrative merchant center of another kind by the middle of the twentieth century. The sand and gravel companies started their extensive operations. They transported their cargo, not in schooners and brigs, but in eighteen-wheel trucks. Many of these leviathan loads went to Logan Airport in Boston to expand the facility, thus contributing to an international commerce of a different sort. In this case, however, although much was removed from Marshfield, no cargo of imported goods was returned. Instead of mighty vessels being built at the water's edge, mighty holes were dug in the landscape of Centre Marshfield.

The first business involved in these operations was the Marshfield Sand and Gravel Company on Clay Pit Road. Established in 1942, it is considered to be the oldest pit operation on the South Shore. The original pit had been dug by the New York, New Haven and Hartford Railroad Company at the time that the nearby railroad bed was being constructed in 1871. It was owned and operated from 1942 to 1968 by Robert T. Ames. John T. Flagg of Marshfield became a partner with Ames in later years. Ames and Flagg sold to the Sylvester A. Ray Company of West Roxbury in 1968. At that time the operation was the largest sand, gravel, and concrete firm on the South Shore. The sale of the buildings and land on Clay Pit Road was one of the biggest sales of property made in the area. Sylvester A. Ray has been very supportive of the Marshfield 350th anniversary.

The so-called Lach Pit on Church Street was also first owned by Bob Ames. This pit was reactivated in the early 1970s by Charles Lach. Another gravel pit was started at about the same time by Kenneth Gauley at the corner of South River Street and Grove Street (now Cranberry Cove). The nearby five acres of cranberry bogs were recently sold by Everett Pearl to Charles Ruisi.

The increased gravel removal caused widespread concern about the general use and operation of gravel pits in the town. Many of the pits were originally opened to obtain sand and gravel for cranberry bog or railroad bed construction, or for use by private contractors. Some pits were closed for periods of time. A discussion ensued over the legality of reopening old pits and claiming continuous use.

By 1972 some residents of Marshfield were seriously alarmed at the extensive earth-removal operations. They were concerned about the

Gravel pit cartoon from the Silver Lakes News, *9 December 1971*

increase of trucking, the size of the trucks, the extended hours of removal activity, and the overall environmental impact. A group of fifteen citizens introduced an article in the 1972 Marshfield Town Meeting, and the town passed a comprehensive zoning bylaw to control the operations of the gravel pits. Called the Earth Removal Bylaw, it gave the selectmen the authority to regulate the sand and gravel operations.

Since the town owns considerable land around the gravel pits between Grove Street and Clay Pit Road, it seemed a suitable place to locate landfill areas. Additional land was acquired by the town in 1961 for this use. In 1974 a large gravel pit was opened for a commercial landfill project, operated by Sylvester Ray. Today there are two sanitary landfill operations in the area, comprising an area of forty acres. Twenty-three acres are for landfill and eleven for septic disposal. A cement operation, called Ray Precast, is located on Clay Pit Road.

Housing developments in Centre Marshfield include Howes Brook and Carpenter Lane, started about 1970; Smoke Hill Ridge and High Beacon Waye, constructed in the early 1980s; and Valley Pasture, begun in 1988. Very much earlier came the housing complexes at Kent Park and Telegraph Hill, both begun sometime after 1903.

Considerable acreage of conservation land has been acquired by the town in the Marshfield Centre area. There are 136 scattered acres of South River marshland, a small acreage called Kent Park Woodlots, and 13 acres known as Shearwater Marsh. Parts of the 707 acres of Carolina Hill conservation land lie within the bounds of Centre Marshfield. The Charles O. Monahan Sanctuary, a little over 11 acres, is owned by the South Shore Natural Science Center, and 15 acres, called the LeBlanc Marsh, is owned by the Plymouth County Wildlands Trust.

Although this peaceful little village at the heart of Marshfield might be called today the center of disruption and disposal, it is still a place of great delight along its easterly slopes, where the river flows at the foot of Snake and Telegraph hills. Here, as the United States Coast Guard watches over the world's oceans, the residents command a spectacular view over the beaches at Humarock and Rexhame to the blue cup of Cape Cod Bay beyond. Gone are the open fields and farms, gone is the church, the railroad depot and the post office, gone are the former generations, but for those who make Centre Marshfield their home, it remains at the center of their hearts.

View from Sea Rivers over the town beach at Rexhame

*White's Ferry Shipyards as depicted in a
mural in the home of Walter and
Margery Frye*
Oil by Carl Blaha, 1935

*Tacking up the South River in a
melonseed skiff skippered by Roger
Crawford*
*Photograph by W. Ray Freden,
courtesy of Roger Crawford*

*Hatch/Keene house on the edge of
Little's Pond, Summer Street, in
Sea View/Littletown
Photograph by Cynthia Hagar Krusell*

*Little's Creek near Bullock's
Boatyard, Sea View/Humarock
Photograph by Gerhard O. Walter*

Nathaniel Phillips house on
Summer Street in Marshfield
Hills. This house was built in
1819.
Photograph by Cynthia Hagar Krusell

Elijah Leonard house, Prospect Street, Marshfield Hills. This house, built in 1803, was lived in by ministers of the Second Congregational Church.
Photograph by Cynthia Hagar Krusell

North River from the Route 3
bridge, looking toward Two Mile
Photograph by Cynthia Hagar Krusell

Adam Rogers house, Highland Street, North Marshfield
Photograph by Cynthia Hagar Krusell

Sunset at the site of Rogers Shipyard near the North River at Gravelly Beach, North Marshfield
Photograph by Cynthia Hagar Krusell

Rogers / Nelson house on Moses
Rogers Hill, Highland Street,
North Marshfield
Photograph by Cynthia Hagar Krusell

Sunset over the Green Harbor
River
Photograph by Cynthia Hagar Krusell

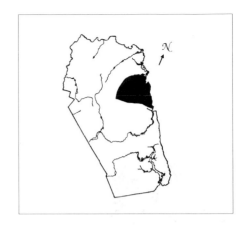

Sea View Village

Marshfield men had lived by building and sailing ships.
— Richard Warren Hatch[1]

SEA VIEW is the "little" village. Settled in the 1650s by the Little family, it was called Littletown for many years. Some still use the name to designate the stretch of Summer Street between Pleasant and Elm streets. This is the heart of old Littletown, where the Littles came and where they stayed until the early years of the twentieth century.

Situated on a flat plain at the edge of the North River marshes and nestled between Carolina Hill and Holly Hill, Littletown is only a part of Sea View. The area also includes Holly and Ferry hills and the part of Humarock that lies on the west bank of the river as far as the Elm and Ferry streets' intersection. The riverside, close against the Ferry Hill upland, was and is the portal to Sea View. Here, near the present site of Humarock Bridge, the great schooners and brigs, barks and sloops of another era were loaded with cargo and crew for world-wide voyages. Here, returning from far-ranging adventures, the stately ships drew up to the dockside with their loads of sugar and spices, coffee and teas, cotton and wool. The Littles, Keenes, and Halls were reunited with their sailor sons, their captains, and commanders, fresh home from perhaps a two- to three-year-long voyage.

The wind blows clean from the sea over this north-facing land. It brings cool east breezes in summer and raging northeast storms in winter. The tops of the hills command a superb 180-degree view of the wide marshes and rivers and of the ocean beyond. The flat plain at Littletown contains excellent soil for farming, while the brook that flows between the hills has been, long since, "flowed up" to provide water power for milling. It is aptly named Little's Creek.

Thomas Little came to this gentle place in 1650. He built a house by the stream and "got about" farming. In 1633 he had married Anne Warren, daughter of Richard Warren of the *Mayflower*. Thomas was a lawyer and served Marshfield as a constable in 1662. He died in 1671. Seven generations of Littles lived here, worked the land, and served the community. Some sailed the seas in merchant enterprise. Others became representatives to the legislature, moderators of Marshfield town meetings, and ministers. Many went to Harvard College. One shot his cousin and then himself while hunting for wild pigeons on Belle House Neck, Scituate. All farmed and fished and grew to love this place at the side of the river and the sea.[2]

Perhaps the most famous and memorable of the Littles are the brothers Luther and George Little, patriot naval heroes of the American Revolution.

Sons of Lemuel and Penelope Eames Little, they grew up at the family homestead in Littletown with their eight siblings. They went to sea as young boys on merchant ships, leaving the docks at White's Ferry Shipyards bound for the Kennebec, the Carolinas, and the Carribean. It is not surprising that, after a childhood spent on the North River and the sea, they chose careers as shipping merchants, becoming ship captains and later, naval commanders.

Captain George Little, eldest brother, was born in 1754. At the age of twenty-four he was commissioned an officer of the Massachusetts navy on 30 November 1778. He served as second lieutenant on the brigantine *Active* and then on the brig *Hazard*. The latter was pressed into service during the American Revolution for the so-called Penobscot Expedition of July 1779. His brother Luther, serving as commander of the sloop *Pidgeon*, was also ordered into action on this ill-fated naval expedition. The British were well entrenched with one thousand troops on Penobscot Bay in the vicinity of present-day Castine, Maine, from which they were preying on American merchant activity. Determined to oust them from this strategic position, Dudley Saltonstall, commander of the armed frigate *Warren*, commandeered and outfitted a fleet of nineteen merchant ships at Boston. There were twelve hundred militiamen and one hundred artillerymen, the latter under command of Lieutenant Colonel Paul Revere. The American troops outnumbered the British. Though it appeared a formidable fleet and was the largest naval force assembled by New England during the Revolution, it failed utterly in its attempt to defeat the English and was itself totally destroyed. Due to poor strategy and leadership, the American fleet was trapped by the British fleet at the head of Penobscot Bay, near the present city of Bangor. Fearful of capture by the British, the Americans burned many of their own ships, abandoned the expedition and, escaping on small boats, made their way back to Boston, some traveling by foot.[3]

Luther Little, in his journal of the Penobscot Expedition, wrote:

My sloop lay above where the fleet was destroyed and was left unharmed. Many suffered and died in travelling across the woods from fatigue and want of food ere they reached the Kennebec. During the journey the Commander was shot at twice but without success. Myself and ten others proceeded in a barge down the Penobscot near to the English fleet where we left the barge and proceeded into the woods. We then pitched a tent for the night carrying provisions. The next day we travelled to Belfast where we arrived at noon. The inhabitants had fled. We entered a vacant house. From a field adjoining we gathered some green corn, killed a lamb and cooked us a dinner. Then we left the house and traveled toward Broad Bay. Here we purchased a boat and came up to Boston.[4]

The next year, George Little was appointed first lieutenant of the *Protector*, the largest ship of the Massachusetts navy, carrying twenty-six guns and two hundred men. Her captain was John Foster Williams of Boston. George served for ten months on the *Protector*, from October 1779 to August 1780, and again for fourteen months, until November 1781. On 9 June 1780 the *Protector* was engaged in battle off Newfoundland with the British privateer *Admiral Duff*, thirty-two guns. The privateer caught fire and blew up with the loss of all but fifty-five men who were rescued by the *Protector*. Only six Americans were lost. A year later, in May 1781, the *Protector* was captured by the *Medea* with a crew of one hundred thirty men. Lieutenant George Little was taken to England and imprisoned at Plymouth, Devon, the very place from which some of his ancestors had departed one hundred sixty years earlier in search of freedom in the new world. George scaled the prison walls, escaped in a wherry to France, and made his way back to Marshfield.[5]

In March 1782 George captained the *Winthrop*, a thirteen- gun sloop of the Massachusetts navy, on several voyages until June 1783. The *Winthrop*

Sea View/Humarock, about 1895, looking west across the river to Holly Hill. In the distance can be seen the Governor George W. Emery estate on Holly Hill.

captured two English privateers and "sent into Boston nearly the whole force they (the British) possessed at Penobscot." This must have compensated somewhat for the disastrous Penobscot Expedition just three years earlier.[6]

During the war with France in 1799, George was appointed captain in the United States Navy and given command of the United States frigate *Boston*, carrying twenty-eight guns, two hundred thirty men. In March 1800 the frigate engaged in several battles in the West Indies and in October 1800 captured the French corvette *Le Berceau* and four other French vessels.[7]

George was discharged from the navy on 22 October 1801 under the Peace Establishment Act and retired to his farm at the corner of Summer and Main streets, Marshfield Hills. His house was located east of the present Massachusetts Audubon South Shore Regional Center. He died in 1809. His wife was Rachel Rogers of Marshfield Hills. They named their second son Edward Preble Little after Commodore Edward Preble of Portland, Maine, who had been midshipman on the *Protector* and first lieutenant on the *Winthrop* with George Little. It is this branch of the Little family for whom the so-called Little's Bridge over the North River to Scituate is named.[8]

George Little's brother Luther, born in 1756, went to sea at age fifteen in 1771. He shipped out on a merchant sloop carrying lumber and rice between the Kennebec River and Martinique. Subsequently he served on a number of coastal vessels and was commander of the sloop *Pidgeon* in July 1779 when it was pressed into service on the Penobscot Expedition. The army was under the leadership of General Solomon Lovell, whose daughter was later to become Luther's bride. The naval transports were loaded with soldiers and provisions and the fleet headed north to oust the British.[9]

In 1780 Luther was midshipman on the *Protector* with his brother Lieutenant George Little. Luther was severely wounded in the jaw and mouth in the encounter with the British *Admiral Duff*. Back in Marshfield he was soon bored with life on the farm, declaring that he was "weary of the monotony of a farmer's life." Undaunted, he went to sea again, serving on a number of coastal ships, making in all twenty-four trips to the West Indies for sugar and molasses.[10]

In 1791 Luther began a series of six trips to Russia, starting every year in January. His ship waited in Lisbon for the ice to go out of the Baltic Sea. About the first of March he would continue to St. Petersburg in Russia with freight. He had many fascinating adventures on his various voyages.

Luther recalled that:

The first of these voyages I arrived in the Baltic Sea too early in the spring. I found great fields of ice. I got by them and succeeded in getting up the Gulf of Finland as far as abreast of Reval (now Tallinn, Estonia). Here I was frozen in solid. The next day a sleigh with four horses came alongside. The gentleman who was in it offered to take me up to the city. He was the clerk of a German merchant. He advised me to send my bills over by mail to Petersburg. I stayed at that merchant's house that night and he sent me on board my vessel in the morning.

I was invited while in Reval by the gentleman, to whom I sold my cargo, to the wedding of his niece given by her grandmother. The ceremony was performed in the Assembly House. The guests were three hundred in number, some coming a great distance. I was the only foreigner among them. The parties married were Mr. John Fessay to Miss Catherine Dubray. They had a band of German musicians who struck up a lively air as every carriage drew up to the Assembly House. The bride was a beautiful girl dressed with taste and splendor. Her gown was of white satin spangled with a rich gold

Luther Little, 1756-1842, naval commander and maritime merchant
Photograph courtesy of Eleanor Magoon

border round the bottom. Her brow was ornamented with diamonds valued at three hundred guineas. The bridegroom was dressed in a superb suit of black, white satin vest ornamented and spangled with gold.

After the ceremony which was of the Church of England, all were seated and took coffee. By this time supper was announced which consisted of one hundred and ten different dishes of meats besides every variety of jelly tarts, etc. There followed a very elegant desert. The meats were all carved and handed by the servants. We were three hours at the table. The bride was placed on an eminence from which she could overlook the company. The bridegroom's father proposed drinking her health in a glass of champagne. It was gracefully done by all rising and touching their glasses at once.

After supper the room was immediately cleared, the musicians placed and then began the leading dance by the bride and groom and all their relatives. The set dancing fifty couples at a time. The dancing continued 'til twelve the next day when the gentleman's father invited all the company to his house the next evening. Then followed the gifts. Every guest had a present of some kind, many of them very valuable. Mine was a pair of large silver spoons P.D. (Peter Dubray). The company then all withdrew.

I stayed in the city of Reval six weeks. When the ice opened we sailed for Petersburg and got into Kronstadt Island the 28th of May. I found sending my bills by mail very much to my advantage. We loaded and returned to Boston. By this voyage I cleared the Vessel and five hundred pounds sterling for the owners. [11]

Luther Little spent seventeen years on these merchant voyages. On one of his return trips from Norway in 1795, his brother William Little died of consumption aboard ship. Luther was stricken by this, declaring that his own brother was the "only man I ever lost in all my West Indies and Russian voyages." [12]

In 1788 Luther had married his cousin Susannah White, thus uniting not only the leading merchant families of Marshfield, but also the two major settlers of Sea View and Centre Marshfield. He and Susannah had three children. In 1798, after Susannah's death, he married Hannah Lovell, daughter of General Solomon Lovell, as his second wife and had eight more children. Luther bought out the other Little heirs and continued to live in the old Little homestead, still standing near Little's Pond (58 Summer Street, owned today by Thomas and Ellen Rooney). Captain Luther Little had several sons, two of whom were Solomon and William. Solomon lived in the homestead and William built the house (later owned by the Gerald O'Donnells), now 90 Summer Street, in 1834. [13]

Solomon's son Luther Little continued to live in the old house (58 Summer Street) with his sister Joanna. He spent the winters in Boston where he was in the steel business. During the summer Luther was at his Littletown farm where he had cows and horses, a big barn, a chauffeur, and hired help. The estate was beautifully maintained, and he was known for his elegant formal dinners. Joanna died in 1938 and, at Luther's death in 1941, the house passed out of the family.

The schooner *Luther Little* was built in 1917 and named for him. Now a derelict ship, the *Luther Little* and another old ship, the *Hesper*, are at Wiscasset, Maine, on the bank of the Sheepscot River. They are the subject of many photographs.

George and Luther had another brother, Jedediah Little, who stayed in Littletown. He built the elegant square brick-end Federal house at today's 119 Summer Street (owned by William and Mary Gill), across from what is

now called Captain Luther Little Waye. Jedediah was in the business of running a chaise between Boston and Marshfield in the early 1800s. He would drive the route to Boston one day and come home the next. Jedediah was badly injured in an accident and had to have his leg amputated. He undertook the operation with great fortitude, refusing any painkiller.[14]

Jedediah Little married into two Marshfield families, his first wife being Betsy Tilden and his second wife, Bethia Hatch. Jedediah tried in vain to have the town divided into a north and south section. His was not the first attempt to make two towns of the 28.32 square miles of Marshfield.[15]

Like the Littles in Sea View/Littletown, the Halls at Sea View/Humarock were a prominent shipbuilding family. They lived along the riverside on the end of Ferry Street between Rogers Wharf (at foot of Ferry Hill) and today's Humarock Bridge. The present North River House and the old house, which stood where the Bridgwaye Inn is today, were the homes of William and Luke Hall. Other homes belonging to the Halls from time to time were scattered along Ferry Street between Centre Marshfield and South River Street.

First-comer was Adam Hall, who married Sarah Sherman in 1725 and built the house at 712 Ferry Street about 1750. The land belonged to Sarah's father, William Sherman. Adam and Sarah had seven children. A son, Adam, married Keziah Ford in 1752 and their son Luke Hall married Anna Tuels in 1794 and was shipmaster at the ferry. Luke was described by one of his shipbuilding sons, William, as "a large, well proportioned man who stood all of six foot high. I have known him to weigh 244 pounds. He was of a sandy complexion, had light hair and always wore short side whiskers. . . . His dress on Sundays and upon special occasions, as long as he lived, consisted of cream colored knee britches, silver buckles, and white stockings. He wore long white-topped tassel boots, ruffled bosom. He was a noble, a gentlemanly, a fine-looking man."[16]

Luke Hall was the first of the Hall family to be connected with the White's Ferry Shipyards, around 1790. He acquired great wealth in the merchant trade and died of yellow fever on Staten Island, New York, in 1815. He left a considerable estate, including three farms in Marshfield and interests in a number of ships.[17]

There were, from time to time, several shipyards at White's Ferry including the Halls' and Keenes' yards, sometimes referred to collectively as White's Ferry Shipyards. This area was the harbor of Marshfield, with access to the ocean at the river mouth. From the crests of the hills and along the river bank could be seen the tall ships as they arrived or departed from the wharfs. The earliest record of any shipbuilding here was in 1705.

Luke Hall's three sons — Luke, William, and Samuel — started shipbuilding at White's Ferry about 1825. Sam left by 1828 to seek his fortune elsewhere. Luke and William worked the yard together until 1837. Then Luke carried on alone for many years.[18]

The Hall brothers' shipyard was known far and wide and was the largest shipbuilding operation in Marshfield. The master-carpenter brothers built schooners, brigs, and sloops, from 72 tons to a 283-ton whaler. These ships traveled all the world's major trade routes and went whaling as well. Most of the ships were sold out of the family to owners up and down the eastern seaboard.[19]

The Halls also built some of the famous North River packet ships which traded locally between the river and Boston, carrying farm produce and timber and bringing back items from the China and Mediterranean trade, as well as staple products for the stores along the river towns. These small

Sign erected by the North River Historical Society in 1919, indicating the location of one of the shipyards at the edge of the river at Ferry and Sea streets

packet ships were often owned by as many as twenty-four men, all of whom reaped profits from this local trade. The only steamboat ever built on the river was built here. A 21-ton vessel, she was built in 1839 and named the *Mattakees*. At about the same time, the schooner *Orleans*, last ship built at the Halls' shipyard, was launched.[20]

The old ferry crossing at the foot of Ferry Hill

In addition to the shipbuilding at the White's Ferry Shipyards, there was also the business of making spars, cordage, sails, and rigging. The great ships built at the many shipyards along the reaches of the North River were hauled down to the White's Ferry yards to be rigged and outfitted. Here they drew up to the docks to have the masts stepped and the rigging assembled before putting out to sea.[21]

Of the three Hall brothers, Samuel Hall brought the greatest fame to the family, not in the Marshfield shipyards, but in the great East Boston shipbuilding business. Sam was born in 1800, at the dawn of the nineteenth century. He attended school for about six months. At the age of fourteen, he went on a voyage to South Carolina with his father, Luke Hall. On the return trip, they were both stricken with yellow fever at Staten Island, New York. His father died and was buried there. Sam made his way back to Marshfield and apprenticed at the Barstows' shipyard, up the North River in Hanover. At the age of twenty-one, with twenty-five cents in his pocket and an ax, he went to work at the shipyards at Medford, Massachusetts. Later he studied the shipbuilding craft at Camden, Maine, returning to Marshfield to build ships with his brothers at White's Ferry. For a while, Sam worked for the Duxbury shipbuilder Ezra Weston, and then established his own yard in Duxbury in 1837.[22]

After a financial depression began to damage the shipping industry, Sam left his native area to found his famous yard at East Boston in 1839. With his ambition and skill, Sam helped to make shipbuilding the chief industry of East Boston and became himself one of the major builders and one of the most outstanding naval architects in America. He built a total of 170 large merchant vessels. Perhaps his most famous was the clipper ship

The Waverly, *a 232-ton brig built in 1827 by Samuel Hall at White's Ferry*
Unsigned oil painting from collection of Peabody Museum

Surprise, which broke all records for speed on a voyage to San Francisco in 1850. She sailed 16,308 miles in just ninety-six days, the greatest run being 284 miles in twenty-four hours, and "she reefed her topsails but twice during the entire voyage."[23]

Among the ships that Sam Hall built was the schooner *Lapwing* for Daniel Webster. In a letter to Webster from East Boston 11 August 1849, Sam Hall wrote:

> *You express a desire that I should visit your place and ascertain how well the* Lapwing *sails, and also what these waters yield in the way of cod and haddock. Sir, nothing would give me greater pleasure than to pay a visit to your mansion and my native town, which is Marshfield, and take a trip to Brant Rock, where I have spent so many hours, in days gone by, with Seth Peterson, Chandler Oldham, William Barstow, Captain Samuel Baker, and Uncle Charles Baker, as we were wont to call him and many others that I could mention, in shooting coots and loons, and catching the cod and haddock; but I am doubtful if I shall be able to do it this season, as the business is very pressing, and, together with my private affairs, makes it difficult for me to leave even for a few days.*[24]

Sam Hall not only made a fortune, but became an important businessman of Boston. He served as alderman of the city and in 1850 was responsible for seeing that water was piped from Cochituate reservoir to East Boston. He was a member of the Massachusetts State Legislature from Boston and, for one term, from Marshfield. He was president of the Boston Dry Dock Company, as well as president of the East Boston Ferry Company and of the Maverick National Bank. Most important for Marshfield, Sam Hall was responsible for the legislation that enabled the Duxbury and Cohasset Railroad to extend their tracks to Marshfield in 1871.[25]

Sam Hall married Christiana Kent. After her death, he married Huldah B. Sherman, and they had four children. At his death in 1870, Hall owned 170 acres of "home farm and meadow" in Marshfield. Some of this land was on Holly Hill. Hall's land extended along Elm and Ferry streets and included the old John Phillips saltbox house (100 Ferry Street) and farm near present Napier Road. A 40-acre parcel on the west side of Holly Hill was owned by the Keene family in 1879. At the foot of Holly Hill was a town pound near the intersection of Elm Street and Ferry Hill Road..[26]

Sam Hall's daughter Marcia Ives Hall, born in 1836, married George W. Emery, governor of Utah, in 1866 and opened another chapter of Sea

The Dispatch, *a 139-ton brig built in 1795 by Simeon Keene at White's Ferry*
Watercolor by Michele Felice Corne from collection of Peabody Museum

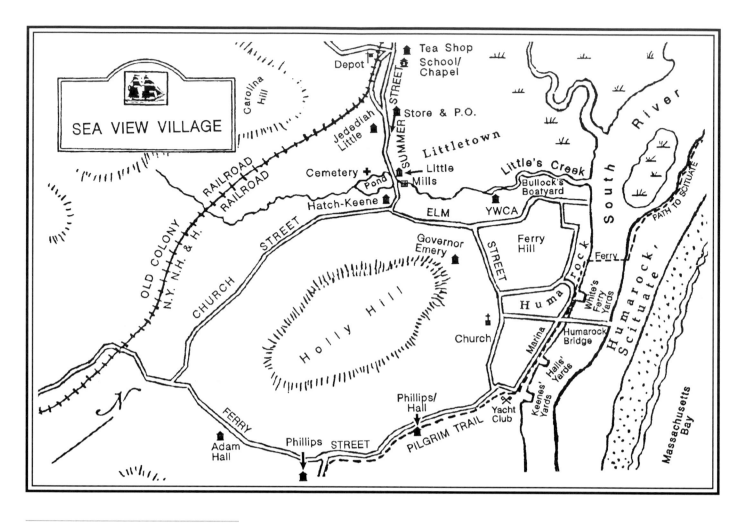

Sea View Village

View/Humarock history. In 1885 they built a mansion on the Hall property on Holly Hill. Sam Hall's widow, Huldah B. Hall, lived nearby until her death in 1879. The Governor Emery house was razed in the late 1940s. Later the land was acquired by the William Grahams and their daughter Virginia and her husband, William Gill, who were responsible for building the present Christmas Tree Lane. Large houses have recently been erected on this spectacular ocean-view property.[27]

George Emery was born in Corinth, Maine, in 1833, later moving to Medford, Massachusetts. He went to Dartmouth College and received a law degree at Albany, New York. George was appointed supervisor of internal revenue for six southern states in 1869. In 1875 President Ulysses S. Grant appointed him governor of Utah, which was then a territory where all elective offices were held by Mormons. With absolute veto power from his seat at Salt Lake City, Emery built Utah into a financially and politically viable state. Retiring to his farm at Marshfield, he became president of the Marshfield Agricultural Society. Emery died a very wealthy man in 1909. The value of his real estate was $26,555, a large amount for that era. His estate included six horses, ten cows, two heifers, and three carriages. He owned four houses, stables, a tool house, a barn and shed, ice house, beach house, windmill, and tower, and some 475 acres of land.[28]

Edwin W. Dwight of Auburndale, Massachusetts, bought the Emery estate sometime before 1922. He was the son of William Dwight and Mary

Jane Winslow, a Kenelm Winslow descendant. Dwight was responsible, along with Robert S. Boles, for starting the development of Holly Hill in the 1920s. Dwight lost his mansion at the time of the 1929 crash and died in 1931. At that time there were still horses and cows grazing on Holly Hill.[29]

Building in the area was continued by Bob Boles in the 1930s and 1940s. Emery, Dwight, and Upland roads were laid out and houses built in the early thirties. Juniper Road followed in the forties, Napier Road in 1958, and Indian, Buttonwood, Holly, Cedar, and Boles roads were developed in the early 1960s. Some of these roads have been extended and further built on in the 1980s. Birch Road began to develop in 1984. Roads near the Julian Street Bridge, including Ridge, Blueberry, and Bayberry roads, were laid out and began to develop in the late 1950s and early 1960s. The Julian Street Bridge was temporary for a while, then made permanent in 1942 to accommodate the Coast Guard personnel at the Fourth Cliff station during World War II. It provided an additional exit from the beach area.

Among other activities, Dwight gave the property for St. Teresa's Church on the side of Holly Hill off Dwight Road. The mission church grew out of St. Mary of the Nativity parish in Scituate and was built about 1930. From 1925 to 1930 Catholic services and Masses were held at Katherine Donovan's shop in the ell of her house in Sea View/Littletown. Pews and an altar were installed for the worshippers.

Although the Littles and the Halls may be considered the leading families of Sea View, mention should also be made of the Keene and Hatch families. The Keenes were shipbuilders at White's Ferry by 1787, a little before the arrival of the Halls. Simeon Keene and his sons Simeon and Benjamin built and operated the Keenes' Shipyard. Family members lived in houses along Elm Street from Sea Street to Ferry Hill Road.[30]

Apparently Captain Noah Hatch was the first of the Hatch name to settle in Sea View. He married Alice Little, daughter of Ephraim Little, in 1767. They lived on her family land in a house (no longer there), which stood at Summer Street across from the present Marshfield Auto Body shop. Noah is listed as having a 70-ton vessel in 1771 and was probably engaged in the merchant trade. He attended the Episcopal church and was a Loyalist at the time of the Revolution. Other Hatches married into the Keene family, thus contributing to kinship ties in Sea View.[31]

The large square colonial house (27 Summer Street) that stands grandly on the edge of Little's Pond in Sea View/Littletown near the Elm Street intersection was home to the Hatches for many generations. Charles Hatch, of the North Marshfield Hatch family, settled here at the time of his marriage to Joanna Winslow in 1787. Charles was one of the drivers of the two-wheel chaise for Jedediah Little's transportation business. Charles and his brother Benjamin Hatch owned a 27-ton sloop, the *North River*.[32]

Charles's son Charles, Jr., ran a store in this neighborhood, possibly in the old house. Supplies for the store were probably brought down from Boston in the sloop. An old ledger kept by Charles, Jr., from 1822 to 1830 lists some of the items sold at the store. These included molasses, sugar, lemons, tea, flour, corn, eggs, beans, raisins, ginger, nutmeg, seeds, red flannel, cotton cloth, buttons, candles, rice, and hides. Interestingly, the current owner of the square house, Joan Mahoney, and her late husband, John, restored the old 132-foot Boston pilot ship as the windjammer *Roseway*, which sails out of Camden, Maine, today.[33]

Although the Hatch family was no longer living in the area by 1903, Alfred Jener Keene was living in the old Hatch house on the pond. His son was Horace Keene, known to many generations of Marshfield schoolchildren as the bus driver for the North School. He had an ice-cutting business from 1920 to 1945, taking ice from the pond and storing it in a barn on Church Street. One of his summer workers was neighbor Bertram O'Donnell. Horace also had wood lots from which he cut and sold wood as a business, employing a hired man. Horace was president of Kiwanis, secretary of the Marshfield Fair for seventeen years, and co-organizer, president, and secretary of the Marshfield Board of Trade. He and his wife, Alice Apollonio, had two daughters, one of whom, Constance (Connie) Keene Lambert, lives in Marshfield Hills today.[34]

Although shipping and shipbuilding were central to life at Sea View/Humarock after 1700, the farmers at Sea View/Littletown were busy with other activities as time went on. The pond on Little's Creek was "flowed up" for milling, and by 1838 the Littles were operating a gristmill. In 1871 William and George Randall purchased the mill from Solomon Little. The Randalls made organ parts and violin cases at a shop at the mill site. In 1884 the shop burned. George rebuilt it in 1885 and continued to manufacture organ parts until 1903.[35]

After George's death, the building was occupied by A. Lincoln Creed, who did house finishing and other woodwork manufacturing there until the early 1940s. He enlarged the building to a three-story structure with an apartment on the top floor. The Posners purchased the mill in the 1940s from Creed. The building was later vacated and allowed to deteriorate. It burned to the ground in 1960.

Over the years the center of Sea View/Littletown saw the arrival of a post office, a number of stores, shoe shops, a school, the railroad depot, two religious organizations, a tea shop, and later, the Langille Garage and Insurance Company. Houses were built along Summer Street, Station Street, and Sea View Avenue. Much later, in 1953, Cedar Acres Road was built by Allan R. Wheeler on the old Luther Little farm land. Wheeler also built the roads off Dog Lane on David Seager's land. These include Deer Hill Lane (1954), Idyl Wilde Circle (late 1950s), Cotton Tail Lane (1960), Pinehurst Road (1969), and Oakleaf Drive (1970), all predating Captain Luther Little Waye (1974), which was the last road to be developed in the old Littletown area.

Mill at Keene's Pond, Sea View.
This mill was built in 1885 and
burned down in 1960.
Photograph courtesy of Philip Randall

The Lost Art of Icing

In the 1930s and 1940s my dad [Horace Keene] was an iceman in Sea View. One could not know upon looking at the placid pond known as Keene's Pond that every winter, for about a week, it was the scene of orchestrated frenzy.

The ice had to be thick enough to make it worthy of harvesting (minimum of eight inches) and contain a balance in black- or clear-frozen water and the minimum of snow-frozen ice. This was due to the fact that ice made from frozen snow melted a good deal faster than black ice. After watching anxiously and finally making the decision to "go icing," my father would put out the word and men and older boys would gladly apply for the work of harvesting. There were always the "regulars," men who helped year after year and knew their jobs well. We could always count on Lyman Kent, who knew every facet of the operation, to keep it under control. Our hired man Russ Williamson, known for his inspired and loud cussing, took care of the

layout and quality of the ice field. A horse-drawn saw carved out the approximately twenty-six-inch wide channels through which the floes were guided. The icehouse crew, the energetic and good-natured Italian farmers (Rugani, Biagini, Bandoni, Castiglioni, Frugoli, Doroni) from Pleasant Street, manned the distribution pattern of the ice floes in the icehouse. I think they had the best time of all, if the peals of laughter which echoed from the icehouse meant anything. Charlie Randall kept the cantankerous oil-fired motor going so it would pull the floes up the ramp without conking out. Lin Creed and Manuel Lopes guided the ice floes through the channels into the ice run, and a myriad of other good neighbors scored and sawed the floes as they were guided through the channels by long-handled wooden shafts, known as pikes. Usually there were two to three "cakes" to a floe.

It was a well-run and smooth-working procedure from ice field to

icehouse except when the motor, which pulled the floes up the ramp, coughed and quit. No one minded, however, because this provided time for hot coffee and doughnuts, made by my mother Alice and served by her good friend Anna Nourse.

The icehouse on Church Street is long gone, but served many years to keep the much-needed ice throughout the summer. This was made possible by about eight inches of sawdust insulation in the walls and layers of straw that were packed between the carefully jigsawed layers of ice. This was an art practiced, year after year, by our Italian friends with much camaraderie and blood-warming good red wine. Ice cutting on Keene's Pond, dubbed by my father as "the pond of the constant flow," served as a positive example of how communities worked together for a friend, though being remunerated at about twenty-five cents an hour.

— Constance Keene Lambert

A post office was located in Littletown as early as 1838. Known as the East Post Office, it was in the cape-style house now at 272 Summer Street. (This house was originally situated across the street but was moved when the railroad was built. In the 1920s and 1930s Dorothy King ran a gift shop here called the Little Green Light. Today it is the home of Moyra and Earl Banner.) By 1879 the East Post Office had moved to a store owned by George Currell on the south side of the present intersection of Captain Luther Little Waye and Summer Street.[36]

About 1884 William W. Randall built a post office and store at 112 Summer Street. He was appointed postmaster in 1886. He sold the store to his clerk, Chester Ewell, in 1893. Ewell sold to Alonzo Stevens. In 1920 Lyman Kent bought the store. Sea View had no post office after 1926, but the store continued to operate until the late 1930s. After a fire in the 1960s, the building was razed. About 1849 George H. Weatherbee owned another store in this area. It stood on the west side of Summer Street across from what became the site of the Randall/Ewell/Kent store.[37]

Delivery wagons made door-to-door deliveries throughout the town for many years. Henry I. Carver delivered groceries once a week in a horse-drawn buggy. Cushman and Hathaway Bakery companies brought bread and baked goods. Horace Keene and Russ Williamson delivered ice and Nathan Carp of Boston came around with a dry-goods cart. The Rockland Trust Company had a mobile unit until 1945. People left a "B" card in a window and the bank car would stop. Some people remember when a hurdy-gurdy man with a monkey would, upon occasion, walk the length of

Alonzo Stevens's store on Summer Street at Sea View, in the early 1900s. William W. Randall built the building about 1884. It served as a store and post office over the years. The building was razed in the 1960s.

Photograph courtesy of Philip Randall

Summer Street playing music. Summer Street was a state road and a main thoroughfare before Route 3A was built in 1927.

From 1865 to 1879 the Gardner and Arnold shoe shop operated in what had been the Weatherbee store. The shop employed twenty men. In a large two-story ell there were one hundred shoe-making machines. Beginning in 1879 the shoe business was run for about three years by George H. Pecker, a summer resident. With the development of shoe-making machinery and the coming of the railroad, it was more profitable to enlarge and centralize the shoe industry, which soon moved to Abington and Rockland. The small local shops that had employed only one or two people, as well as larger shops such as Pecker's, were closed. The building once used as a shoe shop by George Pecker was vacant from 1920 to 1930 when Gould Crosby rented it to assemble model boats made by the Randalls in their shop next door. The Crosby shop employed about six people. For a short time a raincoat factory occupied the building which was later razed. Another shoe shop at Sea View was the Doane and Peleg Stevens shop, located on Station Street in 1903.[38]

George Leonard wrote about early shoemakers:

They had small shops in which they did custom work. None did sale work. They made their own pegs out of maple blocks. The thread which they used was home-made; and also the wax. They generally made their own lasts. The soles of the shoes were always sewed; the heels only being pegged. What are called pegged shoes were unknown in those days; ladies' cloth boots and shoes were also unknown. There were no shoes called rights and lefts. They were made straight so as to fit one foot as well as the other.[39]

For many years school sessions in Marshfield were held in individual homes, but town records indicate a schoolhouse in Littletown as early as 1715, one of the earliest school buildings in the town. It was first located on the west side of Summer Street near the old intersection with Dog Lane (old Pleasant Street). Later it was at the southeast corner of the north end of Sea View Avenue at Summer Street. The Littletown school (District 4, sometimes referred to as the East school) was in session until 1909. The 1908 town report states that "the Sea View school has nine pupils and part of these could very easily go to the Hills. There are three grades with one pupil each, one with two and one with four." With too few children, there seemed no reason to continue the school. A suggestion was made at the time that there be only two schools in the town, a North and a South school.[40]

Later the school building (not the original 1715 building) was converted into the Sea View Mission Episcopal Chapel. Shirley O'Donnell writes that "in 1916 Charles and Mary Louise Randall invited the Reverend Howard Barstow to come from the Cohasset Episcopal church to baptize their son John. When the Reverend Barstow learned that there were other Episcopalian families in the area, he arranged to have services in their homes once a month. The families were the Barkers, Josselyns, O'Donnells, Randalls, Smiths, and Whittens. Dr. Henry Nelson of North Marshfield became interested and rented the East schoolhouse for the services. A woman's guild was formed and in August 1922 Luther Little acted as an agent in the purchase of the schoolhouse from the town." In 1948 the chapel was moved to the grounds of the present Trinity Episcopal Church on Highland Street, Marshfield Hills, and used as a parish house.[41]

The railroad arrived in Sea View/Littletown in 1871. The depot on Station Street was the largest on the Plymouth to Boston line and had an apartment on the second floor that was occupied by the stationmaster. The William Freden home at 53 Station Street is built on the site of the old depot. The depot was the social center of Sea View, the place of goings and comings until the track was removed in 1939. The gracious home (189 Summer Street) of Rosemary and Richard Martinez is where a stationmaster once lived. The railroad bed now belongs to the Town of Marshfield and is used by the North River Ride and Drive Club as a foot and bridle path. All motorized vehicles are prohibited.

Near the depot site is the former Sea View Garage, now called the Marshfield Auto Body. It was started as a summer business by Edgar Willey and bought by Charles C. Langille on 28 May 1919. He opened it as a year-round operation. James Lambert of Station Street was a familiar helper in the Langille garage for many years. Charlie sold the garage to Edward Soule in 1946. Soule built the Route 139 Sea View Garage and later sold it to James Gillespie. In the late 1950s Albert Melchionno bought the Langille Sea View Garage and opened the Marshfield Auto Body, now owned by Edward McDonald.

The Langille family has been operating an insurance business in Sea View since 19 August 1926. It was originally located in the garage building, but was moved to the Langille home (211 Summer Street) in 1946 when the garage was sold out of the family. After Charlie Langille died in 1962, his daughter and son-in-law, Eula and Jerry Kroupa, continued to run the Langille Insurance Company. This year the business has been turned over to their daughter and her husband, Gail and Francis Hartnett, the third generation of Langilles to do business in Sea View/Littletown.

The Langilles have been very active in town affairs over the years. Charlie was selectman of Marshfield from 1940 to 1953. He served in the

Massachusetts House of Representatives from 1936 to 1938. He was a veteran of World War I and belonged to the American Legion, the VFW, the Masonic Lodge, and the Elks. He also served many years on the Marshfield Board of Trade and was general manager of the Marshfield Fair. Charlie was a popular and energetic figure about Marshfield from the 1930s to the 1950s. His wife, Gladys Weston Langille, was equally active as a member of the Women's Committee of the Marshfield Fair. She also served as president of the Women's Club, the Marshfield Garden Club, and the Republican Club.

In the Sea View/Humarock area, along the river's edge where the shipyards and wharfs once were, there came stores and restaurants, boat yards, and a yacht club. This is the place where the old path to Scituate, known today as the Pilgrim Trail, ran along what is now Ferry Street from near the intersection with South River Street to the river crossing. A ferry boat operated between Marshfield and Scituate at the narrowest place in what was, before the storm of 1898, the North River. The first ferryman was Jonathan Brewster, son of Elder William Brewster of the *Mayflower*. Once across the river, the traveler continued up the beach along the sand bar which connected the Fourth Cliff with the Third Cliff. The path led to the Scituate First Church on Meetinghouse Lane. There was no bridge in the Humarock area before 1892, when the present bridge was built.

There have been a number of inns and eateries near White's Ferry crossing. Two large square colonial houses stood at the river's edge from probably as early as the 1750s. The North River House is still there. The other house, which burned about 1963, stood where the Bridgwaye Inn is today. The Bridgwaye was once called the Surprise Inn and in 1903 it was the Sea View House, later the Riverside Inn. It has been owned over the years by the Burkhardts, Calloways, Reynolds, and Vickers. It is now owned and operated by John and Francis Polcari. It has in recent years been the site of the meetings of many of the service organizations of Marshfield. These include the Chamber of Commerce, Kiwanis, Rotary, and Lions Club. These

Across the River, Sea View. *This etching, made in 1912 by Sears Gallagher, shows the two colonial houses near White's Ferry. Gallagher, a well-known artist, was born in 1869 and died in 1955. He visited Sea View frequently during the early 1900s.* Etching courtesy of Katherine Gallagher Burr

organizations carry on a spirit of brotherhood and world-wide concern which the merchants and sea captains of old would have understood.

A modern-day descendant of the small neighborhood stores of the nineteenth century might be the grocery and liquor store at Sea and Ferry streets. Now called the North River Beverage, the store was for many years owned by Howard Stedman, then by Jim Sachetti, and later, by Bob Farley. It is presently owned by Richard Ricci and his son Christopher. In the small building just west of North River Beverage, there used to be the Davis bakery, where one could buy baked goods, baked beans, and fish cakes. Now called Dockside Donuts, it is operated by Bob and Jean Huntoon. Across the street at 20 Sea Street is the Headways Beauty Salon. This building was the Miramare Pizza in the 1950s and 1960s. Around the corner, on Ferry Street at the waterside, is the Fourth Cliff Seafood, a fish market owned by Louise and Herb Kemball and run by Barry Gregory. There has been a fish market and bait shop at the site since the mid-1950s. At one time it was run by Warren Pearson.

A little further south along the riverside, there has been a restaurant since the 1950s, although there is none there today. In the 1950s this restaurant was called the Shack, then it was the White's Ferry Restaurant run by Theo Hicken, and later, the Net Result operated by Steven Craig. It closed in 1985. Nearby, from 1955 to 1960, there was a barbershop called the Clip Joint.

Perhaps the boat yards are the most appropriate replacements for the shipyards and spar yards of another era. There have been a number of boat yards on the site of today's Humarock Marina (1240 Ferry Street). Robert S. Boles started a marine business there in the early 1930s. He sold boats, inboard and outboard motors, and marine hardware. He had one of the first Johnson-motor franchises on the South Shore. Boles was a boat builder as well, and his specialty was a kind of racing outboard boat known as the Humarock Baby. Another Boles boat was called the Humarock Husky. Bob Boles was responsible for having the river channel dredged in the Humarock area. He served as selectman for the town.

In the early 1950s the boat yard was purchased by Eben G. (Duke) Townes, Jr., who added more buildings In 1968 it became the Humarock Marina and was owned by Herb Kemball and son. The business was expanded and boat slips were built. The marina was later owned by John Dennehy. There are now seventy-five slips and it is a complete service marina, owned by Jack Baker. Herb Kemball tells of an old schooner hull that lies buried at the riverside. He has scavenged the dead eyes and chain plates from this Humarock wreck. No clue has surfaced as to its identity.

Across Ferry Street from Humarock Marina, near the site of the old Ferry shipyards, is Crawford Boat Building (1245 Ferry Street). Roger Crawford and his assistant John Dietenhofer build ships of another sort today. Roger constructs fiberglass reproductions of eighteenth- and nineteenth-century boats. The Swampscott dory is a replica of a 16-foot vessel used for fishing off the beach. The 13′ 8″ Melonseed skiff reproduces a vessel once used for duck hunting in the central Atlantic states. It is a sleek, fast-sailing, seaworthy little boat. Roger combines an interest in reproducing the older quality-built boats with a skill in using modern materials to produce an unusually elegant craft. The shipbuilding craftsmen of the nineteenth-century Ferry shipyards would be pleased to see the Crawford reproductions, so very much in the tradition of the old shipyards.

Two other Sea View craftsmen dedicated to the fine art of woodworking typical of another era are Ray Freden and Philip Randall. Ray carves wooden bird decoys, a craft which evolved here on the Atlantic coast. Whittling his birds with a Stanley knife, he makes twenty-four different types of birds in many poses. He then paints them with a cracked, weathered finish resembling antique decoys. Phil Randall uses antique power and hand tools to craft unique and beautiful moldings, clock cases, raised paneling, cupboards, turned finials, and urns. Woodworking is in the family tradition.

Phil's grandfather, William Randall, sold his Sea View store in 1893 and built a shop at his house at 91 Summer Street in 1906. He also manufactured organ parts in his shop. The equipment was powered by a gasoline engine. The turbine was purchased in Boston and transported by train to Sea View. Randall adapted a 1904 Rambler to truck the barrels of gasoline to his shop. He soon had a business selling gasoline to automobile owners. The first year he sold 874 gallons of gasoline. In 1910 he had the first gasoline filling station on Summer Street. His son Charles carried on the family business until the Sea View Garage opened. He was also a carpenter and continued his own woodworking business in his shop. He also made organ parts, model boats, and reproductions of colonial furniture.

A cabinetmaker, Phil uses not only the same workshop today, but some of his grandfather's tools which date back to the 1880s as well as the original gasoline engine which had belonged to his grandfather. Phil started his shop in 1946. He bought the old machinery from Creed's mill. Phil's custom millwork done in his one-man shop is in so much demand that he has never had to advertise. He formally retired in 1988 but still works in his shop.

The special craftsmanship of today's Roger Crawford, Ray Freden, and Phil Randall is in the finest tradition of the old Sea View/Humarock shipbuilders and woodworkers.

Bullock's Boat Yard at 81 Grandview Avenue on the north side of Ferry Hill is owned now by John Zarella, who bought it from Lilian Bullock in 1989. Richard and Lilian Bullock began hauling and storing boats in 1946. When Richard Bullock died in 1973, Lilian continued to operate the yard

until 1979, when she leased it to Zarella. Fill for the extension of the boat yard came from the widening of Elm Street.

Richard Bullock was the harbormaster and clam warden of the North and South rivers from 1950 to 1973. Bullock followed Guy Keith in these positions. When Bullock died, Larry Bonney was appointed harbormaster and shellfish constable, serving until 1988. The present officer is George Burgess.

Westerly of Bullock's and off Ferry Hill Road there is the Marshfield YWCA, housed in what was once Mr. Thurber's barn. The branch director is Linda O'Callahan. The organization serves women and children and offers classes in crafts, yoga, and other activities. These include a day camp, a child-care service, a program for early teens, an early-childhood education series sponsored by the Marshfield schools, and evening programs.

The first plan for the development of Ferry Hill was laid out in 1888 by H. N. Ford. The G. W. Ireland plan included Ireland Road, Preston Terrace, and Carlton Road. The A. B. Gehman plan for the back side of the hill included Pollard and Columbia roads, Grand View Street, and Ferry Hill Road. Prior to 1903 there were only three or four houses on Ferry Hill, owned

Looking north from Ferry Hill to the present mouth of the North River
Photograph by Gerhard O. Walter, 1988

by the Josselyn, Hall, and Harrington families. By 1930 the hill was almost entirely built up with summer houses. The only winter home was Mary Murray's at 117 Carlton Road. It now belongs to Nils and Martine Anderson. Martine is a Marshfield schoolteacher and advisory board member.

Two other early homes were those of Delia Sweetland at 51 Carlton Road and the Frank J. Tuttle's at 110 Preston Terrace, built in 1905 by Daniel Webster Clark. Later this house belonged to the High family; Natalie High Loomis and her husband, Aaron, now live there. Aaron creates beautiful sturdy wooden toys, an occupation in the tradition of the old craftsmen of Sea View/Humarock. His toys are known the world over and he is fondly called the "toymaker of Marshfield." Natalie is a retired Marshfield schoolteacher. She remembers summers at Ferry Hill:

We swam in the river and spent endless hours exploring it by boat. We also swam nearly every good day at Humarock beach and sunned on its warm sand. On cool but sunny days we all played our free-wheeling brand of tennis on my family's tennis court. A Mr. Chandler drove his horse and buggy over our hill to sell vegetables and eggs to the families. The Davis bakery at 17 Sea Street near the bridge to Humarock sold us home-made baked beans for Saturday night and fish cakes for Sunday breakfast. The Fourth of July stands out in my memory. I was allowed to spend five dollars on fireworks. What an exciting day at Humarock for everyone of every age! Tennis tournaments, races of all kinds, swimming, three-legged relays, topped off at night by a display of family fireworks.

The Marshfield Yacht Club (80 Ridge Road) was established in 1952 by a group of Marshfield people interested in boating. The land was purchased from Bob Boles. With money raised by fairs and water shows, a clubhouse was built by volunteer labor. The facility was enlarged in 1975 with floats and a mooring basin. The building was enlarged in 1985. There are presently 350 members. Warren W. Carlin serves as commodore. The club sponsors social events and hosts the U.S. Coast Guard Auxiliary public boating classes, the meetings of the U.S. Power Squadron, and a local diving club.

The blizzard of 1978 ravaged the Sea View/Humarock area, flooding Ferry Street, the boat yards, and the Bridgewaye Inn. The gale-force winds and excessively high tides damaged property all along the river waterfront.

Two small parcels of land have been acquired by the Marshfield Conservation Commission in the Humarock area. These include a piece of the South River marsh near the Julian Street Bridge and six acres, known as the Ferry Hill Thicket, with a 0.3-mile trail off Ferry Hill Road.

To live in Sea View today is to be in a place with a rich tradition of sea captains, shipbuilding, and craftsmen. Here more than anywhere else in the town are the old homes of the seafaring men of Marshfield. Up and down Summer, Elm, and Ferry streets, the captains' houses can still be seen. Two hundred years ago one might have met Captain Luther or Captain George coming up from the ferry, or perhaps have seen them wave from Jedediah's two-wheel chaise as they passed by. Not much more than one hundred years ago, shipbuilder and financier Sam Hall might have been seen arriving from Boston at the riverside wharfs. After 1871 the Sea View depot on Station Street would have been the scene of constant activity. Many new homes have been built, streets constructed, and businesses come and gone over the years. Today's Sea View residents still enjoy their special place at the side of the river and the sea. Boat building goes on at the riverside, fishing and lobstering continue, pleasure craft arrive and depart, and the sun rises from the Atlantic every morning to spill the light of another day over Sea View.

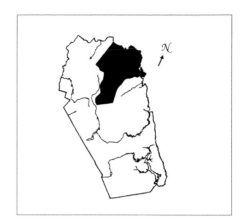

Marshfield Hills Village

Tomorrow I'll remember yesterday
Time's such a player of tricks.
— Cynthia Hagar Krusell

MARSHFIELD HILLS is the hill village, known until 1890 as East Marshfield. It sits high above the winding course of the North River and commands an expansive view over the New Harbor marshes to Fourth Cliff and the new mouth of the old North/South rivers. It is a place of hills and valleys, brooks and swamps, salt marshes, and tidal creeks. It is a timeless village, a village that grew slowly in a quiet backwater of the town.

The settlement of Marshfield Hills began at the foot of Prospect Hill. This skirt of flat land was easily reached up Branch and Macomber's creeks from the North River and served as a doorstep to the hill area. Here along Summer Street, at the edge of the North River marsh, the first grants of land were made. Joseph and John Rogers, sons of Thomas Rogers of the *Mayflower*, were each granted fifty acres by the Plymouth Colony Court in 1640. The Rogers brothers never lived on their land, but deeded it to Richard Beare and William Macomber. Other early settlers on Summer Street were Anthony Eames, Stephen Tilden, and Morris Trouant. Soon the land was cleared and the farms laid out from what is now the foot of Pleasant Street to the intersection of Summer Street and Route 3A.

Richard and Grace Beare acquired fifty acres of land from Joseph Rogers in 1654. They built a house the following year on the site of today's elegant Federal house (758 Summer Street) which stands on the northerly bank of Murdock's Pond. Today this house is owned by Bonnie and Jack Hobbs. The Beares sold their house and farm to Joseph Tilden in 1668. Richard Beare, however, continued to live there until 1670 when Joseph Tilden deeded the property to his son Stephen Tilden. After this time Richard Beare's name does not appear again in Marshfield records. His memory is preserved, however, in the name of Beare's Brook, which flows through the valley between Prospect Hill and Hagar Hill.[1]

Joseph Tilden was the son of Nathaniel and Lydia Huckstep Tilden of Scituate. The Tilden family were among the original "Men of Kent" settlers of Scituate. They came from Tenterden, Kent, England, sometime between 1625 and 1629. Many members of the Tilden family eventually settled in Marshfield, married into Marshfield families, and their descendants are still in the town today.[2]

The 1720 Rogers house at Little's Bridge on the North River. A ferry crossing for many years, the first bridge was built in 1825. Tolls were collected from travelers until 1865. The flat-bottom gundalow at the right was used to transport salt hay from the marsh meadows to the waiting farmer's wagon (center). Here the Rogers family built merchant ships that traded in ports around the world.

Joseph Tilden's son Stephen and his wife, Abigail, had eight children, all born before they came to live at Beare's farm. Stephen built an addition onto the original Beare house before his death in 1732. His son John Tilden, and then his grandson Deacon John Tilden, inherited the farm.[3]

Deacon Tilden died in 1800, having made provisions in his will for his children and grandchild. The homestead passed to his son Joseph. To his daughter Deborah, he stipulated that "so long as she shall live a single life as much bread, milk, butter, cheese, sugar and tea of the same kind of quality as she shall want for her own use and also one cord of oak wood and one cord of pitch pine wood both cords of wood to be brought to the door and cut fit for the fire and three pounds of good sheep's wool and said wool to be paid annually. Further I give unto my daughter Deborah Tilden after the death of my wife the use and improvement of half the front chamber where I now live with privileges to pass and repass for wood and water." Deborah was fifty-three and unmarried at the time. Her mother, Rachel Hall Tilden, died one year later. Deborah presumably lived another year in one-half of the front chamber with staple foods, wood, and wool provided by her brother Joseph.[4]

Over the years the Tildens acquired additional land. They owned a gundalow, a flat-bottomed boat used to harvest salt meadow hay. English grass and blue grass grew in the upland areas of the marshes. This was cut and harvested as fodder for the cattle. Cows, pigs, sheep, oxen, and horses, all mentioned in a 1727 inventory, were raised on the Tilden farm. The Tildens worked this land for one hundred thirty-four years until 1802 when Joseph Tilden, great-great-grandson of the first Joseph Tilden, sold the 100-acre piece of property to Daniel Phillips of Marshfield for six thousand dollars. The farm was described as being bounded "beginning near the bridge at Bear's [sic] Brook, so called, which is about 10 rods below the dwelling house, from thence bounded by said Bear's Brook down stream until it comes to Bear's Creek, so called, and bounded by said Bear's Creek downstream through the cut, so called, until it comes to the marsh owned by Wales Tilden."[5]

Daniel Phillips was of the Centre Marshfield Phillips family. It was he who inherited the wealth of his brother Nathaniel of St. John's,

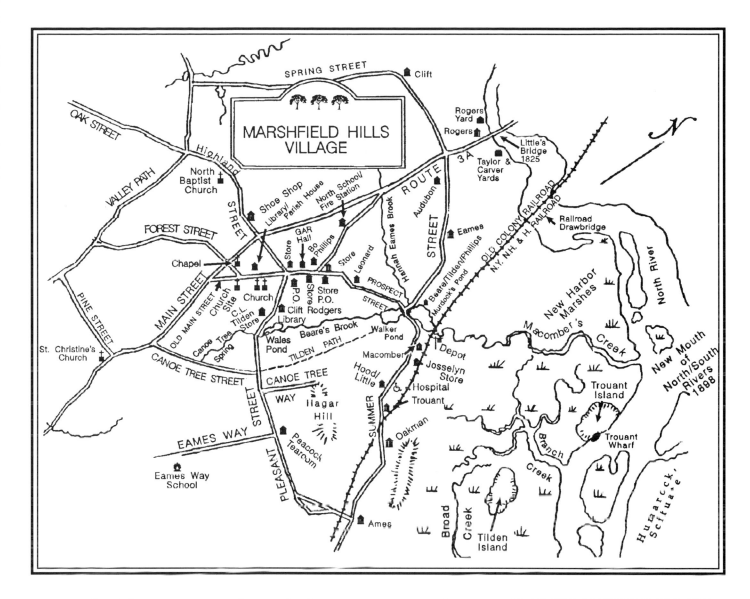

Newfoundland. Between 1802 and 1812 the farm was operated for Daniel Phillips by a tenant farmer. Daniel acquired fifty-six additional acres of land for his Tilden farm before his death in 1812. Daniel's fourteen-year-old eldest son, Nathaniel, inherited the farm. Nathaniel's brother Daniel was given a farm on Highland Street (578 Highland), now owned by W. Torrey and Doris Tilden Little. The farms are twin farms, built by Christopher Oakman. The Phillips brothers were placed under the guardianship of William Macomber and later, of his son Dr. Charles Macomber.[6]

The Macombers kept detailed financial records concerning the Phillips estate. These interesting accounts relate the building of young Nathaniel Phillips's "new" house, the present great, square Federal home overlooking Murdock's Pond. It was built in 1818 on the site of the original Richard Beare house. The building materials for the house were shipped in the Phillipses' 35-ton sloop *Sophia*, built at the Brick-Kiln Shipyard in Pembroke in 1811. This was a North River packet ship, captained by David Church of Marshfield. Items in the Macomber accounts included 17 posts, 251 feet of "bords," and 1000 "bord nails." Some of the labor costs were: "carting sand from my wharf to my house. Two men employed nearly two days with two carts, oxen and horse, 14 loads, $5.34; $140 to pay stone cutters; $3.89 for 432 bricks; $100 for masons; $3 for sand for mortar; and $280.89 to Christopher Oakman, builder." Difficult as the work of building a house was in those days, the expenses involved seem minimal by comparison with today's prices.[7]

In the 1886 inventory of the Nathaniel Phillips estate made two years after his death, there are listed some of the items typical of a small East Marshfield farm of the late nineteenth century. These included three cows, a harrow, plow, old harness, farm wagon, horse wagon, sleigh, covered wagon, horse plow, stone drag and ladder, axes, rakes, twelve tons of blue grass standing, ten tons of English grass standing, and two pews in the Congregational meetinghouse.[8]

The farm stayed in the Phillips family for one hundred twenty years. In 1923 Abbie Phillips sold the place to Elson Blunt and the estate was divided. Interestingly, Abbie's probate inventory includes "a canary, a Panama parrot, and a green head parrot," but no farm animals. In 1958 the marsh area adjacent to this land was dammed up to create Murdock's Pond. It is named for John A. Murdock who developed the adjacent area known as Hidden Acres.[9]

The Duxbury and Cohasset Railroad bought a right-of-way through the Phillipses' land in 1870 when the railroad was extended into Marshfield. The East Marshfield/ Marshfield Hills depot was built on Macomber land at Macomber's Island Road. A standpipe was constructed to hold the water for the steam engines. The water was piped down Beare's Brook valley from Wales Pond on Pleasant Street. Created for this purpose in 1870, the pond is one of the few in Marshfield not originally used as a millpond. Rail service through Marshfield was discontinued in 1939. A section of the old railroad bed became Damon's Point Road.

There are a number of other early Tilden houses in Marshfield Hills. At one time the Tilden family owned most of the village. Joshua Tilden, brother of John above, was given land on Prospect Hill at what later became known as the Batcheller place (29 Prospect Street). His son Joshua married Phebe Wales, daughter of the Reverend Atherton Wales of the Marshfield Hills Second Congregational Church. A 1783 document tells of Joshua selling his negro slave Rozza to Benjamin Hiland for three Spanish milled dollars. Joshua and Phebe had three sons. Atherton Tilden married Mary Wales and inherited the house. Their son Corrington Tilden, born in 1804, continued to live in the home. For many years Prospect Hill was called

The North River railroad bridge, about 1910, on the Old Colony line at today's Damon's Point
Photograph courtesy of Barbara Lincoln

Corrington's Hill. Later owners of the house were the Batchellers and the Savages. Alice Batcheller Savage and her daughter Bettina Savage Brown and the Brown family were well-known occupants of the old Tilden house for many years, until the 1970s.[10]

Another son of Joshua and Phebe Tilden was Wales Tilden, who moved up the valley and built a house near the present intersection of Pleasant and Canoe Tree streets. His son Wales Tilden, Jr., bought the Levi Ford house at today's 543 Pleasant Street. Present owners are Rose Anne and Brian E. Concannon. Wales Tilden, Jr., married Susannah Little, the daughter of Sea View's Captain Luther Little. It was their son, Charles L. Tilden, who built a "new" house next door at today's 535 Pleasant Street and opened a general store in the 1890s in a separate building near the street.[11]

The land between all these Tilden places was cleared and opened for pasturage. From Pleasant Street to Prospect Street, down Beare's Brook valley and along the high ridges, open grazing land remained until the early 1900s. Stone walls crisscross the wood lots to this day, marking the old pasture lots. Brooks and springs provided water for the cattle. The cart path leading from Joshua Tilden's farm on Prospect Hill to his son Wales Tilden's farm on Pleasant Street is still used as a foot and riding path.

The Macomber family arrived in East Marshfield in the 1650s. John Rogers deeded fifty acres to William Macomber at the edge of the marsh along what is now Summer Street and Macomber's Ridge. A house was built on the property between 1654 and 1675 when a record was made of its designation as a garrison house for the town. This original Macomber house was on the site of today's cape-style house at 672 Summer Street (now owned by Joan and George R. Humphreys). William Macomber was a cooper and there is mention of a cooper's shop in 1654. The cooper's shop was still being used over one hundred years later when it was mentioned in the will of Deacon Thomas Macomber, who died in 1771.[12]

A second Macomber house (1 Macomber Ridge, now owned by Barbara Place), built about 1835, was located further along the ridge or island. The Macombers married into the Tilden, White, Phillips, and Hatch families. William Macomber of the fifth generation and his son, Dr. Charles Macomber, were the aforementioned guardians and accountants for Nathaniel and Daniel Phillips. Bookkeeping seemed to "run in the family," since four successive generations of Macombers served as treasurers of the town, the last one being Herbert I. Macomber, who also served as county treasurer.[13]

Still remembered in the village is Herbert I. Macomber, born in 1866, and one of the last of the family to live in the house on Summer Street. He kept a livery barn where horses were stabled for the Marshfield Hills railroad commuters. The depot stood just east of the house where Damon's Point Road is located today. Village people drove their horses and carriages down to the station, leaving them at Macomber's stable for the day. Milk from the Macomber farms was shipped directly to Boston from the Marshfield Hills station. Herbert owned considerable land along Summer Street. He was in the real estate business and erected signs which read "HIM." People would ask, "Who is Him?" He died in 1932, just seven years before the railroad tracks were removed and the train discontinued.

When his wife, Sarah Christie Macomber, died in 1944, the house passed to their son Charles Warren Macomber, who sold the place out of the family on 14 May 1945. The Macombers had lived on this land for two hundred ninety-one years, from 1654 to 1945, setting one of Marshfield's records for length of continuous occupancy of an original home by the same

She heard the train whistle at the East Marshfield depot, a sign of life.

— Richard Warren Hatch[14]

family. How sad the old house must have been to lose the last of the Macomber family!

Railroad stationmaster and telegraph operator Eddie Hitchcock and his wife, Rose, lived at today's 185 Pleasant Street (now owned by John and Nellie Ulanowski). He walked home for lunch every day from the Summer Street depot. Later he built a house at 663 Summer Street across from the old Macomber place. He was related to the Macombers and to the famous preacher, Gad Hitchcock, of Hanson. He served the Old Colony Railroad Company for forty-seven years, working Sundays and holidays, until the last train ran the tracks in 1939. It was the custom for the children of the area to ride the train to attend high school in downtown Marshfield. Present owners of the Hitchcock house on Summer Street are Gail and Reed Stewart. Reed has been chairman and long-time member of the Board of Appeals and is currently on the Growth Management Committee.

Another settler family of Summer Street was the Trouant family, still remembered by the name of Trouant's Island. Morris Trouant came to Marshfield about 1650. He purchased property from Francis Cooke and John Cooke, Jr., who had been granted the land by the Plymouth Colony Court in 1640. Trouant's daughter Hannah married Jonathan Eames of another early East Marshfield family. Courting Hannah would have meant only a short walk up a rough cart path. Trouant had a 25-acre parcel with marsh, bounded by Beare's Brook, Tilden's Island, and Cooper's Island (Macomber Ridge). Trouant's son John Trouant had descendants who continued to live in the area. John's son Samuel had interests in a schooner. John's grandson Church Trouant was a sea captain who owned Trouant's Island. There was a Trouant's Wharf on the island from which goods were

View from Trouant's Island
Watercolor by Robert W. Davis, 1990

The old South Shore Hospital on Summer Street, once the home of the Trouant family. The building was abandoned and later burned in 1934.
Photograph courtesy of Eleanor Magoon

shipped in and out of the area via the river. North River shipping passed by this island, and ships often docked here on their way up or down river. This was the portal to East Marshfield in the days before the coming of the railroad and the improvement of the roads.[15]

In 1879 the seventeenth-century Embankment House at 530 Summer Street belonged to Church Trouant. The house at 460 Summer Street, today owned by Thomas J. O'Neil, Jr., was also owned by the Trouant family, although it had been built by Tobias Oakman in 1702. A large old house across from the recent Torrey Little Auction Barn (575 Summer Street) was a Trouant house in 1838 and still owned by the family in 1879. It was later bought and remodeled into a hospital by Dr. Seth Strong and called the South Shore Hospital, the name perpetuated by today's hospital in Weymouth. In 1926 it was "a home for convalescents and chronic cases" and the superintendent was Carolyn Winona Boliver. The abandoned hospital burned in March 1934.

Just south of the site of the old hospital there lived for over thirty years the nationally-known New England adventure-story author, Edward Rowe Snow. He came to Marshfield in 1950 and wrote nearly one hundred books about shipwrecks and buried treasure. Edward and his wife, Anna-Myrle Haegg, and daughter, Dorothy Caroline (Bicknell), lived at 550 Summer Street. They were active in sports, especially tennis and other outdoor activities, including canoeing on the North River, as well as involved in community enterprises over the years. Always interested in New England maritime history and United States Coast Guard activities, Snow enjoyed his role as Flying Santa for the lighthouse-keepers of the New England coast. He died in 1982 but, as his widow Anna-Myrle writes, "he lives on in his many books and in the memories of his friends."

Another of the early Summer Street settlers was the Eames family. They lived on the end of Summer Street near today's Route 3A. Anthony Eames and his son Mark bought a large 100-acre farm with a dwelling house in December 1650 from Francis Godfrey who, in turn, had bought the land from original grantees Constant and Thomas Southworth. This piece of land

For a few moments I stood atop the sand dune — the only human being within a mile — breathing deeply of the salt air which the sea breezes wafted inland. The blue of the ocean was in vivid contrast to the white sands and the even whiter foam of the breakers offshore, and the only sounds to be heard above the dull boom of the distant surf were the weird cries of the sea gulls as they settled back to their usual pursuits. In any direction I might face there stretched a road to adventure.
— Edward Rowe Snow[16]

Marshfield Hills Village   161

stretched from the North River to Summer Street and from Prospect Street to Route 3A. After Anthony moved to Marshfield, he served as a representative to the Plymouth Colony Court from 1653 to 1661. Mark was born in England about 1620. During his years in Marshfield, he was active in town affairs, serving as a representative to the Plymouth Colony Court and as a member of the town's first Board of Selectmen in 1667. He and his wife, Elizabeth, had eight children.[17]

Mark's land in Marshfield was divided between his two sons, Jonathan and Anthony Eames, in 1699. Jonathan received land along the north side of Summer Street. Anthony was given the land lying south of Summer Street, extending across the valley to Prospect Hill. Jonathan built a "new" house (882 Summer Street), perhaps as early as 1682, when he married Hannah Trouant. The brook that runs through the valley from present Route 3A to Summer Street retains the name of Hannah Eames to this day. This brook is also referred to in early deeds as the "winter brook," an apt name for this intermittently flowing stream which has its headwaters in the swamp between Route 3A and Spring Street. The Jonathan Eames house replaced the early seventeenth-century house mentioned above. A part of the beautiful double cape-style house which stands on the site today is thought to be a 1699 house. This colonial period house was lived in by the Eames family continuously for two hundred twenty-two years, almost as long as the Macomber residency in their house further down the street. The Eames homestead evolved to meet the changing needs of successive generations. It was enlarged into a double house to accommodate pairs of Eames brothers, whose families shared the house. The Eameses were farmers and, until the 1730s, they attended the First Congregational Church downtown. Their way to the meetinghouse was via a path, which today still retains their name, Eames Way.[18]

Successive generations of Eameses married into the Oakman, Tilden, Clift, Rogers, Hatch, Damon, Hall, and Carver families. Thus was woven the kinship network of Marshfield Hills. Jedediah Eames, son of Jonathan, married Mary Oakman, daughter of Tobias and Elizabeth Doty Oakman, of the nearby Summer Street family. Elizabeth Doty was of the *Mayflower* Doty family. Jedediah's son Jedediah married Bethia Tilden and was a Tory at the time of the Revolution. He was listed in the 1771 Tax Valuation as owning an interest in a gristmill on Beare's Brook at the Summer Street pond. One of his sons, John Tilden Ames, married Sarah Rogers in 1792. This was a turning point for the Eames/Ames family, since John chose to shorten the name, which has remained with the spelling "Ames" in this branch of the family.[19]

Edward Ames, son of John Tilden Ames and Sarah Rogers Ames, served on the building committee of the Second Trinitarian Congregational Society in Marshfield Hills in 1835. This church is now the North Community Church. It was Edward's son, Willard Ames, who sold the old 1699 Jonathan Eames house in 1872. Some of the later owners of this unique house were Joseph and Jennie Parker, Cleora and Claude Marvin, and Ernest and Elizabeth Dragon.[20]

Edward's brother Tilden Ames, born in 1795, married Betsy French Hatch in 1818. He built a house around 1827 at what is today 316 Summer Street, the elegant Federal house at the foot of Pleasant Street. He received the land from his grandmother Bethia Little. Being a housewright, he probably built the house himself. Tilden Ames was one of a group of men who formed an express company about 1820. He made deliveries in area towns from the Cape to Boston and became a wealthy man.[21]

In addition to his other interests and activities, Tilden Ames was a noted farmer. He once drove Daniel Webster's cattle down overland from his New Hampshire farm, "The Elms." He and his friend and neighbor Nathaniel Phillips were close friends of Daniel Webster. Webster frequently visited the Ames home and was said to have planted a branch from one of his linden trees in the ground near the drive. It grew into the wide and spreading linden tree seen today.[22]

Later, Tilden Ames invested his money in a lumber business in Michigan. Toward the end of his life, Ames tried to establish oyster beds in the tidal North River flats behind his house. He died in 1867.[23]

By 1902 the Tilden Ames place was owned by his daughter Caroline Ames Smith and her husband, Enoch Smith. Caroline bought additional property along Eames Way. The Ames place passed out of the family in 1944 for the first time in one hundred eighteen years.[24]

The Eames family also owned a considerable part of Prospect Hill. Anthony Eames received the other half of the original Summer Street land of his father, Mark Eames, in 1699. This land stretched from Summer Street to Prospect Street across the Hannah Eames Brook valley. Anthony built a house on the property where the yellow, square Federal house at 110 Prospect Street stands today. He soon sold to Jonathan Tilden, and the property was transferred to the Reverend Atherton Wales in 1759. This might appropriately be called the "house of ministers."[25]

Looking from Summer Street across to Prospect Hill and Marshfield Hills village, about 1900

Time out from building a stone wall in Luther Rogers's field, Marshfield Hills, about 1900. The GAR hall on Old Main Street can be seen in the background.
Photograph courtesy of Eleanor Magoon

This house is central to the history of East Marshfield/ Marshfield Hills village. It became the home of a number of ministers who served the Second Congregational Church for long periods of time. This church, organized in 1738, was variously called the Chapel of Ease, or the Church at the Three Pines. It was built at the top of the hill off what is now Old Main Street. It was easier thereafter for the East Marshfield Congregationalists to attend church. Prior to this time, they had no alternative but to walk to the First Congregational Church in Marshfield, or attend the Scituate First Church across the river.[26]

In addition to the downhill East Marshfield families, there were the uphill East Marshfield families — Rogers, Damon, Hall, and Holmes. As time went on, many of the Summer Street people married into these Main Street families and moved up the hill.

For many years the farms of East Marshfield were scattered. There was no central village, no major road passing through, no industry, and no church for the first hundred years. Out of the mainstream, the area grew slowly, held together only by a network of cart paths and family ties. The arrival of a church and a minister in 1738 began to draw the community together.

The story of the "church shuffle" of East Marshfield is very much the story of the village and its people. For nearly one hundred years, from 1738 to 1835, there was only one church in the village. This was the Second Congregational Church or Chapel of Ease. The Reverend Atherton Wales arrived in 1738 to minister to the people, later taking up residency in the "house of ministers" (110 Prospect Street). The Reverend Wales served the church for over fifty years, until his death in 1795. A year later, his daughter Rachel Wales Rogers sold the "house of ministers" to the Reverend Elijah Leonard. Rachel's husband, Amos Rogers, as a token of his devotion to the Reverend Wales's church, had given a Paul Revere bell for the new belfry in 1791. Elijah Leonard built a new "house of ministers" on the old site in 1803. He served in the ministry for the next forty-five years, until his death in 1834. At his death, his son George Leonard inherited the property.[27]

The Second Congregational Church split, in 1835, in a dispute over church doctrine. A vote was taken and the liberal Unitarian faction won by one vote, thus securing to themselves the church building. The following year, George Leonard became the third long-term minister of the Second Church (Unitarian). In 1848 this church was remodeled by the nationally-known architect, Isaiah Rogers, of East Marshfield. He designed a Gothic exterior for the building. The Reverend George Leonard stayed with the Unitarians for twenty-five years. He presented an Aaron Willard clock to the church in 1838. It was known as the clock that was "Unitarian in belief and Universalist in action." Thus one church became two, and a measure of time came to this timeless village.[29]

There was no regular Unitarian minister after 1861. Theological students served as part-time or summer ministers through the 1920s. The church fell into disuse. In 1974 an attempt was made to restore it as a home for the North River Arts Society. A group of Marshfield High School students under a program entitled "Project Enterprise" tried unsuccessfully to renovate the building, but it was finally razed in 1977.

George Leonard's son, Otis Liscomb Leonard, was a Baptist minister and an evangelist who carried the word far beyond East Marshfield. In his later years he lived with his sister, Sarah Leonard, at the "minister's house." Otis died in 1903 and Sarah in 1930. The house was subsequently owned by Edith T. Scars, Alan and Edith Hovey, and Robert and Susan Emerson. It is now the property of Lou Levin-Cutler, recent chairman and member of the Marshfield School Committee, a pulpit of a different sort. Descendants of the Leonard family have continued to be influential in Marshfield. These include Morton Leonard, the late fire department chief; Ellin Leonard, long-time former secretary and member of the Board of Appeals; and Mabel Leonard Nordborg, the late Marshfield schoolteacher and principal of the North School.[30]

The Second Trinitarian Congregational Society, forced out of the Second Congregational Church building in 1835, formed a new church and built what is now the North Community Church in 1837. About 1841 the Trinitarian Congregational Society built a parsonage on Pleasant Street, currently the home of Lyle and Teresa Pollard (520 Pleasant Street). In 1919 the Congregational society bought the Charles L. Tilden store on Pleasant Street. It was moved across the street and used as a church parish house until the Clift Rodgers Free Library moved into the building in 1950. In 1928, due to decreased attendance at the Marshfield Hills churches, a federation of Unitarians, Congregationalists, and Baptists formed the North Community Church. Today's minister is the Reverend Edward F. Duffy.[31]

A Baptist faction organized the North Baptist Society in 1833. Fifty Baptists came from the already existing First Baptist Church at Standish; others came from the Second Congregational Church at the time of the split of the church congregation. In 1835 they built the church on Highland Street that is now the Trinity Episcopal Church. The North Baptists affiliated with the North Community Church in 1928.[32]

The Episcopalians and their Centre Marshfield building arrived in Marshfield Hills village in 1826. Today this building, considerably changed, is the home of the North River Arts Society on Old Main Street. It was used as an Episcopal church until 1853. In 1866 Wales Rogers purchased it and used it as a paint and wheelwright shop. It was enlarged in the 1880s and rented out as Rogers' Hall.[33]

In 1892 the building was dedicated as the David Church Post 189 of the Grand Army of the Republic (GAR). David Church was the first of twenty-six

Services will be continued in the 'little grey church' [Unitarian] on the Hill next Sabbath.
— Lysander Richards[28]

Old Second Congregational Church in Marshfield Hills. The building was razed in 1977.

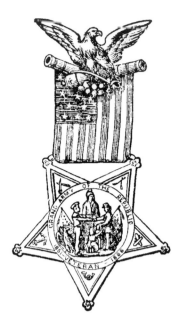

Marshfield men to give his life in the Civil War. One hundred thirty-five men were credited as serving in the war from the town. Of these, twelve were Hatches, ten Ewells, and eight Williamsons. A monument to the Civil War soldiers of the town was erected in the Marshfield Hills Cemetery in 1889. It is the focus of today's Memorial Day services in the village.[34]

The GAR Hall was given to the town in 1919. It was used in the 1910s and 1920s for silent motion pictures with a piano player and in the 1930s for the Marshfield Hills Players, a summer theatre group connected with Leland Powers School of the Theatre. In the 1930s and 1940s the hall was used as a meeting place for various groups, as well as for church dinners, musicals, and plays. In the 1950s it was home to the "Curtain-Timers."[35]

The GAR Hall has been leased from the Town of Marshfield by the North River Arts Society since 1978. The society was organized in 1968 under the leadership of Madeleine Hagar and Brian Doherty, director of art for the Marshfield schools. The original intent of the group was to use the old Unitarian Church, abandoned since 1965, on Old Main Street as their headquarters.

The North River Arts Society was incorporated 17 September 1970 "to promote the exposure, participation and understanding of the arts in Marshfield and surrounding South Shore towns." After an unsuccessful attempt to renovate the church building with the help of the Project Enterprise high school group, the society met at various locations until settling at the GAR. The Morning Subscription Series, offering a variety of cultural entertainment, has continued to be a successful fund-raising activity over the years. Today the society has nearly four hundred active artist members and over two hundred additional members. Jean Horan serves as president.[36]

After the traveling Episcopalians closed their doors (GAR Hall) in East Marshfield in 1853, they attended church in Scituate. In 1916 the Trinity

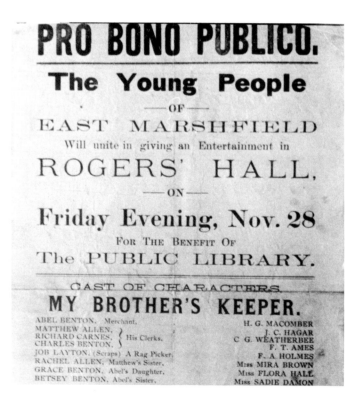

Rogers' Hall playbill
Courtesy of Eleanor Magoon

Episcopal Mission Chapel was established. The old East (Littletown) School building, located at the corner of Sea and Summer streets, was acquired for their meetings. In 1936 the Episcopalians joined the Baptists, Congregationalists, and Unitarians to become a part of the North Community Church, bringing with them their minister, the Reverend L. Snell. They continued to use the mission chapel at Sea View for summer services until 1941. In 1948 the Episcopalians moved to the old North Baptist Church at 228 Highland Street, which became the Trinity Episcopal Church in 1960. The mission chapel building was moved from Sea View and is now used as the parish house of the Highland Street church. The Episcopalians would appear to have found a permanent home at last, after two hundred years of wandering in the wilderness of Marshfield. It is a tribute to their thrift and ingenuity that they wasted not their buildings nor wanted for new ones. Present pastor is the Reverend John Goddard. The popular Steeple School has been located at this site since the 1960s.[37]

A more recent church in the Hills is the Christian Science Church. It began with meetings in private homes in 1906. By 1915 the Scientists were holding regular services in the Clift Rodgers Library at its old location on Old Main Street. The land where the church stands today was given in 1928 by Fred and Helen Lamson and the church built in 1929.[38]

The earliest Roman Catholic church in the village was a chapel remodeled in 1945 from a converted 1732 barn. The barn was moved from Norwell by W. Torrey Little, who dismantled it, numbered the parts, and re-erected it at the northeast corner of Old Main and Main streets, next door to his retail auction business. The chapel is now a private residence (1660 Main Street). St. Christine's Church at 1295 Main Street was built in the 1960s to accommodate the growing Catholic population of the north part of Marshfield. The Reverend Francis A. Regan is the present pastor and the Reverend Arthur O'Leary, the parochial vicar.

This village of the churches grew, in time, into a village with a school, a library, a post office, and stores; small blacksmith shops and shoe shops in homes; a meeting hall; a fire station; a tearoom; and a few small businesses. It is a nineteenth-century village which had its largest growth in the early and mid-1800s. Most of the houses in the village are of this period. For many years Old Main Street was the "Country Way" to Scituate via the North River ferry or, later, Little's Bridge. This way passed directly through the village until 1927, when the completion of Route 3A created a bypass of Marshfield Hills.

There is mention of school sessions being held in private homes in the north part of the town as early as the 1750s. An early school building is said to have been located near the Second Congregational Church at the top of Old Main Street. By 1777 there was a schoolhouse near the present intersection of Pleasant and Old Main streets. The school year was divided into summer and winter sessions. During the spring and fall seasons, the children were needed on the farms for planting and harvesting. The North School was built in 1838. This was a two-room grammar school which at one time accommodated grades one through eight. For many years students wanting further education went to one of the nearby academies, such as Partridge Academy in Duxbury, Derby in Hingham, Thayer in Braintree, or Hanover Academy at Hanover Four Corners. In 1889 the first Marshfield high school was located in the North School. During this time, there were seven grammar school grades and four high school grades in this two-room building. In 1895 the high school grades moved to the new Seth Ventress building on South River Street.[39]

In the 1930s the North School housed six classes, three in each room. There were about sixty students and two teachers in the school. Helen Seaverns (Mrs. Robert Melvin) taught the first three grades, and Gertrude Leighton (Mrs. Edwin Russell) taught grades four through six. There was a remarkable cooperative spirit, with students in upper grades helping those in lower grades, as well as a sense of equality socially, economically, and academically. It was a progressive education in an extended family situation. In 1940 when the "new" high school (later called the Grace Ryder School) was built on Main Street, grades five and six were transferred to the South Elementary School, and on 16 February 1951 the North School held its final sessions. The building was turned over to the fire department and remodeled in 1954 into Fire Station No. 2. Ten years later the district school returned with the opening of the Eames Way School in September 1961. There were 327 students; Wayne E. Thomas was principal. The earlier plan for school centralization had been thwarted by the unexpected rise in population, and local schooling for elementary schoolchildren returned to the village.

Fire Station No. 2 was originally located at the southwest corner of the intersection of Old Main and Highland streets. Later it occupied the small town-owned building, still standing, just south of the GAR Hall. Finally the station was moved into the old North School building in 1954.

The first post office in the east part of Marshfield was the East Post Office, located on Summer Street in Sea View by 1838 (272 Summer Street). This was a convenient place for the downhill Summer Street "Hillers" to pick up their mail. John Tilden was the postmaster. The mail was brought to the post office in Jedediah Little's chaise. By 1847 the post office location had moved to the village and was in the house at the corner of Old Main and Pleasant streets (570 Pleasant Street), presently the home of Priscilla Hall. The old postboxes can still be seen there. The postmaster was Calvin Damon, succeeded by his daughter Sarah Ella Damon about 1865. Assistant was Carrie Damon Carver. In 1926 the post office was relocated to its present site (165 Prospect Street). Marjorie Purdy (Shreiner) was the postmistress for the next forty years, until 1965. Mildred Ainslee served in the position from Marge's retirement until 1979. A long-time and well-known employee was Helen Drake. After Mildred's retirement, Betty Jane (B.J.) Babcock served as officer-in-charge until Joseph Collins was appointed postmaster in 1981.

In 1897 leather-merchant Clift Rodgers left five thousand dollars to incorporate a "library organization" in Marshfield Hills. Lysander Richards, author of the 1901 *History of Marshfield*, incorporated the organization and was the president for thirty years, until 1927. To start the collection, a donation of one hundred books was acquired from the old East Marshfield public library located in the old North School. Today the library has ninety-three hundred volumes. Another example of Marshfield's traveling institutions, the Clift Rodgers Library was originally housed in what is today the new parish house of the North Community Church on Old Main Street. This building was built to careful specifications to provide a meeting hall and a stage for benefit plays. The hall was rented for dances, auctions, services, and lectures. In 1950 the North Community Church and the Clift Rodgers Library swapped buildings.

Now the library is housed in the old church parish house at 540 Pleasant Street. A board of twenty-five trustees oversees this popular village library. It is a nonprofit organization. A consignment shop, located on the second floor, was started in 1955 by Martha Reese to raise funds for the library. It is still in existence today, staffed by a group of loyal volunteers. The late Anne Byam (Dede) O'Neil, popular librarian of the 1950 period, was responsible for arousing renewed interest in the library. She organized an Arts and Crafts Boutique to help support the institution. A Friends of the Library group was established in 1964 by Peggy Beals.

Today the library is open three hours a day, six days of the week. It is an active institution with patrons from far and wide, since, in addition to being a lending library, it holds regular book sales, yard sales, and social events. Clift Rodgers would be pleased to see his library now such a center of Marshfield Hills social and intellectual life, enjoyed by young and old alike.

East Marshfield/Marshfield Hills has had as many stores as churches, and some have "traveled" as well. In the early days, goods were sold from a room or part of a private home. As time passed and the population grew in the early 1800s, there was an increased demand for goods and services. A paper written in 1862 by George Leonard, entitled "Marshfield Sixty Years Ago," states that there was only one store in East Marshfield in 1812.

In 1823 Luther Rogers opened a store at the corner of Highland and Old Main streets (8 Highland Street) in the ell of his house, built by Christopher Oakman. This is the home of Eleanor Magoon and the late Gertrude Lynd. The store remains in its original condition to this day, and Eleanor generously opens it for historical events and for the annual North River Arts Festival. The store has slanted counters to accommodate the hooped skirts of the ladies of that era. The multitude of shelves and cubbyholes as well as the old ledger desk can still be seen.

Tall elms shaded the 1823 Luther Rogers house and store in June 1895. The building still stands at the corner of Highland and Old Main streets in Marshfield Hills. Photograph courtesy of Eleanor Magoon

Luther Rogers married Abigail Little Tilden in 1802, thus bringing together uphill and downhill East Marshfield families. Rogers was a shipbuilder and shipowner. He brought goods for the store on his packet ship, docking at his family wharf near the present Little's Bridge on Route 3A at the North River. The store operated on a barter system typical of that era. Farmers brought in their dairy products and vegetables in exchange for yard goods, coffee, sugar, spices, and other items from the Mediterranean and

The Danforth Hall house, built in 1822 at the fork of Old Main and Prospect streets, Marshfield Hills. The Halls and Weatherbees operated a store in the building for nearly one hundred years, from 1822 to 1918.
Photograph courtesy of Eleanor Magoon

China trade. The Luther Rogers store and inn was a stop on the stagecoach route to Boston. The store closed in 1848.[40]

Another East Marshfield store of the same period was that of Danforth Hall. Son of Luke Hall of Medford, Danforth was the first of this branch of the Hall family to come to the village. He married Betsy Church Trouant of the downhill Summer Street family in 1793. They were married by the Reverend Elijah Leonard in the Second Congregational Church at the top of Old Main Street hill. In 1822 Danforth and Betsy Hall built the gracious Federal house at the fork of Prospect and Old Main streets (190 Old Main Street). Danforth opened a store in the house. Supplies were shipped in his sloop *North River Packet*. In 1833 he sold the property and the business to George H. Weatherbee of Billerica, Massachusetts.[41]

George H. Weatherbee was engaged in cloth manufacturing in Boston. In 1840 Weatherbee put an addition on the house to accommodate his general store. Account books in the possession of the Marshfield Historical Society list the merchandise sold at the Weatherbee store 1847/48, indicating the variety and extent of business carried on in this country village store in the first half of the nineteenth-century. Items include yard goods (8 yards of shirting $1.00), horse blankets (2 for $1.70), flour (1 barrel $7.13), molasses (1 gal. for 30¢), salt (2 bags for 40¢), shot (1 bag for $1.50), boots ($1.12), mittens (48¢), razors (1 for 37¢), cigars (2 boxes for 50¢), padlocks (2 for 36¢), glass (1/2 box for $2.12), tea (1 chest for $3.90), pearl buttons (1 gross for 45¢), and silk handkerchiefs (1 for 88¢).[42]

In 1849 Weatherbee sold the business, but not the house, to Wallace and Calvin Ames, who in 1852 sold the store to Elisha Hall, grandson of Danforth Hall. Elisha Hall and George Weatherbee, Jr., ran the store as a partnership for one year. Between 1849 and 1852 George Weatherbee, Sr., also owned a house and ran a store on Summer Street, Sea View, though he retained the East Marshfield house. Weatherbee bought a house and store in Greenbush in 1857. In 1859 he deeded his East Marshfield house to his son George Weatherbee, Jr., who continued to operate both the Sea View store and the East Marshfield store. George, Sr.'s other son, John, continued to run the Greenbush store. This might be appropriately called the first chain store on the South Shore. George Weatherbee, Sr., died in Greenbush in 1877.[43]

George Weatherbee, Jr., married Martha Bartlett of Plymouth in 1859, the same year that his father deeded him the East Marshfield house. In addition to operating his East Marshfield store, George, Jr., served the town as clerk and treasurer, performing his duties in his store from 1894 to about 1918. Town clerks in those days carried on town business from their own homes, there being no central clerk's office. This was an era when raccoons and skunks were brought to the clerk's office for bounty payment. There are people who still remember the animal skins hanging in the dooryard of the Weatherbee house.[44]

A daughter, Blanche G. Weatherbee, graduated from Radcliffe College and was a teacher for many years in the Boston school system. She continued to live in the Weatherbee house until her death in 1939. Blanche was a highly respected person in the village. She was a fund of knowledge, a learned conversationalist who kept the village and the church alive with her ideas and inspiration. She was one of the original incorporators of the Marshfield Historical Society in 1913 and became its first secretary, a post she held until her death twenty-five years later. On 4 December 1977 the large barn with a cupola that stood behind the old Weatherbee house burned to the ground.[45]

When Elisha Hall left his partnership in the store with George Weatherbee, Jr., in 1853, he set up his own business in a store that he built across the street, the present Marshfield Hills Post Office building. Elisha, who by that time was living in the house (154 Prospect Street) next to the Weatherbees, married George Weatherbee, Jr.'s sister, Sarah Weatherbee, in 1854. They had four children, Winthrop T., Henrietta, Flora A., and Sarah B. Hall. During the Civil War Elisha's store did a great business in selling government uniforms, as well as West Indies merchandise, rum, groceries, dry goods, and grain. This was the heyday of the store, which occupied the entire building. Horses were stabled next door in a barn, which has been remodeled into a house (161 Prospect Street), today the home of Vivian Wills, widow of Dr. Arthur Wills). The Hall family continued to be active in the village and eventually Winthrop T. Hall took over his father's store. The store closed in 1921.[46]

Winthrop T. Hall's son was the late Maurice Hall who was on the School Committee from 1929 to 1953 and was chairman of the water commissioners in the 1960s. He also served as a trustee of the Soldiers' Memorial.

Maurice and Priscilla Rogers Hall's son Richard Hall has been active in town affairs for years, serving on the Martinson Junior High School building committee in the early 1960s, the Charter Commission in the 1970s, the Bylaw and Charter Commission in the late 1970s and early 1980s, and, since 1984, as town meeting moderator. As chairman of the Cable Televison Commission in the early 1980s, Dick was responsible for bringing cable television to Marshfield. Currently he is on the Board of Appeals. He also served on the Steering Committee for the Ventress Library Development Fund and on the Dwyer Farm Committee, which raised funds for the purchase of the farm.[47]

Other East Marshfield/Marshfield Hills stores were those of Henry Tilden at what is today 142 Old Main Street and of Charles L. Tilden on Pleasant Street. The Henry Tilden general store operated from 1857 to about 1886.

The Charles L. Tilden store was located in front of his family house (the old Levi Ford house, owned by the Tilden family from 1818 to 1877) at 543 Pleasant Street. He built and opened the store in the 1890s. He sold groceries, grain, tools, seeds, shoes, and dry goods. Charles L. Tilden captained a North River packet ship on which he transported his goods. In 1908 Guy Frank Drew, his son-in-law, became proprietor of the store and

Some time after the Civil War . . . some civic-minded Hills people planted elms all along Pleasant, Old Main, and Prospect streets. . . . I came along later and those trees are among my clearest memories. They obscured and softened the utility poles and wires that ran under them. They provided an archway for views along village streets. . . . Their high shade kept the Hills cool in summer. . . . Even the leaves weren't too bad in the fall. Small, and coming down from such a height, they bothered our lawn, and my brother and me, only a little. . . . The Dutch elm disease ended all that. . . . [but] the memory of the elms is a sweet one.

— Richard Hall

CHARLES L. TILDEN,

—DEALER IN—

Groceries, Flour and Grain,

Farm and Garden Tools and Seed. Crockery, and Glass Ware
Boots, Shoes & Rubbers, Paints & Oils, DryGoods, &c. Also

Auctioneer & Appraiser.

MARSHFIELD HILLS.

Charles L. Tilden store on Pleasant Street, about 1890. This building, originally on the property at 543 Pleasant Street, was moved across the street and is today the Clift Rodgers Library. Where once people gathered for groceries and foreign goods, today they come in search of knowledge and journeys of the imagination. Photograph courtesy of Eleanor Magoon

continued the business until 1913. In 1919 the store building was moved across the street and converted into the parish house of the Second Congregational Church. It is now the Clift Rodgers Library.[48]

Charles L. Tilden was also a shoemaker. He married Beulah Damon and in 1858 he built the house (535 Pleasant Street) next door to his family's home.[49]

The Henry I. Carver store was located in the house at today's 150 Old Main Street. Present owners of the home are Alden and Constance Mitchell. The grocery store was owned and operated by Henry I. and Carrie Damon Carver from the early 1900s to the late 1930s. Carver's store was known for high quality groceries, which, in the early days, were delivered by horse-drawn cart. Well-known villager Frank Mallory drove the Carver grocery cart for many years. Later, Henry Carver had a Jenny gasoline pump in the yard and served gas to the first generation of automobiles. In the 1930s he specialized in S.S. Pierce goods. Some villagers still remember Henry and Carrie quietly emerging from the back parlor to wait on customers.

Henry I. Carver bought his house in 1900 from Joseph C. Hagar, author of the 1940 town history and member of the Marshfield Tercentenary Committee. Joseph Hagar's father, Doctor Joseph Hagar, came to Marshfield as a country doctor in 1856 and bought the house about 1879. Dr. Hagar was a familiar person around Marshfield in the late 1800s, making his doctor's calls by horse and buggy.

His son Joseph Hagar, fondly known throughout the village as Hijo, or Joe, was town moderator from 1918 to 1921 and selectman of Marshfield from 1922 to 1929. This was a period of great change for Marshfield. Town water was provided and paved roads built for the first time. The town home for the poor and the first high school were both built in 1923. Joe Hagar was president of the Marshfield Fair in the 1920s, founder and president of the Marshfield Historical Society, and president of the Historic Winslow House Association. He was responsible for the formation of the North Community Church in 1928. For many years he was an editor and publisher, founding the Rapid Service Press in Boston in 1914. He and three of his sons, Donald, Stuart, and Malcolm Hagar, operated this printing and publishing business for many years.

Joe Hagar retired in 1951 and the business was carried on under the presidency of Donald C. Hagar until 1975. Donald was president of the Winslow House Association for twenty-one years, from 1959 to 1980, and a member of the Marshfield Historical Commission for twenty years. He also served on the Steering Committee for the Ventress Library Development Fund in 1984.

Another of Joe Hagar's sons, Joseph Archibald Hagar, served on the Marshfield School Committee from 1929 to 1941. He was also chief of the call firemen of Marshfield Hills village, along with other such well-remembered villagers as Freeman Damon, Waldo Phillips, Maurice Hall, Walter Bartlett, Merrill Kinsley, George Reardon, and Frank Mallory. He is most noted, however, for his long service as Massachusetts State Ornithologist from 1934 to 1959.

Donald and Edith Culver Hagar's daughter, Cynthia Hagar Krusell, is of the fourth generation of Hagars in Marshfield. She is present town historian, long-time member of the Marshfield Historical Commission, and co-author of this current history. The Hagars are descendants of two Marshfield settler families: William Thomas and his wife of Green Harbor, and Thomas and Anne Warren Little of Sea View.

Of the many East Marshfield/Marshfield stores, the most beloved and remembered is the store owned by Waldo ("Bo") Phillips, located at what is today the house at 185 Old Main Street. This building was originally a blacksmith shop started by the Ewell family in 1867. Judson Ewell and then his son, Ralph Judson Ewell, were the village smithies for two generations. The Ewells opened a general store in 1911.

Bo's Store

The door creaked open with the familiar tinkling of the bell. It slammed closed like a pistol shot. The room within seemed dim and uninhabited. Presently the shuffling of footsteps betrayed the presence of the storekeeper. A pungent odor of pipes drew attention to a circle of figures gathered around a potbellied cast-iron stove. Flies buzzed about the long sticky strings of hanging flypaper. Somewhere a clock ticked.

Any long-time resident of Marshfield Hills recognizes the scene as Bo's Store fifty years ago. One of two small local grocery stores, it was like countless of its kind across New England, yet unique and special to the neighborhood. Bo was our fond name for Waldo H. Phillips, a native villager, one of those strong Yankee characters of few, but choice, words. From behind the counter of his store, he quietly wielded his influence over the village.

Photograph courtesy of Eleanor Magoon

Bo's store on Old Main Street was the social, economic, and political center of the village. Bo carried the usual line of country store produce and, in addition, sold gas from a hand-cranked tank that stood in the front yard. When a customer drew up for service, Bo emerged, in due time, in his shirt-sleeves and pants held up with elastic suspenders. Limping and sighing, he lumbered across the porch, down the one step, and across the yard. He struggled to unhook the gas hose, inserted it into the tank, cranked the handle, and casually inquired about the amount wanted. Sometimes he'd leave a customer outside to wait on a customer inside, then have to saunter out again to complete the gas sale, then take another trip into the store for change, if he didn't have enough in his pocket. To purchase either gas or groceries necessitated some give-and-take conversation and a lot of patience. Bo was a man to be reckoned with.

Inside the store, Bo was a marvel of inefficiency. The Kellogg's Corn Flakes, Wheaties, and Shredded Wheat were kept on the top shelf. Bo dislodged the boxes with long-handled tongs, then caught them as they tumbled down. It was a real search to find the raisins, rice, jello, or cooking oil. Then he lumbered out back to the refrigerator for "on-ice" items, fetched paper goods from a back room, or circumnavigated the potbellied stove to get an item from the other side of the store. Taking his pencil from behind his ear, he added up the bill on the brown paper bag several times to get it right, then carefully put each grocery item into the bag, selecting the heaviest ones for the bottom.

Bo was in his real element, however, when he got to the ice cream department. He shook out a quart ice cream container from a nest of boxes, banged open the refrigerator chest lid, took a metal scooper from a dish of water in which it was stored, and began to scoop and push and pack. If anyone could get a quart-and-a-half into a quart container, Bo could. He then carefully rounded off the ice cream, being sure that a hunk dropped on the chest top. This he picked up with great relish and popped into his mouth. Munching delightedly, he searched for the proper size top for the container. When he pressed down on the top in an effort to compact further the already squeezed ice cream, some additional pieces would drop or ooze down the sides. Running his finger adroitly around the container, he would quickly consume the excess. Then he reached for a brown paper bag, gently lowered the packed ice cream box

into it, and handed it across the counter, as if parting with a dear friend.

Bo's wife, Edna, helped him in the store. She didn't like it much and she let you know it. She made a herculean job out of the smallest request, all the time bantering with Bo. She'd say, "Oh, Bo, you don't mean that," or "Bo, come 'round here and get that down for me." Edna was quick to close up shop and made a slow-to-order customer feel uncomfortable at about two minutes before closing time. She'd be right there to shut and lock the door when you left.

For the children of the village, Bo's store meant not only ice cream but penny candy. There was a tempting array in the candy cases of mint juleps, orange jellies, marshmallow bananas, Necco wafers, root beer barrels, licorice sticks, raspberry sours, candy canes, lollipops, and bubble gum. Pressing our noses to the glass case, we picked and chose while Bo, with infinite patience, plucked out the individual sweets and popped them into the tiny brown bag.

When we went to the North School, we thought it great sport to make for Bo's store at recess, buy some candy with our few hard-earned pennies, and then race back to school undetected. It was only in later years that we realized that Bo knew just exactly what we were up to. He also knew our teachers and our parents.

The group around the potbellied stove served as the village central

intelligence department. They seldom spoke, preferring to communicate tersely or in silence. There was a bit of shuffling, a muffled cough, a slow creaking of a chair tipping on its back legs. Then someone might say, "Score's two to one," referring to the Red Sox game coming from the radio. Or it might be, "Charlie got two this morning." Charlie was Bo's brother and an incessant and intrepid hunter. He hunted wildfowl, fox, and coons, and his daily catch was often seen hanging limply on his front porch on the main street of the village.

Just before the Fourth of July was the most exciting time at Bo's store. A table was placed in the front yard not far from the gas tank. Out came a great array of fireworks, colorful packages of cherry bombs, rockets, silver sparklers, and long rolls of firecrackers. Everyone converged on Bo's. Then off we'd go down the street to the accompaniment of pops, bangs, and shrieks. The village exploded with excitement and surprise. After the Fourth everything quieted down noticeably, and summer droned on under the high arching elms. But in Bo's store, the flies buzzed, the clock ticked, Charlie's hunting dogs lay about, Edna's knitting needles clicked, the ball game continued, and Bo shuffled about fetching groceries and scooping his ice cream, an unforgettable person in a timeless village.

— Cynthia Hagar Krusell

When Bo Phillips married Judson Ewell's daughter Edna in 1921, he and Edna took over the management of the business. Bo and Edna were unforgettable personalities. This store was the center of activity in Marshfield Hills village for thirty-seven years. When it closed in 1958, an era came to an end.

In the 1930s Everett and Alice Josselyn ran a small store on Summer Street (632 Summer Street today). It carried bread and milk, candy, and cigarettes. Their daughter Hazel Morehardt (Mathers) had built the house in 1925 and ran a luncheon place there before the era of the Josselyn store. Before Route 3A was completed in 1927, Summer Street was the main way from Marshfield to Scituate. There are those who still remember when cows grazed in the fields along this area of Summer Street.

In the 1920s there was a drugstore in the village run by Jennie Sumner, located next to the present house of Dr. William Spitz, dentist (173 Old Main Street). There was a barbershop over the post office and a meat market where the post office is today.

Charlie Phillips with his hunting dogs and display of pelts
Photograph courtesy of Eleanor Magoon

In 1945 Henry G. ("Bud") and Marjorie Purdy Shreiner opened a restaurant, called Bud's Place, where the current Marshfield Hills General Store is located, on the north end of the post office building. Today's owners of the general store are Burton and Sandra Cowgill. Bud's Place became very popular, with its soda fountain, home cooking, and Marge's lobster rolls and delectable homemade pies. Bud's Place closed in 1953. Bud was appointed Civil Defense Director for Marshfield in 1956 and used the store building for related activities and First Aid classes. Bud ran the largest civil defense operation the town had ever known and was area representative to the Southeastern Massachusetts National Civil Defense Advisory Council. He resigned in 1958 and was succeeded by Police Sergeant Robert E. Frugoli. Bud died in 1959, bringing to an end another special era in Marshfield Hills history.

Marjorie Purdy Shreiner, daughter of George A. and Lena Perry Purdy, is an institution in Marshfield Hills village. Postmistress for thirty-nine years, from 1926 to 1965, her presence around the post office, where she still lives upstairs with her sister Irene Purdy, is felt by all villagers. For a while, she not only helped Bud in the restaurant, but also ran a little shop between the post office and Bud's Place, where she sold candy, newspapers, and sewing articles. Her influence has been felt far beyond the village. Very active in town affairs and outspoken at town meetings, Marge is a person both loved and respected.

Blacksmith shops and shoe shops were a vital part of village life in the eighteenth and nineteenth centuries. There was a continuing need for horseshoes and iron utensils, and the sound of the anvil rang through the streets. In addition to the Ewell shop, there were several other blacksmiths

from time to time in East Marshfield/Marshfield Hills. Blacksmiths in the 1789 period were Arunah and Nathaniel Damon and Adam Rogers. Calvin Damon ran a blacksmith shop in the village from the 1830s to the 1850s. Another shop was run in the early 1900s by Mr. Feltis across from the present North Community Church. There was a blacksmith shop at the corner of Prospect Street (130 Prospect Street). In 1903 the F. A. Damon Carriage Factory was operating next to Ewell's (189 Old Main Street). Lincoln Damon and Charles L. Tilden ran small shoe shops in their homes. From 1885 to 1897 Albert Bates had a shoe shop, which employed fifteen to twenty-five men, on Highland Street (88 Highland Street).[50]

Joshua and Deacon Samuel Tilden ran a sawmill on the pond at the foot of Prospect Hill about 1793. Charles Walker had a nail and tack factory at the site by 1838. Later there was a gristmill run by Charles Lewis. In the early 1900s Tom Stackhouse cut and stored ice in a large barn beside the pond, for some years known as Stackhouse Pond.[51]

The Rogers family of East Marshfield not only ran stores and kept school, but also built ships. Their shipyards were located at the North River near the present Little's Bridge and Mary's Boat Livery. Peleg, Luther, and possibly Nathaniel, Jr., and Thomas, Jr., built at this site. Other Rogers family members worked at Gravelly Beach, Corn Hill, in North Marshfield. Skilled shipwrights, they built schooners and brigantines, ranging from 90 to 221 tons, between 1784 and 1809.[52]

Perhaps one of the most interesting of the Rogerses' yards was that of Luther Rogers who had a shipyard a mile from the river on his Highland Street land. This was later the site of the home of historian Lysander Richards and is where Phyllis and George Harlow live today. In 1819 Luther constructed a 20-ton packet, the *Abigail Little*, hauled her down to the water's edge in winter on sleds, and launched her on the ice. Nothing daunted a determined and skilled shipbuilder! There was a shipyard in Norwell which was three miles from the river.[53]

William Taylor had a shipyard just east of Little's Bridge. This yard, operated by William Taylor and Israel Carver, was a later operation where several schooners were built between 1848 and 1860.[54]

There were, from time to time, some twenty-five shipyards along the river. Some of these were small and short-lived operations. Most of the shipbuilders worked at several or all of the yards. The peak year of North River shipbuilding was 1800 when twenty-five ships were built. The area was famous as a training place for master shipbuilders. A North River man was in great demand in the large East Boston, Salem, and Maine shipyards.

The river was a bustling scene of activity in the shipbuilding age, with some men working on the ships, others hauling timber from the wood lots with oxen teams, while others were making the iron fittings, sails, and cordage. Some sailed the packet ships to and from Boston, exporting timber and farm produce and importing staples and goods to stock the stores of the local villages throughout the valley. Almost every family was engaged in some activity related to shipbuilding and the shipping industry.

The first bridge built at the 3A site was Little's Bridge in 1825. It was a toll bridge for forty years. The story goes that the ministers of the Second Church in East Marshfield and those of the First Church of Scituate frequently exchanged pulpits. They would meet early on a Sunday morning at the bridge and swap horses, thus avoiding the toll.[55]

The Rogers house, part of which is believed to date to about 1720, still stands near the old shipyard today. From this spot, the Rogers men not only built ships but sailed them around the world. There have been a number of inventive and famous men in this family. Isaiah Rogers, born in the house in 1800, was the son of Peleg, Jr., and Jemima Eames Rogers. He studied architecture with Alexander Parris and helped to develop the Greek Revival style. Isaiah is known as the "father of the American hotel," having invented a means of piping water to upper floors of buildings. He designed the Gothic exterior for the Second Congregational Church at the Hills in 1848.[56]

In 1838 Isaiah Rogers built the house at 392 Summer Street which, before it was remodeled in 1922 by Louise Regan, was a half-cape style house. Some of the interesting details that were built into the original house can still be seen today. These include paneling and moldings said to have come from the New York Stock Exchange building and the New York Customs House, both of which Rogers designed and built.[57]

Isaiah Rogers sold the homestead (2205 Main Street) to Amos F. Rogers before 1860. Later it passed to the Damon family. Mary Damon ran a boat

Mary's Boat Livery on the North River at Little's Bridge, 1990. The 1720 Rogers house still stands, overlooking the activities of today's recreational boating.

A grandmother's clock made by Samuel Rogers in 1780 when he was fourteen years old. Born on his father's farm in Marshfield Hills village, he became a well-known clockmaker and inventor.

yard there in the early 1900s and gave it the name Mary's Boat Yard. The house was inherited by Mary's nephew Freeman Damon, who sold it to John Duane of Quincy. In 1948 John sold it to his daughter Mary Duane Williams and her husband, George P. Williams. They started a boat livery again in this place so long associated with boats and boat building. After George died, Mary continued to run Mary's Boat Livery until 1986, when she leased it to her daughter and son-in-law, Jane and John Duffy. Presently there are moorings for one hundred boats.

Due to serious pollution, the North River clam flats are closed to shellfishing now. The Scituate Sewer-Water Waste Treatment Plant is believed to be responsible for violating the Federal Clean Water Act by dumping raw sewage into the river. The North and South River Watershed Association, formed in the 1960s, is constantly concerned with the river, which was declared a Scenic River in 1978 under the Massachusetts Scenic and Recreation Rivers Act. Today the watershed association works to preserve this fragile estuary system, so important ecologically and histori-cally to the region.[58]

Samuel Rogers, baptized 27 July 1766, son of Thomas and Submit Hatch Rogers, became famous as a clockmaker. The family lived in East Marshfield village in the house at 197 Old Main Street, currently owned by Willard and Claire Robinson. In 1780, when a boy of only fourteen, Samuel made an exquisite grandmother's clock which incorporated astronomical and zodiacal time measurements based on ancient Caldean and Chinese concepts. He also worked with Ezekiel and Jesse Reed to invent early nail and tack machinery and made grandfather clocks and watches. Sam's brother Isaac was also a clockmaker and inventor. A grandfather's clock made by him, and inscribed across the face "Isaac Rogers," is in a Marshfield home today.[59]

In the 1920s and 1930s Harry Rogers sold fresh spring water from Canoe Tree Spring off Pleasant Street where Rugani Avenue is today. This area was once a cow pasture owned by William Alvin Rogers. The water was stored in five-gallon carboys and delivered to homes in the area, at first by horse and wagon, later by pickup truck. Other door-to-door deliveries in the 1930s included meat from the Gould Meat Wagon, milk from Jack Little's Union Street farm, ice for the ice boxes, bread, and fish.

The Lathrop house at 575 Summer Street was acquired by the H. P. Hood Milk Company in 1934. The barn next door was used for bottling milk that was shipped to this location. Truck drivers for the company were lodged in the enlarged house. W. Torrey Little later acquired the place and moved his antique and auctioning business, originally located on Route 3A near Forest Street (1660 Main Street), to the barn, turning the house into apartments. Today there is a proposed plan for multiple housing on the acreage.

In the early part of this century there were strawberry fields everywhere in Marshfield Hills. Marshall Ewell, who lived on Spring Street, developed an especially large and delectable hybrid specimen, and soon many of the villagers went into the strawberry business. The fields stretched behind the houses along Old Main Street and between Prospect and Bow streets. Everett Ford had extensive fields between Pleasant and Old Main streets near the site of the present Christian Science Church. Many people were employed picking the strawberries. In the late 1930s Bo Phillips grew strawberries on his property on Route 3A at Highland Street, but by this time the Marshall strawberry strain had died out, and this succulent Marshfield fruit was gone forever.

Marshfield Hills Garage in the 1930s
Photograph courtesy of Constance Anderson Benzaquin

The Marshfield Hills Garage on Route 3A was built in 1928 by Thaxter Anderson. He and his wife, Jeannette Perry Anderson, were active and respected villagers for many years. Almost everyone in the surrounding area purchased his or her new car and had it serviced at this local Chrysler agency until the late 1960s. Jeannette was bookkeeper and business manager of the garage, as well as a Girl Scout leader, an avid and life-long birder, and a devoted friend and neighbor. Their son Stephen continued to run the business after Thaxter's death in 1963. Steve moved the business to 975 Plain Street in 1975.

Thaxter and Jeannette's daughter, Constance Anderson Benzaquin, is known in the community today for her many years of singing in the North Community Church choir and in a number of local choral groups. She has also served as a Girl Scout leader. Her husband, Paul Benzaquin, is a well-known Boston radio personality, talk-show host, and author.

There were, from time to time, a number of small restaurants in the Hills. In the 1930s the Peacock Tea Room, at what is now 215 Pleasant Street, was run by Isabelle G. Thayer, assisted by Alma M. Rall and Margaret (Peggy) Anderson, who was renowned for her superb cooking. Peggy's rum cake was a specialty that will be long remembered. Isabelle's sister Gertrude Borland, a pianist for the Cleveland Symphony Orchestra, lived in the house next door at 222 Pleasant Street. This house was built by Warren White in 1836 and is currently owned by Nancy and Richard Thompson.

A small restaurant on Route 3A, behind the old North School, was run by Pat Ford in the 1930s. There was for a short time a restaurant by Walker's Pond. Trout were caught fresh from the pond, and the slogan used to advertise this small eatery was, "You catch it, we'll cook it."

New roads and developments came to the Hills as elsewhere. Glen Road was built in the 1940s, followed by Rugani Avenue in 1955. Damon's Point Road was improved at this same time. Eastwood Lane and Blacksmith Lane were developed in the 1970s. The newest roads are Meghan Way and Andrews Avenue, built in 1989 off Forest Street between Route 3A and Valley Path.

The Marshfield Conservation Commission has a large acreage on Carolina Hill, part of which lies within the Marshfield Hills area, and some scattered North River salt marsh acres. The North River Wildlife Sanctuary is located at the Massachusetts Audubon Society South Shore Regional Center. The society owns a 177-acre parcel with trails, located at the intersection of Route 3A and Summer Street. David E. Clapp is director of the South Shore Sanctuaries.

The Canoe Tree Spring label for water bottled by Harry H. Rogers from springs in the wetland off today's Rugani Avenue

Summer Art Festival, *depicting the North River Arts Society annual event*
Watercolor by Dorit Flowers, 1988, courtesy of Martha L. Morrison

In spite of the changes in other parts of the town, the peaceful village of Marshfield Hills remains little changed today. There is a sense of community. Many of the old families still live in the Hills. The greatest visible change that time has brought is the disappearance of the tall elm trees that once graced this almost perfect New England village. Forming an archway over the main street, like the vault of a magnificent cathedral, they were the pride and joy of several generations. What the disastrous hurricane of 1938 did not destroy, the Dutch Elm disease finally took, so that by the 1970s these trees, lovingly planted by a former generation, were gone. Gone too are the dirt byways, the blacksmith shops, shoe shops, old stores, and tea shops.

But there are two events which carry on the traditions of Marshfield Hills. One is the deeply moving annual Memorial Day Parade, when the bands and marching units proceed with dignity and pride up Old Main Street to the cemetery on the hill to pay homage to those who have gone before. The other is the colorful and popular North River Arts Society Festival which bedecks the village with arts and crafts, sprinkles it with flags and balloons, and peoples it with joyous children and adults. Marshfield Hills is a timeless village that will not die.

Marshfield's Little Italy

Along a stretch of Pleasant Street in Marshfield Hills there is a small community of Italian families who have made a large contribution to the town. These are the families of Bandoni, Biagini, Castiglioni, Cervelli, Doroni, Frugoli, Rugani, and Salvetti. They all came originally from Lucca in northern Italy, where they lived in the village of Moriano, a place very much like Marshfield Hills. They grew up together and many are related to one another.

Karen Biagini writes:

About 1916 the first group of men were hired to work as farmhands at Ruthven Farms (357 Pleasant Street), owned by Fremont Whitten who was in the railroad business. Other Italian families soon followed. Some worked on the D.C. Seager farm where Deer Hill Lane is today. Eventually they were able to buy land and farm for themselves. They survived by farming and doing any job they could find, such as cutting wood, plowing, sanding in winter, and ice cutting. Some of them worked for Horace Keene, who had an ice and wood business near the Sea View pond. The Italians are well known for their beautiful stonework and they constructed many of the stone walls around the town. They also laid most of the town water lines, digging the trenches by hand.

The earliest families lived together in a house that they built at the corner of Pleasant Street and Eames Way. The land was given to Julio Rugani by Mr. Whitten. The house is no longer there. Later another home was built further up Eames Way, and finally the "Big House" was built by Julio Rugani off Pleasant Street. Everyone, including married couples, shared these quarters. When they became established they built their own homes.

The men took evening classes at the South River School to learn English. The Ruganis established a contracting business as did their brother-in-law Frank Castiglioni. Joe Biagini became a partner of Castiglioni and later, upon his retirement, bought him out. Joe's brothers Vieri, Omero, and Sirio joined the Biagini business as time went on. Joe's sons Robert and Paul are the only members of the second generation to stay in the family construction business.

The first generation did not become involved in community activities because of the language barrier and the

Joe Biagini and Donald Doroni at the "Big House" off Pleasant Street, about 1940
Photograph courtesy of Joe and Dora Biagini

necessity to spend their time at hard work. Later generations have been very active in town affairs. Bob Frugoli was on the Marshfield Police Department for twenty-three years, until his retirement in 1977. From 1972 to 1977 he was chief of police. Bill Frugoli has served on the Marshfield Personnel Board and is on the board of directors of the Marshfield Fair. Donna Frugoli has served on the board of directors of the Steeple Preschool on Highland Street. Eileen Biagini is currently serving as treasurer of the Marshfield 350th Commemorative Trust and has previously been on the Council on Aging. Karen Biagini is chairman of the Program Committee for the YWCA and serves on the Country Arts Committee for the Marshfield Fair. Aldo Salvetti continues in the fine masonry tradition of his ancestors, and also in the tradition of his father as a farmer.

These warm, generous families have been a welcome part of the community for the past seventy years. The women have been known and respected by three generations of Marshfield neighbors. Dora, Marianna, and Rita Biagini, as well as the late Eny Biagini, Anna Frugoli, and Olga Salvetti, have a warm place in the hearts of many. The

cheery optimism of Joe, Vieri, and Omero Biagini are familiar throughout the community, followed now by the next generation, Paul and Robert Biagini and their wives, Karen and Eileen.

For some of us who went to the old North School in Marshfield Hills there are the memories of good times shared with Donaldo and Frank Cervelli; Agnes, Arthur, and Louis Rugani; Aldo, Lloyd, and Sergio Salvetti, and others in this special community within a community.

Perhaps Joe Biagini speaks for the Italian community when he tells of how he arrived here in 1929 with one set of clothes, and no knowledge of the English language. Today he is comfortable and appreciative of the opportunity he found here to get ahead and prosper through his own hard work and ingenuity.

The Mounces' barn and orchard in Two Mile

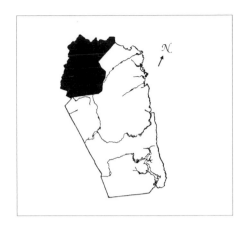

North Marshfield and Two Mile Villages

NORTH MARSHFIELD is no longer a village. It is a large expanse of fields, woods, river, and sky. Still topped by the great white pines and scattered with white oak left from the shipbuilding days, North Marshfield lies along the crest of the hills that border the North River.

The area has two parts but no village center, preferring to give its full attention to the river front. One part is known as Two Mile, a term seldom used today. It was an area set off to Scituate in 1640 that remained a part of that town for 148 years, until 1788. Scituate needed salt hay and early petitioned the Plymouth Colony Court to grant a parcel of land two miles long and one mile wide along the river, running from the midstream to the upland. The Two Mile extends from Oak Street at Union Street south to the Pembroke line and into Pembroke as far as Robinson's Creek. It might have been aptly called the Mill Village or Hatchville. Almost every house was a Hatch house and every mill a Hatch mill. The little Two Mile Brook provided water power for the mills, which supported the Hatches for over three hundred years.

The other part of the area is simply called North Marshfield. It is the section along Union Street from Oak Street north to the Union Street Bridge, Corn Hill Lane (originally Gravelly Beach Lane), and Highland Street to Valley Path. Most of the settlers of both parts of North Marshfield came from Scituate or South Scituate, the old name for Norwell, where their loyalties remained. During the seventeenth and eighteenth centuries, they went to meeting, carried on their trade and crafts, and married into Scituate families across the river.

William Phillips Tilden, who lived at the Block House Shipyard in South Scituate, wrote about his uncle Jotham Tilden's family, who lived near Rocky Reach in North Marshfield:

They attended church with us at Scituate. It was a pretty sight. . . to see them winding along, in their best attire, down the hill to the river, on a Sunday morning, and across in the large, flat bottomed boat made for the occasion.[2]

Sparsely settled to this day and still presenting a cleared, farmed landscape neatly divided by stone walls and graced with colonial houses,

The North River and the meadows of Two Mile, that snug corner of Marshfield was all apiece with the quiet beauty of the place, the beauty of pine woods and level meadows and stone walled fields sprawled upon the hills.

— Richard Warren Hatch.[1]

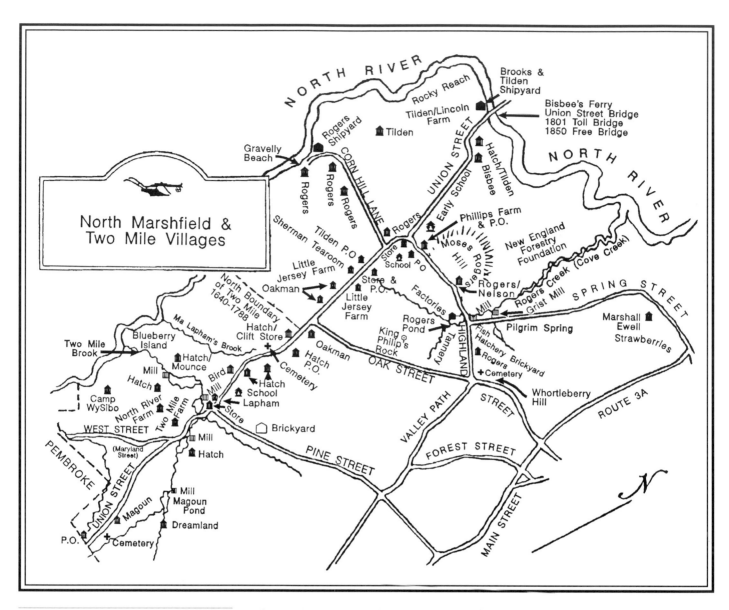

North River

Brooks & Tilden Shipyard

Rocky Reach

Tilden/Lincoln Farm

Bisbee's Ferry
Union Street Bridge
1801 Toll Bridge
1850 Free Bridge

Tilden

North River

Rogers Shipyard

Hatch
Tilden
Bisbee

HatchTilden
Bisbee

Gravelly Beach

Rogers

CORN HILL LANE

Rogers

UNION STREET

Early School

Rogers

Phillips Farm & P.O.

New England Forestry Foundation

North Marshfield & Two Mile Villages

Rogers

Sherman Tearoom

Tilden P.O.

Rogers

Moses Rogers Hill

Rogers Creek (Cove Creek)

Little Jersey Farm

Store P.O.

School

SPRING STREET

North Boundary of Two Mile 1640-1788

Oakman

Store & P.O.

Little Jersey Farm

Factories

Rogers/ Nelson

Mill

Rogers/ Grist Mill

Marshall Ewell Strawberries

Rogers Pond

Pilgrim Spring

Hatch/ Clift Store

King Philip's Rock

Tannery

HIGHLAND

Fish Hatchery

Brickyard

Ma Lapham's Brook

Blueberry Island

Oakman

Hatch P.O.

Cemetery

Rogers Cemetery

Two Mile Brook

Hatch/ Mounce

Bird Mill

OAK STREET

STREET

Whortleberry Hill

ROUTE 3A

Mill

Hatch

Hatch School Lapham

Store

Camp WySibo

North River Farm

Two Mile Farm

Brickyard

WEST STREET

Mill

VALLEY PATH

(Maryland Street)

Hatch

PINE STREET

FOREST STREET

PEMBROKE

UNION STREET

Mill Magoun Pond

MAIN STREET

Magoun

Dreamland

P.O.

Cemetery

N

North Marshfield and Two Mile Villages

this is an area in which to step back in time. Approaching from the north over the present Union Street Bridge, one follows the path of the first English arrivals up from the river. Or one can approach, as some Indians did, by canoe or boat up Rogers Creek (today called Cove Creek) to the land between the hills at Rogers Pond. Much of the modern world arrives by automobile from the expressway, driving through Two Mile and along Union Street. From any direction, North Marshfield is a special experience to the mind and senses. The old people declared it was the loveliest ride one could take on a Sunday afternoon. It still is, although the area is changing rapidly.

At the site of today's Union Street Bridge there was a ferry before 1700, run by Elisha Bisbee. A cart path kept to the lowland near the edge of the marsh by Rocky Reach and continued to the end of Corn Hill Lane. From there it continued on the lowland through the fields to Two Mile Brook, up the hill by the doorstep of the Two Mile farmhouse, along the ridge, and into a shady glen to what is today the Pembroke line at what used to be West Street and is today Maryland Street.

The Rogers Creek approach to North Marshfield led up to the fresh water springs at Spring Street (originally Clift Street), or continued up Rogers Brook and along the old Indian path to the landmark known as King Philip's Rock. Oak Street and Corn Hill Lane were dirt roads sixty years ago and knew only the tread of the horse's hoof or the soft sole of a foot traveler. Valley Path was one of the last roads to be paved, in the late 1950s.

This part of Marshfield is Indian, Quaker, farming, shipbuilding, and river country all rolled into one. The Indians arrived first, paddling up the river and the tidal creek in search of fresh water and protected campsites. The North River valley is rich in Algonquin history. A passageway across southeastern Massachusetts via the North River, the Pembroke ponds, and the Nemasket and Taunton rivers to Narragansett Bay was much used by the local Wampanoags and Massachusetts tribes. Many base camps and lithic artifacts have been found along the hillsides of the river valley, especially wherever the upland dips close to the mainstream of the river. The Indian spirit lingers here when the mist lies over the marshes, or when the great horned owl hunts silently along the marsh at night.

The English settlers came to fish and farm and build ships. John Rogers arrived about 1649 from Scituate. He built a house on a 100-acre farm on the crest of the Highland Street hill. The first record of this house (540 Highland Street) is in 1660. The Rogers family continued to own and live in the house until 1854. Many members of this family were Quakers.

Stephen R. Rogers, who was living in the old house before his death in 1835, sought out his cousin's son, Moses F. Rogers of Danbury, Vermont, to be his heir. Moses Rogers's branch of the Rogers family had earlier moved from Marshfield to Vermont to live in a Quaker community. Stephen willed his house to Moses and to Moses' son Stephen Rogers Rogers. Moses and his son lived in the house from 1835 to 1854 when it was sold out of the family. Stephen Rogers Rogers married Mary Little, daughter of Edward Preble Little and Edy Rogers and moved to Sandwich in 1853.[4]

The Highland Street hill was known for years as Moses Rogers Hill in reference to this Vermont member of the family. The house still stands, keeping watch over Rogers Creek and the pond below. Graced with old barns and outbuildings and flooded with sunshine, it is today the home of Charles and Catronia Case. Once the river and the creek were the only highways to this outlying farm, which was early designated by the town as a garrison house against Indian attack.[5]

In 1872 the 200-acre Rogers farm was purchased by Henry W. Nelson. He stocked the farm with horses, Holstein cattle, pigs, and chickens. He grew crops of all sorts and maintained large greenhouses. He developed an elaborate water system that pumped water up from the brook and stored it in a large tank on the hill. He cultivated the famous Marshall strawberries and had an extensive apple orchard. The farm employed fifty full-time resident farm workers. The property passed to Margaret and Dorothea Nelson, who gave one hundred acres of land between the house and the river to the New England Forestry Foundation before their death.[6]

Henry's great-granddaughter Margaret Milholland inherited the farm and continued to live there during the summers until 1977, when it was sold out of the family. A letter in Mrs. Milholland's possession describes summer on the farm in the early 1900s: the hay barn, the excitement of climbing up to the cupola, the hired hands working in the cow barn, the tree house, grunting pigs in the piggery, and the joy of browsing in the garret among the dusty books on rainy days. Margaret gave another twenty-three acres

The North River abounded in fish. Eels were caught with bobs in the spring from the banks, with pole and line, and in winter through the ice, with spears long enough to reach the bottom and draw them out of their snug winter home. Herring and shad were caught in abundance in seines in the spring of the year. Perch and bass were not very plentiful, but very delicious; and the clam banks in the lower reaches of the river, near the sea, yielded an abundance of very sweet clams.

— William Phillips Tilden[3]

of land to the New England Forestry Foundation in 1977. She also gave an extensive collection of memorabilia to the Marshfield Historical Society.[7]

The Rogers family is still in Marshfield. Through the generations they have been shipbuilders, millers, tanners, and shopkeepers. In addition to the shipyard near Little's Bridge, the Rogers ran a yard at Gravelly Beach, Corn Hill Lane. Many of the Rogers lived along the lane. Mary Eliot's house at 255 Corn Hill Lane, built about 1730, is thought to be a Rogers house, as is Tom and Jan Lydon's at 137 Corn Hill Lane.

The Rogers crossed the North River to attend meeting at the Quaker meetinghouse at Wanton Shipyard in South Scituate. Later there was a Quaker meetinghouse in Pembroke. Its present location is at the top of Schooset, the intersection of routes 139 and 53. Quaker Meeting Way was the old path to Pembroke along the marsh edge through Two Mile. Often Quaker meetings were held in individual homes. Quaker vital records are difficult to find, since they were not a part of town records as were those of the established church. A few meeting records have survived and are at the town hall in Pembroke and at the Rhode Island Historical Society in Providence.

Some of the Rogers men built ships at Gravelly Beach. The heyday of this yard was from 1790 to 1819. There was a large saw pit at this site. Teams of oxen dragged white oak and pine timber from the nearby forests to be sawed here by hand, or at one of the Hatch mills on Two Mile Brook. The white pine made excellent masts, while the white oak was used for ships' knees and hulls. Samuel, Stephen, Joseph, and Captain Thomas Rogers all built at Gravelly Beach. They also worked in most of the yards up and down the river as caulkers, liners, and carpenters.

Many of the earliest shipyards on the North River were run by Quakers who, being outside the control of the established church, were free to turn their attention to shipbuilding and the related crafts of iron making, sail making, and cordage works.

The North River valley rang with shipbuilding activity. Shipping went on continuously, with cargoes going in and out of the river on the sturdy and reliable packet ships. The Rogers built, traded, sailed, and prospered.[8]

Site of Rogers' Shipyard at Gravelly Beach, Corn Hill Lane. At one time the hills along the North River resounded with the sounds of the shipbuilders at work. Large cast iron signs marking some of the shipyards were placed along the banks of the North River in 1919 by the North River Historical Society.

However, Edwin T. Rogers, when a child in 1836, said that he wished he could live to see the day there would be no shipbuilding on the river, because "he had to take his father's dinners across the meadow where the water was sometimes nearly up to his waist and in the winter the snow was very deep and often slushy." Edwin later spent his life building ships.[9]

Like the downtown Quaker Howland family, the Rogers family was persecuted by the authorities. Money was demanded from them for support of the established Congregational church. It was a life of hardship and challenge, but the rewards were great when a newly built schooner slid down the ways. It was then kedged, or hauled, down river, rigged at White's Ferry, and guided over the shoals at the old mouth of the river to put to sea at last off Rexhame.

Other members of the Rogers family were engaged in milling and manufacturing, blacksmithing, and tanning. In 1799 Amos Rogers ran a gristmill on the Pilgrim Spring water system off Spring Street. There was a blacksmith shop near the intersection of Union and Highland streets. A tannery was owned and operated by John Rogers, Jr., as early as 1771 on Tannery Brook (Rogers Brook) near the intersection of Spring and Highland streets. The house at today's 451 Highland Street is on the old tannery property. Rogers sold the 100-acre farm where the tannery was located to Nathaniel Waterman in 1793 and moved to Tinmouth, Vermont. The Watermans continued operating the tannery until the 1820s when Nathaniel's son James sold the property. In 1831 John Sprague, a blacksmith, bought the house and land from the Waterman family and established a rivet factory. He was probably responsible for damming up the so-called Rogers Pond.[10]

The rivet factory was converted eventually to box making, then to shingle production, and finally, to making toy buckets. Henry Nelson owned the water privilege on the pond by 1907, and later it passed to his son George Nelson, in the 1930s.[11]

In 1894 G. D. Damon & Sons operated a catering and ice-cream business on the west side of Rogers Pond. There were outdoor tables, and on Sunday afternoons people gathered to eat strawberry ice cream made with native

Rogers Pond and Moses Rogers Hill, Highland Street. On the hill is the John Rogers house, built in the 1650s. A variety of mills and factories and ice-cream, candy, and ice businesses have been located near this pond.
Photograph courtesy of Eleanor Magoon

Marshall strawberries. Frank G. and Granville T. Damon sold ice cream from Damon's tent at the Marshfield Fair. In the early 1900s Walter Damon made ribbon candy at the factory at the pond. It was shipped by train from the Marshfield Hills depot. Granville Damon had an ice business, cutting and storing ice in a large barn on the east side of the pond.[12]

Around the corner on Spring Street, the Webster Spring Company was selling fresh spring water by 1903. It was later called Pilgrim Springs Company and run by Alvin Vinal. Two truck loads of spring water a day were shipped to Nantasket during the 1920s. Later there was a fish hatchery in this location.[13]

Alden Rogers and his wife, Marjorie, and their son and daughter-in-law, John Alden and Veronica Rogers, live in an old Rogers house at 372 Highland Street. This house holds the record in Marshfield for continuous occupancy by the original family. They descend not only from the Quaker Rogers family, but also from Pilgrims William Brewster, Richard Warren, John Alden, and Priscilla Mullins. Marjorie Rogers counts as one of her ancestors the religious dissident John Sanford, who was expelled from Puritan Boston and went to Rhode Island with Anne Hutchinson. Small wonder that the Alden Rogers have wanted to "stay put."

Alden's grandfather was a carpenter and made shoes in a shop on the second floor of the house. The old shoe-making bench and tools are still in the possession of the family. Alden is an artist and decorator. For many years he and Marjorie designed and made figurines, some fashioned from native clay. These were sold in retail stores across the country. Alden also designed greeting cards for Erle Parker's Wayside Press on Union Street in the 1930s. For twenty-five years he was the interior decorator and furniture buyer for the Welch Company in Scituate. Behind the Rogerses' house is the site of an old brickyard. A Rogers family burying ground is to be found off Highland Street at the top of the hill, once called Whortleberry Hill.

Elijah Brooks and George Tilden operated a shipyard just above the Union Street Bridge. Brooks and Tilden built some seven vessels between 1837 and 1847. Theirs was one of the later yards on the river, the height of North River shipbuilding being around 1800.[14]

Another family that was as much a part of North Marshfield as they were of Marshfield Hills was the Tilden family. Joseph Tilden of the Scituate "Men of Kent" owned all the land from the Bisbee Ferry/Union Street Bridge site to Corn Hill Lane at Gravelly Beach. His son Samuel Tilden, a shipbuilder at Gravelly Beach, lived between Rocky Reach and Corn Hill Lane on a site marked today by only a cellar hole. Samuel's son Hatch Tilden built the magnificent square Federal house overlooking the river near Union Street Bridge in 1808. He was tollkeeper of the Union Street Bridge for forty years.[15]

More recently Robert Tilden and his wife, Dorothy Phillips Tilden, ran a large farm on Highland Street hill. Rob grew tomatoes in several large greenhouses and in the fields. He was a perfectionist about his tomatoes, wrapping each one separately and driving them himself to the Boston market. His daughter, Doris Tilden, married the auctioneer, W. Torrey Little, of the Sea View Little family. The Littles live in the 1819 Federal-style home built for Daniel Phillips at 578 Highland Street.

Elisha Bisbee came from Scituate about 1644 to run the Upper Ferry. Later the ferry was run by the Oakman family until 1770, then by John Tolman, who became the first bridge tollkeeper after the bridge was built in 1801. It was built as a drawbridge by a corporation formed for the purpose. Tolls were to be collected to the amount of the cost of the bridge; then the bridge was to become the property of the town. Hatch Tilden was tollkeeper from 1808 to 1850 when it was made a free bridge. A great jubilee was held on the bridge to celebrate the event. A new bridge was built in 1898. Damaged by a severe winter ice storm on 17 January 1917, it was rebuilt at that time. The present bridge was built in 1971 and opened in March 1972. It was built as a drawbridge, but the draw has never been functional.[16]

Elisha Bisbee lived near the ferry site and his son Elisha later kept a tavern, perhaps on the Norwell side of the river. Elisha, the first settler and ferry keeper, also farmed and was a shoemaker. He left a small estate of only eighty-three pounds at his death in 1688. He willed his farm to his wife and to his eldest son, Hopestill, and left to them "all the fruit of the trees which now grow in my orchard so long as they bear fruit and no longer."[17]

To his two married daughters Elisha gave "bed and bedding," which were considered the most valuable items in a seventeenth- or eighteenth-century home. The term *bed* referred to what we call a mattress. Beds were made of scraps of material and pieces of wool encased in cloth bags. A featherbed, which was a mark of wealth, had a value equal to that of a young cow. Bedding included blankets, bolsters, sheets, pillow beers (covers), and rugs, which were heavier than blankets. Bedsteads were rough wooden frames. Coverlets and bed curtains hung around the bedstead for warmth and privacy. A daughter usually received bed and bedding at the time of her marriage, or by the will of her deceased parent.[18]

The value of Bisbee's beds and bedding was listed at four pounds, nineteen shillings, while his cattle, the most valuable item outside of the house, were valued at four pounds, twelve shillings. Today the Bisbee home (1332 Union Street), which has been much enlarged, is owned by Nancy and William Clark, Jr., and is called Tattenhall.[19]

Another prominent North Marshfield family was the Oakman family. Samuel Oakman came from Scarborough, Maine. His son Tobias was in Plymouth about 1693 and married Elizabeth Doty, granddaughter of Pilgrim Edward Doty. Tobias and Elizabeth moved to Marshfield about 1697 and built a house in 1702 on Summer Street (460 Summer Street). The first Oakman on Union Street was Tobias, grandson of the Summer Street Tobias. About 1748 he built a house on the site of today's 815 Union Street. The present house is lived in by Donald and Janet Gibson. Tobias — yeoman, mariner, and "coaster" — built ships at Wanton Shipyard across the river in South Scituate. He also operated the Upper Ferry and ran a packet ship from the North River to Boston for forty years. The Oakmans were patriots during the Revolution and owned and operated several North River ships. Many of the Oakmans married into the Hatch family, creating kinship ties in this shipbuilding and merchant community.[20]

A number of houses along Union Street were built by Oakmans. In 1827 Hiram Oakman, grandson of Tobias, the mariner, was born in the house at 815 Union Street. After his marriage to Jane Soule Rogers, he built the house at 785 Union Street, owned today by Susan and Samuel Spencer. Hiram's brother Christopher is credited for building many of the houses in the north part of the town in the first half of the nineteenth century. He also built several churches in the area, including the First Church Unitarian in Norwell in 1830. Hiram's son Hiram was a shoemaker and owned a livery stable and a mill privilege at Oakman's Pond in Two Mile.[21]

Henry P. Oakman, housewright, built the house at 710 Union Street, where Jack and Jean Christensen live today. Henry Oakman served in the Civil War and as a selectman for the town in 1864 and 1865. Owners of the house have included John (Jack) and Damaris Hollidge, and Geraldine and

Union Street Bridge before 1917, looking toward the Hatch-Tilden house in Marshfield. Elisha Bisbee ran the Upper Ferry at this site as early as 1644.

North River Packet Sloop
Mayflower — 1823, off Block
House Shipyard, Norwell, Mass.
Drawing by William A. Baker

North River Packet Sloop MAYFLOWER - 1823
off Block House Shipyard
Norwell, Mass.

Alan Stephens. Jean Christensen serves as project manager for the South Shore Coalition and has served on the Marshfield Planning Board. Both Jean and Jack Christensen have been active on the North/South Rivers Watershed Association.[22]

During the 1800s the activities of North Marshfield centered around the intersection of Union and Highland streets, close to today's post office. There was a store, a post office, a blacksmith shop, and a school. As shipbuilding grew at Corn Hill Lane and Rocky Reach, there was a demand for these services and businesses. Prior to 1817 the store was operated by Jotham Tilden, Jr. When he died in 1828, his inventory listed the "store items." His widow, Harriet Chittenden Tilden, married the housewright Christopher Oakman. Jotham Tilden, Jr., built the home at 685 Highland Street, recently owned by John and Verna Harrington and now the home of Matthew and Eileen Byrne. A store was still located in this area in 1879.[23]

The so-called Union or Corn Hill School District No. 6 stood near this same North Marshfield crossroads as early as 1838. The original building was sold in 1847 and a new one built. When the school closed its doors in 1920, there were seventeen pupils in grades one through five. The building, which was located just three feet behind the present house at 645 Highland Street, was acquired by Robert Tilden in 1922 and moved to his farm, where it is now used as a small barn.[24]

The North Marshfield Post Office, like the mail, has seen a lot of travel. In 1838 it was at the Daniel Phillipses' house (578 Highland Street). By 1894 it had moved to Roxalina Hatch's house at 682 Union Street (now owned by attorney David Kozodoy) in Two Mile. By 1901 North Marshfield residents were picking up their mail at Carlton Tilden's (now 945 Union Street, home of Judge Robert Cauchon and his wife, Betty). For a while, Carlton Tilden's sister Cora kept the post office in a little building across the street from Carlton's home and ran a small store as well. From 1935 to 1947 Florence Ewell was postmaster in a building across from the present post office on the corner of Short Street. Verna Harrington became North Marshfield's postmaster in 1947 and served for thirty-two years until 1979. Verna and her husband, John Harrington, bought the old post office and moved it to the site of the present building, then sold it about 1950. The building was

moved to Norwell. The Harringtons then built the present post office at 645 Highland Street. Verna ran a card shop in the post office for many years.[25]

Down Union Street south toward Two Mile, Howard W. Damon had a livery business with a barge, stable, and fifteen horses in 1894. With all the comings and goings to the railroad depots, this was another center of activity for North Marshfield. The livery was located near the Lot Sylvester house (1760), today's 845 Union Street, now the home of Ellie and Dick Hoehn.[26]

Union Street was one of the first streets in Marshfield to be declared a "scenic road" in 1974, when the Marshfield Historical Commission presented an article at town meeting requesting adoption of the scenic road legislation. Since that date over thirty streets have been so designated. The Scenic Road Act of the Commonwealth of Massachusetts protects the stone walls and trees along scenic roads and mandates that a public hearing be held if any cutting or removal of trees or destruction of stone walls is involved in road repair or reconstruction work.

Martha E. Sherman (Mrs. Ashton Sherman) ran a tearoom and gift shop called "Ye Shuttle Craft Shop" in the 1920s at 915 Union Street. She served "tea and toast and trifles, Priscilla Sears sweets, waffles and coffee." She also advertised a "20th Century Lending Library." Her two daughters, Elizabeth and Grace, married, respectively, neighbors Tracy Hatch and John (Jack) Little.[27]

Two North Marshfield farms were operating well into the early 1900s. These were the Lincoln farm (1309 Union Street) at Rocky Reach, and Jack and Grace Little's Little Jersey Farm at 915 Union Street.

George Lincoln, Jr., married Mercy Hall, daughter of William Hall and Sarah Kent of White's Ferry, Sea View/Humarock. George and Mercy's son, Alfred Loring Lincoln, married Edith Whitten Clapp. Edith bought the Rocky Reach property in 1909 and the Lincolns operated a cattle farm on this stretch of high land above the great bend of the river west of Union Street. Alfred had the cattle shipped from Guernsey in the Channel Islands.

He also owned teams of oxen and ran one of the first motor launches on the North River. The farm was dismantled and the buildings torn down about 1919. Alfred and Edith's son, Edwin Lincoln, worked on the family farm as a boy. He became president of the Edwin Clapp Shoe Company in Weymouth. The farm property was owned by Edith Clapp Lincoln until 1963 and is today owned by her granddaughter Barbara Lincoln, daughter of Edwin and Josephine Lincoln.[28]

There are two eighteenth-century Tilden houses on the farm. In 1838 the two houses were occupied by three Tilden families. By 1879 the house nearest the river was occupied by a Henderson family, while the other house was lived in by two Ewell families. In 1909 Edith Lincoln purchased the Henderson house and in 1946 she bought the Ewell property. It was sold in 1980 to Richard Railsback.[29]

Jack and Grace Little (915 Union Street) had a herd of pure Jersey cows at their Little Jersey Farm. They sold milk and cream throughout the South Shore from the 1930s to the 1950s. Before homogenized milk was introduced, the rich cream was concentrated at the top of the bottle. For the generations of people who knew this delight, it is a sweet memory. To get up before sunrise and run the daily milk route for Jack until nearly sundown was an exhausting experience, but one remembered by those who took the challenge. Today the cow barn (904 Union Street) has been converted into living space by Jack's son, Christopher Little, and his wife, Marjorie. He raises beef cattle and pastures them in the fields below his barn and house.

A few new roads and housing developments have come to North Marshfield. Carolyn Circle was developed in the 1950s by the Sweeneys of Holly Hill. Later, Riverside Circle and Edmund Road were built by Steve Wildes, Sr. This area off Spring Street near the home of the Ewells who developed the "Marshall strawberry" was, like Marshfield Hills, once open fields abundant with the rich red fruit. The Oakman and Ewell families in North Marshfield also raised strawberries in the fields along Highland and Union streets. Pickers and toppers were hired to harvest the large berries. Many young people of the day remember working the strawberry fields.

Cape Verdeans in Marshfield

A group of people from the Cape Verde Islands off the west coast of Africa arrived in Marshfield in the early 1900s, three hundred years after the *Mayflower* landed at Plymouth.

The Cape Verde Islands lie in the Atlantic Ocean off the coast of Africa. Most of the Marshfield population come from the islands of Fogo and Brava. Agriculture was the country's major industry, but due to severe droughts much of the land can no longer be farmed. Originally the Cape Verdean men migrated to the United States to Cape Cod to work the cranberry bogs or to New Bedford to work on the ships.

When the Cape Verdeans first came to Marshfield they lived on the Daniel Webster estate, owned by Lincoln Hall, in a house they called the "Big House." They worked on Hall's cranberry bogs near Webster Street, where the Green Harbor Golf Course is today.

Benjamin ("Big Jim") Fernandes, Sr., was one of the first to come, in 1922. After several years he saved enough money to buy a house and over thirty-eight acres of land on Oak Street for $1,000. He married Katherine Gomes.

Joe Roderick and his wife, Olive, came to live on Oak Street in 1939. He built his house for $350. He remembers life on Oak Street when he had a little vegetable garden behind his house and a man (Jim Hurley) came with a truck selling everything from candy to clothing. He came two or three times a week and was paid a little each time he came. This was the first charge account the Cape Verdeans knew."

Other Cape Verdeans who have lived in Marshfield are the families of Andrade, Andrews, Barrows, Correira, DaLuz, Gomes, Gonsalves, Lopes, Nunes, Pinas, Rodrigues, and Rubin. There are today about one hundred and fifty Cape Verdeans in the town.

The Cape Verdeans have served the town of Marshfield in many capacities. One of Joe Roderick's sons, John Roderick, is a well known retired Marshfield police chief. He was captain, and then chief of the police department, from 1960 to the 1980s. A current member of the police force is Captain James Louis Lopes. Benjamin Fernandes has

The Fernandes house on Oak Street. Standing in front of the house are members of the Roderick family. The house burned in 1932.
Photograph courtesy of RuthAnn Fernandes Weinberg

been with the fire department for fourteen years. Domingo Andrade has worked for the town DPW. James Gonsalves owned and operated Marshfield school buses for about ten years. Edward Fonseca was postmaster at the Brant Rock Post Office for eight years and is now postmaster of the Marshfield Post Office, where he has been for the last five years. Joseph DaLuz and Domingo Nunes worked for many years as caretakers for the Marshfield State Game Farm. Visitors going to the Ocean Spray Cranberry Museum in Plymouth can see a film of Domingo Fernandes working Marshfield cranberry bogs.

The islanders continue some of their native customs, such as the celebration of christenings and St. John's Day. At christenings people bring food and put money on a cake as a gift to the new baby. St. John's Day, a festival honoring the saints, is celebrated on 24 June. A "mast," shaped like a cross, is placed in an open area and food, fruit, and beverages tied to it for three days. There is music and dancing. Finally the mast is knocked down and food handed out in thanks to the saints for riches, health, and survival.

The Cape Verdeans have house parties where they sing and play instruments. They serve their native foods, including canja, kâcupa, and Olive Roderick's gufongu. For a while, a Portuguese American Club held social functions until, as Diane Martin Fernandes says, the club grew too large to govern.

A tragedy occurred in the home of Laura and Antonio Gonsalves on 12 February 1955 when their house on Clay Pit Road was destroyed by fire and

their thirteen-year-old daughter, Roberta, was burned to death. Laura Gonsalves (also mother of Beatrice Amado) recalls how Harold Stanton, Marshfield town moderator, and Harold Scott, chairman of the local Red Cross, started a fund to help the family. Feinberg's Department Store, Marshfield Sand and Gravel Company, Rand-Handy Oil Company, Gino Rugani, Taylor Lumber, and many others donated materials and talents to rebuild the Gonsalves' home. About sixteen months later, Mr. Stanton handed Laura Gonsalves the keys to her new home. Children in Roberta's eighth-grade class planted a Norway spruce in front of Marshfield High School [later Grace Ryder School] in her memory. After a storm destroyed the tree, a plaque was placed in the school corridor. Mrs. Gonsalves is grateful to the many Marshfield people who helped her.

Dr. Joseph Fortunow is fondly remembered by the Cape Verdeans. Laura Gonsalves recalls that he was "a real country doctor, who would come to the house whether you had a stomach-ache or were about to deliver a baby."

The Cape Verdeans consider Marshfield their home and would choose it if they "had to do it all over again."

— Beatrice Gonsalves Amado

There is a certain place known to all the people and the older birds and four-footed creatures as Two Mile. It is a country place, where you can see a good deal of land and woods and sky all at once.

— Richard Warren Hatch[30]

Two Mile is that part of North Marshfield that belonged to Scituate until 1788. The area was settled by Scituate people, many of whom were among the "Men of Kent" who originally came to Scituate from Kent, England. One of the first to come to Two Mile was Thomas Bird, who arrived in 1649 and built a house at the site of today's 499 Union Street beside "Ma Lapham's" brook. This family did not remain in the area.[31]

Two Mile has been the domain of the Hatch family for over three hundred years. This family so dominated the area that for many years it might have been called Hatchville. Walter Hatch was the first of the family to settle in Two Mile, where he built a house next to the Two Mile Brook, possibly as early as 1647. Present owners of the house at 385 Union Street are Dr. Ronald Messer and his wife, Patricia.

Because of the vague boundary designations, the changes in location of roads, and the duplication of Hatch family names, the exact chronology of houses and mills in Two Mile is difficult to unravel. Almost every colonial period house on Union Street from Oak Street to the Pembroke line was originally a Hatch house. Some are gracious square colonials, others cape-style houses, all scattered over the hills and fields of Two Mile. They once belonged to Joseph, Benjamin, Israel, John, Abijah, Deacon Joel, James, Jonathan, and Walter Hatch.[32]

When Walter Hatch wrote his will in 1698, he left to his two sons, John and Israel, "all my lands I live upon and the two mills the corn mill and the fulling mill with all my housing and barns." Israel and John divided the property in 1712, and Israel's son Jonathan built the house at 352 Union Street, probably in 1733 when he married Agatha Phillips. Five generations later, the house was owned by Clinton Hatch, who lived there for ninety-six years, until his death in 1939.[33]

Clinton's mother, Lucy Harding Hatch, kept a diary that reflects life in the year 1859 in Two Mile. She talks of visits with neighbors and records birthdays, marriages, and deaths, purchases for the farm, and farm events. On 21 March 1859 she wrote, "Got two geese on 26 eggs on the 15th." On the 31st, "Hatched 28 chickens. Had 42 dozen eggs." On 3 and 4 April, "Both turkeys commenced laying. Hatch and Doll had each a lamb." And on 18 April, "Uncle Emmons commenced shingling the house and the cider house. About four and one-half thousand on the house. Both finished."

In the 1940s and 1950s, Norman and Dorothy Skillings Thompson restored the old house, later owned by their daughter Charlotte Lane. It has recently been owned by William Last.

The Hatches were all, by necessity, farmers in this isolated area. Many were also millers, operating a series of mills on Two Mile Brook over the years. The little brook was dammed up into four ponds and water used to operate sometimes as many as two mills on each pond simultaneously. There were gristmills, fulling and carding mills, sawmills, shingle mills, and boxboard mills. These were part of the timber cutting, milling, shipbuilding complex of activities that once prospered the whole ten-mile length of the North River.

Of all the many North River mills, the only sawmill left today is the Hatch Mill on Union Street at Two Mile, located on the lane opposite Pine Street intersection. There was an early gristmill on the site. The long, low shed part of the present structure dates to 1812, the larger barn part to 1859 when it was enlarged as a sawmill. For over one hundred and fifty years the mill was owned and operated by the same Hatch family, father to son, until 1965. In 1968 the Marshfield Historical Society purchased it from Robert

Reed, who had acquired it from Franklin Decker Hatch, last of the Two Mile millers.

Decker Hatch had been running the mill for fifty-four years and his father before him for forty-nine years. The Hatches replaced the original up-and-down saw with a circular saw, and a turbine was installed in 1872. A familiar site in the early 1900s was Decker with his helpers, Elmer and Burt Fish and Peter Whynot, driving his team of horses and hauling huge pine logs down from his Pine Street wood lots. Pine slabs were taken from the mill to the Welch Company in Scituate. Tracy Magoun drove the sometimes frozen slabs in an open wagon across to Scituate and remembers that, by the time he arrived at Welch's, his pants would be frozen to the pine slabs. Decker was also a farmer, raising rhubarb for the Boston market in underground pit houses and hoeing his own garden until the age of ninety-eight.

There was a satinet factory on the lower, or David Hatch mill site in 1838, two mills on the Jonathan Hatch Pond east of Union Street, and a boxboard mill on the upper pond, or Magoun Pond. Some of the boards manufactured at the mills were used for making shoeboxes. There was great demand during the Civil War for these boxes to ship shoes to the soldiers. Before 1830 there was a nail factory, operated by Ambrose Magoun on Magoun Pond. By 1879 there were gristmills, sawmills, and boxboard mills at all four mill sites. All these mills were still operating into the early 1900s.[34]

Coffins were made at the satinet factory. In the early 1900s a plain pine coffin could be had for four dollars and, if stained, for $4.50. Clinton Hatch told Charlie Gleason that he had attended funerals when the odor of freshly stained coffins was so strong that the house doors had to be opened. The entire cost of a funeral, including the digging of the grave, would not exceed six dollars.[35]

The Magouns were a family much involved in milling on the upper pond of the Two Mile Brook. The family is related to many of the founding families of Marshfield and Pembroke, and to the Pilgrim settlers at Plymouth. The Magouns were involved early in shipbuilding at Magoun and Turner's Yard and the Brick Kiln Yard in Pembroke. There were many Magoun houses near the Pembroke line in both Marshfield and Pembroke. The jagged "M"

A winter afternoon at the Jonathan Hatch house, built about 1733. It is one of many Hatch homesteads in old Two Mile.

boundary line of Marshfield near the present expressway bridge and ramps represents the Magoun family lot lines.

Ambrose, Andrew R., Andrew T., and Isaac Winslow Magoun were all mill owners and operators. They had nearly one hundred acres of woodland, which was cut over for logs for the mills. Isaac W. and his brother Andrew R. Magoun began the boxboard business about 1870. Eventually these mills were put out of business by the Lot Phillips Company of Hanover. The Phillips Company was located on the Hanover branch of the New York, New Haven and Hartford Railroad and had easier access to transportation for their lumber.[36]

Andrew T. Magoun served on the first Marshfield School Committee in 1857 and was a Latin teacher at Hanover Academy. He also operated a tin business, making deliveries by horse and wagon. He was one of a number of local millers who, unfortunately, lost one of his hands in the milling operation.[37]

Later, in the 1920s, Isaac Winslow (Winnie) Magoun built a miniature mill on the upper end of Magoun Pond. Around it he created a little park that he called Dreamland. The park, which included a small water wheel and gristmill, a wooden owl perched lifelike in a tree, a natural rustic bridge, and benches and picnic tables, was a great attraction for visitors for many years. Magoun was described as a peaceful and serene man, who had created a haven of woodland beauty that reflected his own love of nature. In the tradition of his shipbuilding, milling, and woodcrafting family, he fashioned beautiful antique reproductions and worked on the repair of the acquired furniture collection of the Historic Winslow House Association in the 1920s. He also cut ice and ran an ice business on Magoun Pond.[38]

The nearby Magoun cemetery, situated deep in the woods, was laid out by Ambrose Magoun about 1840. The beautiful stonework was done by

William Rideout of Pembroke, a stonemason and blacksmith. The obelisk is decorated with an acorn, symbolic of the oaks used in shipbuilding. Rideout collected boulders from the pastures and split them with wedges and drills. This process was called "laying up stonework." He also did the gateposts and doorsteps for the Daniel Webster estate.[39]

There are some members of this old Two Mile family still in the area. On Union Street live grandchildren of I. Winslow Magoun: Edith Magoun Shepherd and Betty Magoun Bates, co-author of this book and long-time member of the Marshfield Historical Commission.

Joseph Clift, Sr., another Two Mile settler, was born on Spring Street in the old 1702 Clift house near today's Riverside Circle. He ran a store in the Spring Street house from 1765 to about 1800. A still earlier Clift family home, which burned in the early 1900s, stood on the northwest corner of the intersection of Spring Street and present Route 3A. In 1797 Joseph Clift, Sr., moved to Two Mile and remodeled the old 1704 Joseph Hatch house at today's 687 Union Street, now owned by Frank and Janet Sambuceti. During some recent restoration work, the old gambrel-roof house was discovered under the present two-story, hip-roof Federal house. Joseph Clift, Sr., married Mary Hatch. He served in the Revolution as a captain of the 10th Marshfield Company under Colonel Anthony Thomas from 1775 to 1778. In 1804 Joseph, Sr., deeded the house to his son Joseph Clift, Jr. There is a tradition that Joseph, Jr., ran a store in the Union Street house for a short period. By 1849 the house had passed to Wales Clift.[40]

During the nineteenth century, the center of activity at Two Mile was at the intersection of Pine and Union streets. Not only was this a milling and factory area, but it also had a school, a store, and a blacksmith shop. The blacksmith was Charlie Church, who ran a shop from 1879 to 1923 in a little building still standing behind the house at 361 Union Street. This

Two Mile Farm
Etching by Sears Gallagher, about 1912, courtesy of Katherine Gallagher Burr

old Hatch house is presently owned by Gail and James Whelan and known as Two Mile Farm. Charlie Church had a windmill, barns, and a stable and, with his assistant Joshua T. Paulding, did the smithy work for Two Mile.

The store was operated by Henry Tilden at today's 431 Union Street, present home of Priscilla and Leonard Fagan. Priscilla is currently secretary of the Marshfield Historical Society. Tilden had bought the 1819 Joel Hatch, Jr., house in 1845 and ran his store there until 1857, when he moved to Marshfield Hills and opened a store at today's 142 Old Main Street.

The Two Mile School near the corner of Pine and Union streets was built in 1839 for $175. Isabelle Paulding Magoun, who attended this school around 1900, remembered that the boys brought in the wood and water, and that the pupils all drank from the same water dipper. Scholars brought their lunches in tin lard pails. Isabelle walked to school, during the spring and fall sessions, from her home on School Street and knew every neighbor along the way. There was a strong sense of neighborhood. In 1906 when the Two Mile School closed, there were only nine children in attendance. The children in grades one through five were sent to the Union School, while the older students went to grammar school in Marshfield Hills. Originally located back from the road in a field, the Two Mile School was moved nearer the street and remodeled into the house at 470 Union Street, lived in today by the Rhodes family.[41]

The people of Two Mile used the post office at Roxalina Hatch's house, now 682 Union Street, near Oak Street. This post office was operating at least as early as 1879. By 1903 a post office, known as the Standish Post Office, served the south end of Union Street and the east part of Pembroke. It was located in the home of Andrew R. Magoun at 11 Union Street, near the Pembroke line. The postmaster was Alice Magoun. Later this house was owned by Ruth and Allen Magoun. The building was moved in the 1970s to 425 Main Street and is today owned by the Brandt family.[42]

Some of the old Two Mile farms remained operating until quite recently. Brothers Harry and Larry Mounce had extensive gardens and orchards. People came for miles around to buy apples, sweet cider, peaches, and pumpkins from them in the fall. Harry once remarked that "people used to live off the land, now they live on it." The Mounces lived in their family home off Union Street at the site of the old David Hatch house, near where Two Mile Brook flows into the North River.

North River Farms, about 1900. On this farm Tracy Hatch raised flowers for the Boston market from the 1930s to the 1950s. Girl Scout Camp Wy Sibo was located behind the house on the hill and overlooked the North River.

Tracy Hatch, a direct descendant of Walter Hatch, the settler, operated a flower-raising and bulb-forcing business on the farm of his father Harris B. Hatch. In several greenhouses he grew gladioli, dahlia, and Easter lilies that he sold to the Boston market. The fields around his house at North River Farms (381 Union Street) were filled with daffodils in the springtime. The house is now owned by Fred and Nancy Frazee.

Both Tracy and Elizabeth Sherman Hatch (Martinson), his wife, were involved in Marshfield civic activities over many years. Tracy was a member of the Advisory Board from 1931 to 1938, a selectman from 1938 to 1943, chairman of the Highway Commissioners, and chairman of the Board of Assessors. Between 1938 and 1955, he served on various school building committees and on the committee to investigate the town-manager form of government. He was also on the Veterans' War Memorial Committee in 1947/48. Elizabeth Sherman Hatch, who later married Edwin A. Martinson, was secretary and member of the School Committee in the 1950s and 1960s. It was during this period that many parcels of land throughout the town were acquired for future school building, and two new schools were built. Elizabeth was also involved with starting Girl Scouting in Marshfield.

A farm still in existence in Two Mile is that of John R. DuBois at 539 Union Street. Where formerly Paul Cretinon raised and sold vegetables from his farm stand, DuBois raises registered Polled Herefords.

There was a brick factory on Pine Street operated by Henry ("Pete") Bernier from 1926 to 1940. Water was piped from a spring to use in the manufacturing process. The better bricks cost three cents apiece.

Around the turn of the century Calvin Joyce had a cobbler's shop in a small building behind the house at 63 Union Street, now owned by Sarle and Anna Mellyn Krede. People would bring their worn shoes there to be repaired. When a new pair of shoes was needed, people bought them from a shoe wagon that peddled shoes around the area.

A printing company, called the Wayside Press, was located in the Ambrose Magoun house (94 Union Street) from 1923 to about 1943. Its inspiration was Erle Parker. He and his wife, Clara, began coming to Marshfield for the summer in 1923 and moved here permanently in 1929. Erle had been associated with Rust Craft cards in Boston, but started his Wayside Press as soon as he came to Marshfield. He was something of a Renaissance man, who wrote verses and was an artist and editor. The printing was done by Buddy Wilde and Alton Olson. Alden Rogers and Emily Foster designed the greeting cards, while Mr. Parker chose the ones he wanted printed. The business was in the upstairs of the big barn that stood south of the house. Parker had a one-man offset printing press and packaging equipment. Artists worked at easels hand painting the cards, which were printed in black and white only. It was a neighborhood business, employing nearby people. Workers included Ruth Magoun, Edith Magoun Shepherd, Mabel Backus, Barbara Ela, Marion Hubbard, Margaret White McCarthy, Catherine and Bill Mellyn, Betty Walsh, and Bertha Reske. To be at the Wayside Press was not only to work, but to enjoy the other activities Parker provided. He had clay tennis courts, a small golf course, a toboggan run, a pavilion, and a poolroom. The yard was landscaped like a park.

A greeting card designed and printed by the Wayside Press

A business that still thrives in old Two Mile is the Village Lantern, run by David R. Williams in an old Hatch house at 598 Union Street. Dave reproduces original colonial lantern designs. He handcrafts the heavyweight pewter plate reproductions. Some are antiqued in a soft pewter finish. Painted items have four coats of lacquer. This business is truly in the tradition of the old Two Mile craftsmen of another era.

For a while in the 1930s and 1940s there was a Girl Scout day camp in Two Mile. It was started in 1932 and run by the Marshfield Girl Scout Council at the farm of Tracy and Elizabeth Sherman Hatch (Martinson) at what is today 381 Union Street. For those who were fortunate to be of scouting age at that time, the experience of going to Camp Wy Sibo, as it was called, was a rich experience in outdoor living, river swimming and boating, camp lore, and comradeship. The staff was unusually dedicated and talented. Leaders included Elizabeth Sherman Hatch (Martinson), Rosella Ames, Laura ("Cappy") Day, Josephine and Marion Ford, Julia Peterson, Jeannette Anderson, Betty Killam Rodgers, and Olive Keene.

The main building was a log cabin built about 1927 from timber brought from Maine by Tracy's father, Harris Hatch. It sat high on the hill above the North River in a great stand of white pine. Tracy taught swimming to a generation of young girls who learned the reward of hard work trying to swim against the current of the river, and to master the skills necessary to pass the series of swimming tests. There were games and sports, nature walks and talks, reading and rest time under the tall white pines on the hill above the river. There was the Indian lore and the discovery of Indian artifacts just beneath the surface of the ground; the box turtles, snakes, butterflies, and birds that were found, seen, or heard. Best of all were the last moments of the day, the singing of "Peace I ask of Thee, O River" around the campfire, the holding of hands, the Girl Scout vows, and the moving notes of taps echoing across the North River valley. Then all the campers would depart in silence, like the Indians of another age.[43]

Canoeing up Two Mile Creek

Sawmill at Two Mile
Watercolor by Cynthia Hagar Krusell,
1956

Girl Scouting in Marshfield was started by Susan Delano MacMillan in the early 1930s. There were two troops: the Holly Troop and the Pine Cone Troop. Today Marshfield has twenty-five Girl Scout troops and a membership of more than four hundred girls. The number of scouts has quadrupled over the last twelve years. The groups include the Daisies, Brownies, Cadets, and Senior Girl Scouts. The director of volunteer services for the Plymouth Bay Girl Scout Council is Margaret Cain, and in charge of the Marshfield Service Units are Jean Alexis and Laurie Harrington.

There are two Boy Scout troops in Marshfield today. In 1989 Troop 101 had fifty-one scouts. Scoutmasters were Rick Rooney and Ray Joyal. Troop 212 had twenty-four scouts with scoutmaster Paul Harrington. There were three Cub Scout packs with about two hundred boys.

Even in rural Two Mile, however, time has brought changes, and the inevitable new roads and housing developments have appeared. The wood lots on Pine Street were disturbed for the first time by building in the 1980s, although Forest Street began to be developed in the 1950s and 1960s with Earldor Circle. In the 1980s came Woodland Hills, then Page's Lane, Prince Rogers Waye, Arrowhead Drive, and Hampstead in 1988. George Williams's development called Eagle's Nest, which was started in the mid-1980s around Magoun Pond, was the first disturbance of the old Magoun 100-acre woodland.

Land acquired by the Marshfield Conservation Commission in the North Marshfield/Two Mile area includes the 41-acre Union Street Woodland, the 123-acre Corn Hill Woodland, the 35-acre Mounce's Meadow, the 4-acre Blueberry Island with 12 acres of surrounding marsh, the 21-acre Oak Street Woodland, a 5-acre Highland Street field, 15 acres at the old site of Brooks & Tilden Shipyard, and the large 130-acre Henry and Thomas Nelson Memorial Forest, owned by the New England Forestry Foundation.

North Marshfield and Two Mile still retain a feeling of another era. Although modern development has intruded upon the stretches of fields and wood lots, and the extension of Route 3 has brought teeming traffic to its borders, this area of colonial houses and millponds still remains relatively quiet, a few farms are under pasturage and cultivation, and the sun still sets in spectacular crimsons and mauves over the curving ribbon of the upper North River valley. It is but a moment of time since the Indian "drove his birchen boat along the woodhung shore."[44]

The New Calf

The calf came two days ago.
I left the plumber standing in the kitchen
when I heard the news
and ran across the yard,
my shoes catching dew from the long grass
in the neighbor's field
where I'd picked daisies and Queen Anne's lace
for my daughter's wedding.

I found him in the trampled place —
sleeping, curled loosely,
his soft face tan and white —
and bent to pat the infant bull
while Abby,
devouring cornstalks
as if it were her last supper,
raised her eyes at me across the wire
and the farmer pronounced
in the accent of all his New England ancestors,
If you don't pat the newborn
early and often,
they're apt
to grow up
hostile.

— Frances Downing Vaughan[45]

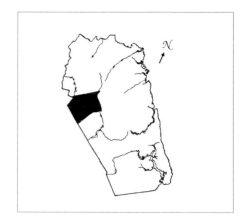

Standish Village

STANDISH is the lost village. Once a small neighborhood on the border of Pembroke at School Street and today's Route 139, this special place has been almost obliterated by the industrial and business zoning that began along Plain Street in 1958. The only remaining landmark is the brave little First Baptist Church, which itself rose from the ashes of a disastrous fire in 1940 to stand watch once again over this outlying area of Marshfield.

The village may have been named Standish after the Pilgrim Myles Standish, who did much of the surveying and laying out of land for the Plymouth Colony. The inland areas, such as Standish, were considered valuable pieces of land to hold for speculation and settlement by later arrivals to the colony. Standish village sits on the watershed between the North and South rivers in an area of wetlands and stands of tall white pine. It stretches from the Pembroke border along the southwesterly edge of Marshfield to Forest and Furnace streets as far north as Pine Street, including School Street.

For many years Standish was thought of as the village on the Mattakeesett Way, the way to Pembroke. The road from the Marshfield First Congregational Church led up Puddle Wharf Way (the valley route along Furnace Brook) to School Street, past what was later the site of the First Baptist Church, across what is today Route 139, followed Lone Street (opposite School Street and now a dead end) to the old Randall house in East Pembroke, keeping to the high land and avoiding the swamps. The Pembroke settlers used this route to come down to the Marshfield First Congregational Church for services. Later, when Furnace Street was laid out, the path followed that way and continued across the "burnt" plain (where Route 139 is today) to Lone Street.

Route 139, as we know it today, was widened and improved about 1935 when James Michael Curley was governor of Massachusetts. It was referred to as "Curley's red road" because of its original red surface. The federal government allotted $450,000 to build the road and mandated that it have a sidewalk. Frank Sinnott, selectman at the time, had proposed the broad boulevard, and the project developed with the cooperation of the town of Pembroke.[1]

Later, Sinnott stated that he felt unhappy about the extra expenditure of $40,000 for the sidewalk, "the greater portion of which went through

No stars, no moon, only heavenly light and silver brightness on the snow.

— Betty Magoun Bates

The First Baptist Church at Standish. There has been a church on this site since 1788. The present church was built in 1941 after a fire destroyed the original building.

forest and vacant land." Today the sidewalk provides the only safe route for pedestrians along this heavily trafficked route from the expressway to downtown Marshfield.

There is currently a Route 139 corridor study underway to develop long-range plans for the still undeveloped land south of the town's industrial park, between Route 139 and Route 3. In 1936, the year after the building of Route 139, Furnace, Pine, and School streets were paved for the first time, using WPA labor. That left only three miles of dirt roads remaining in the town at that time.

Land on the other side of Standish, in what is now Pembroke, was originally owned jointly by Duxbury and Marshfield. In 1662 Major Josiah Winslow purchased a large area of land around the Pembroke ponds for the town of Marshfield. It was known as the Major's Purchase, or the Marshfield Upper Lands. The remaining area of present-day Pembroke was owned by Duxbury until 1698. In 1712 both Marshfield and Duxbury gave up their holdings and Pembroke was incorporated as a separate town.

A large piece of Standish was set apart by the early settlers of Marshfield as common land. This was eventually divided, in what was known as the Division of the Common Lands, in 1710, and each of the then residents of the town was given a parcel, or a share of a parcel. The piece divided included land along the Furnace Brook valley and the Burnt Plain as far as what is now School Street, Pine Street, Valley Path, and easterly as far as Eames Way. It was the least desirable land in the town and the last to be parceled out. The soil was arid and sandy, with little opportunity for agriculture or grazing, and the land had no river or water frontage.[2]

The village of Standish looked to Pembroke and Pembroke to Standish. Families in the bordering land intermarried, weaving kinship networks between the two towns. In time, the Joyce, Sherman, and Eames families came to settle in the area, and eventually there were nine houses, the First Baptist Church, Samuel Keene's store, and a district school. There were no blacksmith shops or shoe shops, and there was no stream for a mill. It was a quiet area of small farmers, many of whom worked at the Brick-Kiln Shipyard in Pembroke. They were not involved in Marshfield town affairs, being in this remote area oriented toward Pembroke.

First to come were the Joyces, next the Shermans, and finally, the Eameses. The center of village activities by the eighteenth century was the church. The first recorded gathering of the Baptists of Standish village was at the home of Jonathan and Abigail Holmes Joyce, which stood just west of the present church. The house has since been moved and is today's 15 Cross Street. Present owners are Donald and Karen Welinsky. The Baptists signed the church covenant on 11 June 1788. Original members were Jonathan and Abigail Joyce, Zenas Thomas, Thomas Joyce, Prince Hatch, Ichabod Sherman, Abigail Thomas, Lucy Joyce, Rebecca Chase, Mercy and William Curtis, Rachel Joyce, and Lydia Ford.[3]

The Baptists had built a church in Centre Marshfield earlier, in 1734, but had been forced to abandon it to the Episcopalians because of lack of funds. No meetings were held at the Centre Marshfield church, but there are records of six Marshfield people being baptized in a Baptist church in Boston before this period. Some Baptists went to Middleborough where the preacher, Isaac Backus, was an inspiration for the entire Plymouth County. Many early services of the church were held in private homes. Finally a plain, barn-like church was built in 1788 on land owned by the Joyces. At first the church was unpainted and unplastered, with no pews. There was no spire, no bell, nor a chimney until 1836. Tradition says that on one spring Sunday morning during service, a skunk wandered through the open doors of the little church, creating an event that left its permanent record in the name forever-after attached to this church, the "Old Skunk Church." Like other early churches of Marshfield, the Baptist church was sometimes used for town meetings until the building of the first town hall, in 1835.[4]

In 1818 the land was deeded to the church by the Joyce family. Many Baptists walked miles to attend this church. Records tell of Polly Little, who lived near Little's Bridge at the North River. She walked to church in snow and rain. People who lived along her route would know that there was no service held if Polly failed to pass by. She and others eventually agitated for the building of a church nearer their area of town, and in 1833 the North Baptist Society was formed. Fifty members of the church left to attend the new church on Highland Street, now Trinity Episcopal Church. This number represented over half the members of the Standish congregation, and the little "Old Skunk" was left with only forty-five members.[5]

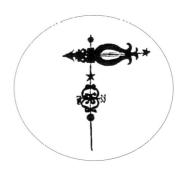

Weathervane on the Standish Baptist Church
Pen and ink drawing by Anne Philbrick Hall

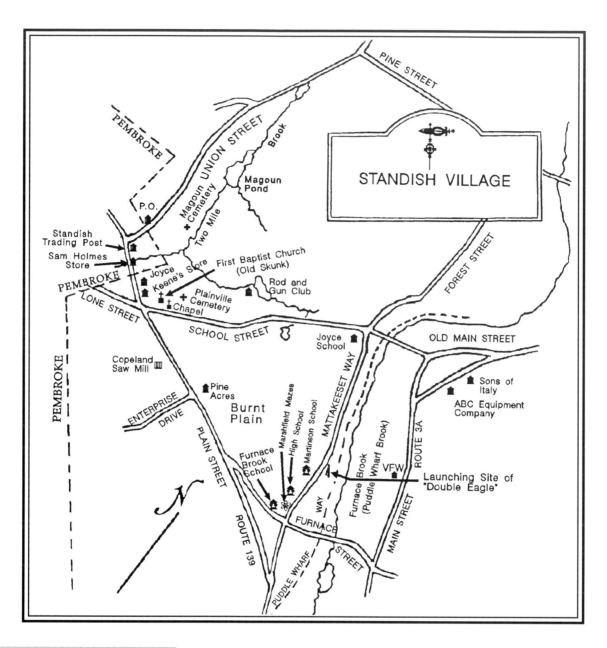

Standish Village

As recently as 1931, open-air baptisms were performed at either Job's Landing at the edge of the North River in Pembroke, or in Two Mile Brook off Union Street, behind Magoun cemetery. Tradition says that the first Baptist Sunday School in Plymouth County was held in the Standish church. In 1796 the Plainville Cemetery, a private burying ground adjacent to the church, was established. The first marked burial was that of Huldah Jones. The interred are largely Baptist church members.[6]

The Magoun family of Pembroke and Two Mile have been associated with this church since the 1800s. They have served as benefactors and deacons of the church. In 1883 Celia Magoun gave the church eight hundred dollars to build a small chapel in honor of her deceased sister. Still standing today, the chapel is used for church activities. Until 1989 the popular summer Wednesday luncheons (started in 1941) were managed by Ruth Kinsman Ames Melvin and Helen Seaverns Melvin, who are experts in "old

Yankee" cooking. Proceeds of these luncheons have served the church in many ways.[7]

Elizabeth Magoun once planted a "missionary apple tree" to raise money for the missionary work of the church. The tree survived for over a century.[8]

A popular minister for many years was the "Scottish Reverend," William Barclay. It was during his ministry that the 1940 fire burned the church to the ground. The present church, built in 1941, is a small-scale replica of the original. Today's minister is the Reverend Irving Beveridge.[9]

Sam Keene's general store was the first and only store in the Marshfield part of Standish. Located near the corner of School and Plain streets where Parish Pathe is today, it was built by Keene in the late 1850s. Sam bought his supplies from the old Ford store in Duxbury. Goods were shipped from Boston and Medford to the Duxbury store by packet ship and delivered overland by horse and wagon. Ford's store was a wholesale as well as a retail store. As time went on, goods were delivered to Keene's by packet ship to Job's Landing on the North River at Water Street in Pembroke, then carted overland. Butter and milk were purchased directly from the farmers in the area. In 1860 Ben Hopkins operated the store. One particularly hot summer when all the wells ran dry, Ben was said to have remarked that he'd never before known a time when "rum was more plentiful than water." For a period of time, Daniel Simmons ran the store. By 1903 Keene's daughter Clara was living in the old store building, which had closed as a store about 1876. Clara sold penny candy from her house. The building was taken down and removed in the 1970s.[10]

Samuel Holmes ran a general store in the late 1800s on his farm near the corner of Oak and Church streets (Route 139) in Pembroke, next to today's Gulf Station. Sam was said to have passed the time between infrequent customers asleep on the store counter. Villagers who needed a tooth extracted would hang a white cloth on a post at the store to notify the itinerant dentist. Many a tooth was extracted without benefit of painkiller in this little Standish store. The so-called Standish Trading Post that stood just west of Holmes's store was first operated by Howard Taylor and, from the 1940s to the 1960s, by well-known Josephine ("Auntie Jo") Backus.

Joyce School, built before 1838 and closed in 1886

Later, Roger Melvin joined in the operating of this famous local store, gas station, and auto repair shop combined.[11]

A post office that served both the Standish and North Marshfield neighborhoods was at first located at the home of Alice and Andrew R. Magoun at 11 Union Street. Later, the location of the post office was moved to the store at the corner of Route 139 and Union Street in Pembroke.

At the southwest corner of School and Forest streets there once stood the small, one-room Joyce School. It was built before 1838 and closed in 1886. (The building was later moved to Hummy Lane and is used as a garage.) The children were then transported by barge and sleigh in winter to the Sea View School. In 1903 the few children on School Street were attending the Two Mile School. In the spring and fall the children walked to school, but during the winter Israel Hatch transported them in his horse-drawn barge. Isabelle Paulding Magoun, who went to school in the early 1900s, remembered the horse up to his belly in the snow pulling the sleigh to Two Mile. "But," she said, "we always got there."[12]

Not far from the site of the once remote Joyce School, there stands today the extensive Marshfield High School and Marshfield Junior High School complex. The story of these schools is the story of yet another shuffle of the use of buildings.

The first school built on the flat, sandy plain near Forest and Furnace streets was the "new" high school (now the Furnace Brook School) in 1959. With a rapidly increasing school population, the need for a larger high school to replace the 1940 high school (later called the Grace Ryder School) was evident. A new building was proposed in 1957 for $1,685,000 and built by 1959. Ten years later an addition was constructed, and in 1972 the present high school was built. James P. Romeo was principal of Marshfield High School for twenty-five years, from 1949 to 1974, serving first in the 1940 school, then in the 1959 building, and finally in the 1972 high school, a feat not likely to be accomplished by any future principal. Several innovative programs were started under Romeo, including the National Honor Society and the Guidance Department in 1954 and the Adult Education Program in 1958. Romeo was succeeded in 1974 by John Erickson. Today Peter Deftos serves as principal of Marshfield High School.

The Edwin A. Martinson Junior High School opened in 1965. Prior to this date, the junior high school students had been housed in the "old" 1940 (Grace Ryder) school after the 1959 opening of the "new" high school. James McLaughlin, principal since 1960, was replaced by Richard Burgess in 1967 followed by Robert Marshall and then Daniel Kehoe. In 1973, after the opening of the new high school, the old high school became the Furnace Brook Middle School. Principals of this school have been Paul Kelleher, Richard Burgess, and Daniel Kehoe. The Martinson School became the Martinson Middle School. Today, Furnace Brook houses only grade six and Martinson, grades seven and eight. Principal of both schools is Harvey Horwitz.

School enrollment began to soar in 1966 and was rising at an "alarming rate" by 1969, due to the rapid development of the town after the extension of the present Route 3 to Marshfield in 1965. A public kindergarten program was inaugurated by state mandate in 1973. The school population began to decline in 1982.

The story of the Marshfield school superintendency began in 1888 when the town joined Duxbury and Scituate under a joint superintendency. Before this date the schools were run by the school committee. Duxbury dropped out in 1926, but Marshfield continued in a joint superintendency with

Marshfield's winning marathon softball team, 1981. The team set a world record for the longest continuous softball game, as recorded in the Guinness Book of World Records *in 1983.*

Scituate until the 1940s. Since long-time (twenty-seven years) superintendent Harold Wingate retired in 1953, the position has been held by Edwin Martinson (1953-64), Laurence Greene (1964-68), Richard Burgess (1968-72), Robert Peebles (1972-75), Donald Sipe (1975-79), Daniel Bresnahan (1979-90), and today's William Hurley.

A number of landmark events have happened in the vicinity of the high school complex over the last few years. On 9 September 1977 the Double Eagle, a helium balloon, took off from the gravel pit across Forest Street from the Martinson Middle School. Ben Abruzzo and Maxie Anderson of Albuquerque, New Mexico, attempted to make a transatlantic flight in a massive ten-story-high helium balloon. Caught in storms and blown off course, they were forced down over Ireland 65 hours and 30 minutes after take-off.

The launching was a big event for the community. Five thousand people gathered to watch the balloon lift majestically above the hills of Marshfield and disappear over the northerly horizon between eight and nine o'clock in the evening. The balloonists' second attempt from Presque Isle, Maine, to Miserey, France, in 1978 was successful. The adventure took 137 hours, 5 minutes, and 30 seconds, which set a world record. Abruzzo and Anderson were determined to be the first balloonists to cross the Atlantic, and their success catapulted them into international fame. Tragically, both Abruzzo and Anderson were killed later in airplane and balloon accidents.[13]

In 1981 a group of Marshfield softball players, after several years of marathon game playing, made the *Guinness Book of Records* for the longest softball game ever played while raising money for charity. This event engendered tremendous community spirit. It began in 1978 with the suggestion of Steve Anstatt of the Marshfield Jaycees, who were looking for a spring fund-raiser. A committee including Lenny Williams, John Colley, Dave Richardson, and Frank Cole was established. Beneficiaries of the first game, played on 25 May 1979, were the March of Dimes and the Jimmy Fund. The record game at that time was 72 hours, so the participants knew that they would be playing for at least three days nonstop. They were forced

to stop at 62 hours, 32 minutes when one of the players became ill. A second attempt was made in May 1980 and the playing continued for 83 hours. In the meantime, two teams from Virginia had set the new record at 90 hours, 5 minutes. The third game was set for 2 September 1981 and the beneficiary was the Muscular Dystrophy Association. The Marshfield Softball Marathoners played 284 innings in 91 hours and 3 minutes nonstop, setting the new world record for the longest softball game in history. The record was published in the 1983 edition of the *Guinness Book of World Records*.

A third event of great community interest and support was the building of the Marshfield Mazes by the Marshfield Community Playground, Inc. in 1988. The idea came from Kathy Burokas, Janet Gibson, and Mary Beth Southerton. In 1987 Robert Leather's architectural firm was chosen to design the playground. Funds were raised and building materials solicited. A children's committee, consisting of two children from each grade at each of the four elementary schools, was selected to help with the design of the playground, as well as with the publicity. In order to be central, visible, and near an active school complex, a site in front of the high school was chosen. Ideas for the playground were solicited from two thousand schoolchildren.

Many individuals helped to coordinate the project. The Taylor Lumber Company generously gave $25,000 worth of lumber. Construction took place from 12 to 16 October 1988. Fifteen hundred volunteers worked on the playground project in some way, including contractors, carpenters, and the high school's Industrial Arts Department, Child Care Department, and Video Department. The Marshfield Mazes is considered to be one of the most extraordinary volunteer efforts of families and friends ever undertaken in Marshfield.

Another exciting event for Marshfield was the participation of the high school Marching Rams Band in the Cotton Bowl Parade of 1988 in Dallas, Texas. The Friends of Music put on an extensive fund-raising campaign to send this deserving and top-rate music group to Texas. The following year the band attended the Fiesta-Val music competition in Williamsburg, Virginia, where they won, along with the Marshfield High School Jazz Band, a total of fifteen first awards. Another musical achievement for Marshfield was the gold medal won by the Jazz Band (under director Steve Benson) at the 1981 International Music Festivals in Canada. The next year, the Jazz Band performed as the representative from the United States in the Paris, France, Jazz Festival. Steve Benson, who had been with the music department since 1974, was Director of Music for the Marshfield schools until 1990. President of today's Friends of Music is Charlene Petrizzi.

The Marshfield Rod and Gun Club was started in the late 1920s by a group of men interested in hunting and fishing. For a while they met in the old Marshfield Fire Station No. 3 on South River Street. They used a field located off Parsonage Street near the present town barn for skeet shooting. The group was incorporated in August 1930. After World War II, about 1947, a membership drive was conducted by the club and a letter sent to local residents who held a hunting or fishing license. In the early 1950s the club bought land from Fred Hall off School Street and purchased some adjacent land from the town. Later, Helen Hall gave the Rod and Gun Club additional land. Today the club owns about one hundred acres, including some land in the Green Harbor River valley. The clubhouse was built in 1952 and an addition added in 1960. The brook was dammed up and the pond dug in 1953 and 1954.

The Rod and Gun Club has a trout-stocked pond, where an annual Fishing Derby Day is held every May for children under fourteen. Two trophies are given in honor of Francis ("Dash") X. Gowen and Herbert ("Skip") Hunt. There are one indoor and two outdoor archery ranges and an indoor and outdoor soft rifle- and pistol-shooting range. The club sponsors two teams of rifle and pistol shoots in competition matches. In addition, the club has an outdoor skeet field. Regular cribbage tournaments are held. The club sponsors Helen Hall Scholarships at Marshfield High School, Conservation Camp scholarships, and a Cub Scout pack. There is a Safety Shooters Program under the National Rifle Association. A course in Home Firearms Safety and Responsibility is mandatory for new members. Membership is open to any "true sportsman." Today's president is Allen Burchell.

There are several long-standing businesses on Route 139. These include the complex of stores at Pine Acres, Davenports' Marshfield Cleaners (now Anton's), Lou's 139 Restaurant, and K.E. Copeland Lumber Company.

There was once a large chicken farm called Pine Acres where the Pine Acres Package Store (776 Plain Street) and Tedeschi's Food Shop (774 Plain Street) stand today. For a while it was operated by Eddie and Anne Martorana, who sold eggs and chickens from a small building in front of their house. Then Eddie ran a small grocery and liquor store and added a laundry. The Martoranas sold the Pine Acres complex to David Gregory and his partners in 1967. He built the present store buildings. He also constructed the apartments now known as Fox Run (760 Plain Street). These are luxury one- and two-bedroom apartments and condominiums, managed by Al Phinney. There are twenty-three buildings with twelve units in each and four condominium buildings.

Davenports' Marshfield Drive-In Cleaners was started by Anne and Dave Davenport as a small dry-cleaning business at the old Pine Acres building in 1957. The popular couple soon added two people to their operation. The business grew rapidly and, by 1964, they bought land and moved the business to 668 Plain Street, eventually employing twenty-two people. A disastrous fire destroyed the building and contents in 1972, but thanks to great community support and the determination of the Davenports, the building was rebuilt in a few months. The Davenports sold the business in 1984 to Anton's.

Lou's 139 Restaurant at 459 Plain Street was at one time a small bar and eatery called the Candlelight. Lou and Margery Bournazos acquired it in 1960 and have greatly expanded it over the last thirty years. The restaurant now seats two hundred people and is a popular family dining place. There are provisions for banquets and small weddings. Lou and Margery's son, Charles Bournazos, has been the manager since 1986. Lou is well known as an activist in town affairs, and both he and Margery have given much to the community.

K. E. Copeland and Sons Lumber Company at 887 Plain Street is reminiscent of the old milling tradition of the North River valley. Built about 1963 on five acres of land, the mill has operated with both diesel and electric power. Devastating fires in 1979 and 1989 totally destroyed the equipment and the building each time. But not to be defeated, Ken has rebuilt his mill and today is well known for his custom sawing of native pine lumber. His son Dean is a sawyer and another son, Arthur, handles customer relations. Ken, whose wife is June Macker Copeland, has served long and loyally on the Hatch Mill Committee of the Marshfield Historical Society.

The Marshfield Family Skateland (790 Plain Street) was a popular place during the 1960s and 1970s. Vincent Cohee built the roller-skating arena in 1959. Hockey, speed, and art-skating competitions were featured. The professional was David Tassinari, who was a state and national champion in free-style and dance skating. He taught classes as well as private students. Skateland was one of the few community entertainment centers for young people of that era. Cohee sold Skateland to Paul Telland about 1967, and Telland ran the business until about 1985. The building was subsequently remodeled and made into a restaurant.

Marshfield's own radio station, WATD (With Antenna at The Dump), was opened on 28 November 1977 by Edward Perry. It is a commercial station that provides local, regional, and national news, plays music for easy listening, and broadcasts some town events. It also provides a noncommercial, nonprofit radio-reading service for the blind and print-handicapped in Massachusetts. Talking Information Center (TIC) was started in 1978 by Ron Bersani and presently has a full-time staff of three, assisted by some one hundred fifty volunteers. TIC is now connected with cable WGBX — TV Channel 44.[14]

One of the seven branch offices of the Myles Standish Federal Credit Union, chartered in 1977, is located at 560 Plain Street in old Standish. The first office of the credit union was opened in the Assumption Church hall in Green Harbor. In October 1989 a Marshfield High School branch of this institution was started. It is operated by students, a credit union employee, and a teacher.

At the intersection of School Street with Old Main Street at Route 3A, there is a small complex of business and service organizations. In the 1930s George Lantz, a mason, had a cement block business there and later a state DPW garage was at this location.

The Herman Maynard Fire Equipment Company was founded in 1956. The company could assemble one fire engine truck every two weeks and produced as many as twenty-five trucks in a year. These were pumpers, forest fire trucks, rescue trucks, and airport crash trucks. Each was built to custom specifications and they were shipped all over the world. The first fire engine that the company made for the Town of Marshfield was in 1969. The ABC Equipment Company (844 Main Street) sells fire equipment, snow blowers, and other machinery at this same site.

The Order of the Sons of Italy in America, Marshfield Lodge 2345, a fraternal organization, was organized in 1975 and moved into the building at 870 Main Street in 1985. The founder and first president of the Marshfield Sons of Italy was the late Anne B. Marmai and today's president is her daughter, M. Sugar Young.

On the west side of Main Street between Furnace and School streets, at 655 Main, there is the Daniel Webster VFW Post 8345. The present commander is David Brown, and Teresa Collins is president of the Ladies' Auxiliary. The focus of the VFW is on veterans' activities and scholarships.

New streets and housing developments in Standish began as early as 1956 when Arthur Macker (Rock Realty Trust) bought the land at Joan Way. Houses began to be placed along School Street as far as Forest Street. In 1966 and in 1969 the Williams brothers built Tilden and Flames roads off Forest Street. At about the same time, houses were built along Eames Way at Carolina Hill off Furnace Street. Enterprise Drive and the Industrial Park began to be developed about 1972.

In addition to the Fox Run apartments, other housing complexes have come to Standish. Royal Dane, one of the first apartment house groups (now condominiums), was built in the 1960s. This was followed by the development of Castle Green off School Street and more recently, Stage Stop Village condominiums. The building of apartment complexes in the 1980s was a turning point in citizen participation in town affairs, since it awakened many people to town issues. The recent April 1990 Town Meeting passed a landmark bylaw permitting apartments in single family dwellings. To implement it, however, requires a special permit process.

Some conservation land has been set aside in Standish. This includes parts of the 283-acre Furnace Brook Watershed land, "a chain of parcels covering 3 miles, protecting 5 town well sites and acquired for protection of town water supply, including Town Forest and 1.5 miles of trails and fishing in the ponds." Another small 8.3-acre parcel of land runs along the upper reaches of Two Mile Brook and is called Edgewood Forest. The Marshfield Rod and Gun Club has about one hundred acres of private wooded land with a fishing pond. The Marshfield Conservation Commission and other private conservation groups own nearly three thousand acres of land throughout the town.

There are current attempts to protect the town's precious water supply. An aquifer protection bylaw was passed at the 1990 Town Meeting. One of the large aquifer systems, known as Magoun Pond Aquifer, is in the Standish area.

The commercial development along Route 139 took its toll on the little village of Standish. Route 139 was zoned for business as far as the Pembroke line in 1958. A second phase of development was proposed in 1960. This area

Shall we take the old Mattakeesett Way through Standish to Pembroke?

of Pembroke, adjacent to the Marshfield line, was zoned for business in 1965. One by one the houses were either moved away or torn down. By 1985 there was only one house remaining (1025 Plain Street) and it was moved to 143 Furnace Street. This cape-style house was the 1835 home of William Hall and was later owned by Edgar and Lillie Bates Simmons. Their son Frank Simmons was a member of the Marshfield Fire Department for forty years. He was appointed chief in 1966 and retired in 1972.

In 1964 a box turtle was found by Stephen Bates about one-eighth of a mile from this old Hall/Simmons house site. It was initialed ENS on the plastron, having been marked thus by Edgar N. Simmons in 1896. The initialing of turtles in this fashion was an old custom, and the children of former days often found such marked specimens. Now it is rare to find a box turtle anywhere in Marshfield, marked or unmarked.

Only the First Baptist Church remains as a reminder of this little village on the outskirts of Marshfield, where once foot travelers and carriages passed on their way to Pembroke, and the Pembroke people filed by on their way to church at Marshfield. The Baptists came and stayed. The houses were built and disappeared — some burned, some were razed, and some were moved — but a few of the old families still remain near old Standish.

Notes

Green Harbor Village

1. Maria Louise Pool, *In a Dike Shanty* (Boston: L.C. Page and Company, 1898), 31.

2. William Bradford, *Of Plymouth Plantation 1620-1647*, ed. Samuel Eliot Morison (New York: Alfred A. Knopf, 1966), 104, 106, 229.

3. Ibid., 253.

4. Ibid.

5. W. Sterry-Cooper, *Edward Winslow* (Birmingham, England: Reliance Printing Works, 1953), 59.

6. Marshfield Tercentenary Committee, *Marshfield. The Autobiography of a Pilgrim Town* (Marshfield: Marshfield Tercentenary Committee, 1940), 22 (hereafter cited as MAPT).

7. Nathaniel B. Shurtleff and David Pulsifer, eds., *Records of the Colony of New Plymouth in New England* (Boston: William White, 1855-61), 1:58.

8. Marshfield, Mass., Records of the Historical Commission.

9. MAPT, 12, 239.

10. Marcia A. Thomas, *Memorials of Marshfield* (Boston: Dutton and Wentworth, 1854), 48.

11. Ruth C. McGuyre and Robert S. Wakefield, *Mayflower Families in Progress, Edward Winslow of the Mayflower and His Descendants for Five Generations* (Plymouth: General Society of Mayflower Descendants, 1988), 1.

12. Cynthia Hagar Krusell, "The Winslows of 'Careswell' in Marshfield," in *The Winslows of "Careswell" Before and After the "Mayflower"*, by Quentin Coons and Cynthia Hagar Krusell (Marshfield Hills: By the authors, 1977), 16.

13. Ibid.

14. Lucy Mary Kellogg, ed., *Mayflower Families Through Five Generations* (Plymouth: General Society of Mayflower Descendants, 1975), 1:99, 101.

15. McGuyre and Wakefield, 1.

16. Krusell, *Winslows of Careswell*, 19; Thomas Church, *The History of Philip's War* (Boston: Thomas B. Wait and Son, 1827), 63.

17. Krusell, *Winslows of Careswell*, 22.

18. Marshfield, Mass., *Town Records of Marshfield*, 1:451, 548.

19. Plymouth County, Mass., *Plymouth County Registry of Deeds*, 48:155, 55:236-37, 57:173-75 (hereafter cited as PCRD).

20. Doris Johnson Melville, *Major Bradford's Town: A History of Kingston, 1726-1976* (Kingston: Town of Kingston, 1976), 350.

21. MAPT, 29; Vera Thomas, "Marshfield, Gwent," typewritten manuscript sent from Wales to Joan Scolponeti, Marshfield.

22. Cynthia Hagar Krusell, *Of Tea and Tories* (Marshfield: Marshfield Bicentennial Committee, 1976), 7, 20.

23. Anna Green Winslow, 1773 Diary, Historic Winslow House, Marshfield, 16.

24. William B. Clark, ed., *Naval Documents of the American Revolution* (Washington: U.S. Government Printing Office, 1964), 1:65.

25. Krusell, *Tea and Tories*, 15; John Cushing and Jeremiah Hall to Major General John Thomas, Hanover, 21 April 1775, John Thomas Papers, Massachusetts Historical Society, Boston; Richard B. Johnson, ed., "The Diary of Israel Litchfield," *New England Historic and Genealogical Register* 129 (July 1975): 250-69; Justin Winsor, *History of the Town of Duxbury, Massachusetts, with Genealogical Registers* (Boston: Crosby & Nichols, 1849), 130.

26. Krusell, *Tea and Tories*, 19-20.

Green Harbor Village *(continued)*

27. MAPT, 200; Daniel Webster, *The Papers of Daniel Webster: Correspondence*, ed. Charles M. Wiltse et al. (Hanover, N.H.: University Press of New England, 1974-), 3:138; PCRD, 175:238; Information about John Thomas and his family was obtained from papers owned by William Thomas, Marshfield.

28. Pool, 60.

29. Joan Scolponeti, *Daniel Webster Bicentennial Celebration* (Marshfield: Marshfield Historical Society, 1983).

30. Walker Lewis, ed., *Speak For Yourself, Daniel* (Boston: Houghton Mifflin Company, 1969), 41.

31. Cynthia H. Krusell, "Daniel Webster Wildlife Sanctuary, 1986," Cynthia H. Krusell Papers, Historical Research Associates Library, Marshfield Hills (hereafter cited as HRA Library).

32. Lewis, 467.

33. Maurice G. Baxter, *One and Inseparable: Daniel Webster and the Union* (Cambridge: Harvard University Press, 1984), 298.

34. Daniel Webster, 6:269.

35. Rachel Moorehead, Letters and Poems, comp. George H. and John W. McElroy, Trustees-Historical Room Papers, Ventress Memorial Library, Marshfield.

36. Information about Walton Hall was obtained from papers owned by Stephen Hall, Marshfield; MAPT, 306.

37. *Quincy Patriot Ledger*, 29 January 1990.

38. Pool, 9.

39. Moorehead; PCRD, 239:59-60.

40. Ibid., 284:135, 309:12.

41. Moorehead.

42. Mrs. R. C. Waterston, *Adelaide Phillips* (Boston: A. Williams and Company, 1883), 108-9, 115, 121; *Boston Sunday Globe*, 24 January 1960; *Quincy Patriot Ledger*, 9 January 1990.

43. Lysander Richards, *History of Marshfield* (Plymouth: Memorial Press, 1901), 1:192; Krusell, "Dwyer Farm"; article from untitled newspaper 6 April 1945, Trustees-Historical Room Papers, Ventress Memorial Library, Marshfield.

44. *Marshfield Mariner*, 2 August 1973.

45. Waterston, 123; PCRD, 477:252.

46. Margaret Brown, Interview by Cynthia H. Krusell, 13 January 1988, Cynthia Hagar Krusell Papers, HRA Library.

47. Ibid.; The hotels were variously known over the years as hotels, houses, inns, or cottages.

48. Brown.

49. Ibid.

50. Massachusetts, Joint Board Consisting of the Harbor and Land Commissioners and the State Board of Health, *Report of the Joint Board upon the Restoration of Green Harbor in the Town of Marshfield, Mass.* (Boston: Wright & Potter, 1898), 31; Brown; Plymouth County, Mass., *New Topographical Atlas of Surveys: Plymouth County Together with Town of Cohasset, Norfolk County, Massachusetts* (Springfield: L.J. Richards Co., 1903).

51. *Directory of Scituate and Marshfield Mass 1926* (Boston: Harold Howard Directories, 1926).

52. Joan Scolponeti, "Assumption Church Latest in Long List of Churches," *Marshfield Mariner*, 10 August 1983.

53. Brown.

54. Marshfield, Mass., Vital Records, 1850-.

Green Harbor Village *(continued)*

55. Marshfield, Mass., *Annual Reports of the Town Officers*, 1971.

56. Ibid., 1958.

57. Ibid., 1973.

58. Charles Lanman, *The Private Life of Daniel Webster* (New York: Harper & Brothers, 1852), 80.

Brant Rock and Ocean Bluff Villages

1. Maria Louise Pool, *In a Dike Shanty* (Boston: L.C. Page and Company, 1898), 147.

2. Ibid., 28, 57.

3. Marcia A. Thomas, *Memorials of Marshfield* (Boston: Dutton and Wentworth, 1854), 43; Cynthia Hagar Krusell, *Plymouth County 1685* (Plymouth:Pilgrim Society and Plymouth County Development Council, 1985), 60; Plymouth County, Mass., Commissioners, *Plymouth Colony Probate Records*, 4, pt. 2: 61-62.

4. Thomas, 42; Lucy Mary Kellogg, ed., *Mayflower Families Through Five Generations* (Plymouth: General Society of Mayflower Descendants, 1975), 1:100-101; Marshfield, Mass., Records of the Historical Commission.

5. Marshfield Tercentenary Committee, *Marshfield. The Autobiography of a Pilgrim Town*, (Marshfield: Marshfield Tercentenary Committee, 1940), 81 (hereafter cited as MAPT); *Marshfield Mariner*, 9-11 May 1989.

6. *Marshfield Mariner*, 9-11 May 1989; MAPT, 61, 256-57.

7. Lysander Richards, *History of Marshfield* (Plymouth: Memorial Press, 1901), 1:203,205.

8. Plymouth County, Mass., *Plymouth County Registry of Deeds*, 196:243, 200:240, 268:104, 557:263 (hereafter cited as PCRD); Plymouth County, Mass., *Plymouth County Probate Records*, Docket 22274 (hereafter cited as PCPR).

9. Edna McClellan Blauss Howland, "Major's Island," Historical Research Associates Papers, Historical Research Associates Library, Marshfield Hills (hereafter cited as HRA Library).

10. Richards, 204.

11. Jeannette Hixon Avery, "Brant Rock," Historical Research Associates Papers, HRA Library.

12. Edward Rowe Snow, *Ghosts, Gales and Gold* (New York: Dodd & Mead, 1972), 225; Shipwrecks Folder, Trustees-Historical Room Papers, Ventress Memorial Library, Marshfield.

13. MAPT, 222.

14. Edward Rowe Snow, "Sea and Shore Gleanings," *Quincy Patriot Ledger*, 10 November 1967.

15. Richards, 1:203; Massachusetts, Joint Board Consisting of the Harbor and Land Commissioners and the State Board of Health, *Report of the Joint Board upon the Restoration of Green Harbor in the Town of Marshfield, Mass.* (Boston: Wright & Potter, 1898), 11.

16. MAPT, 216; Marshfield, Mass., *Annual Report of the Town Officers*, 1981 (hereafter cited as MAR).

17. Fairview Inn, Newsletter, Fall/Winter 1989, Historical Research Associates Papers, HRA Libary.

18. Richards, 1:204-5.

19. *Diamond Jubilee Seventy-Fifth Annual Marshfield Fair 1941* (Marshfield: Marshfield Mail Print, 1941).

20. Carol Funderburk, "Helen Peterson: Brant Rock Expert," *Marshfield Reporter*, 28 April 1988.

Brant Rock and Ocean Bluff Villages *(continued)*

21. "75th Anniversary of the Brant Rock Union Chapel 1895-1970," Historical Research Associates Papers, HRA Library.

22. *Marshfield Reporter*, 28 September 1989.

23. [Evelyn Cecil], "Marshfield Matters," *South Shore Mirror*, 23 November 1967.

24. *Diamond Jubilee*.

25. Avery.

26. Ibid.

27. *Directory and History of Cohasset, Scituate, Marshfield, Duxbury and Norwell, Mass 1894* (Quincy: J.H. Hogan Company, 1894), 187.

28. Avery; Faith Jean, Estes Candy Kitchen Paper, Historical Research Associates Papers, HRA Library.

29. Faith Jean.

30. Funderburk.

31. *Diamond Jubilee*.

32. Marshfield, Mass., *Valuation of the Town of Marshfield*, 1907; Plymouth County, Mass., *New Topographical Atlas of Surveys: Plymouth County Together with Town of Cohasset, Norfolk County Massashusetts* (Springfield: L.J. Richards Co., 1903).

33. Lucy Maglathin Stein, Letter, Betty Magoun Bates, Marshfield; *New Topographical Atlas*.

34. Avery.

35. *Report of the Joint Board*, 32; Avery; Funderburk.

36. MAPT, 298-99; MAR, 1907.

37. Helen M. Fessenden, *Fessenden, Builder of Tomorrows* (New York: Coward-McCann, Inc., 1940), 126-27.

38. Ibid., 130, 153-54.

39. Ibid., 154.

40. *Marshfield Mariner*, 21 April 1977.

41. Avery, 6.

42. MAR, 1923, 1931-32.

43. *Marshfield Mariner*, 9-11 May 1989, South Look section.

44. *Boston Sunday Globe*, 7 January 1990, South Weekly section; James Haddad, Interview by Faith Jean, 1989, Historical Research Associates Papers, HRA Library.

45. *Quincy Patriot Ledger*, 8 December 1989; *Marshfield Mariner*, 9-11 May 1989, South Look section.

46. MAR, 1941.

47. Ibid.

48. John Taylor Paper, Historical Research Associates Papers, HRA Library, 4.

49. *Quincy Patriot Ledger*, 8 December 1989.

50. *Marshfield Mariner*, 9-11 May 1989, South Look section.

51. MAR, 1956, 1958-59.

52. *Marshfield Reporter*, 22 February 1990.

Rexhame Village

1. Maria Louise Pool, *In a Dike Shanty* (Boston: L. C. Page and Company, 1898), 82.

2. Mrs. B. M. Sherrill, *The Story of Rexhame* (Rexhame: Rexhame Country Club, 1915), 10; Marcia A. Thomas, *Memorials of Marshfield* (Boston: Dutton and Wentworth, 1854), 42; Robert Blair St. George, *The Wrought Covenant* (Brockton, Mass.: Brockton Art Center, 1979), 26.

Rexhame Village *(continued)*

3. John Kent House Study, Janet Peterson, Marshfield; Marshfield Tercentenary Committee, *Marshfield. The Autobiography of a Pilgrim Town* (Marshfield: Marshfield Tercentenary Committee, 1940), 13 (hereafter cited as MAPT); Sherrill, 11.

4. Massachusetts, *Reports of the Supreme Judicial Court*, 13:240; MAPT, 256-57.

5. John Kent House Study.

6. Sherrill, 13-14; MAPT, 281-83.

7. Thomas, 29-30; Eugene Aubrey Stratton, *Plymouth Colony, Its History & People 1620-1691* (Salt Lake City, Utah: Ancestry Publishing, 1986), 69, 375-76.

8. Thomas, 29-30; MAPT, 27-28.

9. MAPT, 76-77; Ruth A. Bradford, "Marshfield and Its Historic Houses," *The New England Magazine*, June 1901, 435; Stratton, 375-76.

10. MAPT, 77-79; Thomas, 27-29; Stratton, 376-77; Bradford, 437; Sherrill, 9-10.

11. Stratton, 376-77.

12. MAPT, 24, 26, 30, 58; Stratton, 376-77; St. George, 26-27.

13. Thomas, 28-29.

14. Lysander Richards, *History of Marshfield* (Plymouth: Memorial Press, 1901), 2:39.

15. Thomas, 38-39; MAPT, 24.

16. Plymouth County, Mass., Commissioners, *Plymouth Colony Probate Records*, 4, pt. 2: 89.

17. Thomas, 40; MAPT, 77.

18. Green Harbor Path Papers, Historical Research Associates Papers, Historical Research Associates Library, Marshfield Hills.

19. Shipwreck Folder, Historical Research Associates Papers, Historical Research Associates Library, Marshfield Hills.

20. Sherrill, 13-14.

21. Ibid., 15.

22. *Diamond Jubilee Seventy-Fifth Annual Marshfield Fair 1941* (Marshfield: Marshfield Mail Print, 1941); *Scituate and Marshfield, Mass. Directory 1926* (Boston: Harold Howard Directories, 1926).

23. *Reports of the Supreme Judicial Court*, 13:240.

Marshfield Village

1. Cynthia Hagar Krusell, "Pointed Cedars", *Boston Magazine*, December 1966, 86.

2. Marshfield Tercentenary Committee. *Marshfield. The Autobiography of a Pilgrim Town*, (Marshfield: Marshfield Tercentenary Committee, 1940), 19, 27 (hereafter cited as MAPT); Lysander Richards, *History of Marshfield* (Plymouth: Memorial Press, 1901), 1:69-70.

3. Richards, 1:27, 69.

4. John Ford Jr., surveyor, *Map of Marshfield, Mass. 1838* (Boston: Thomas Moore's Lithography, 1838); *Directory and History of Cohasset, Scituate, Marshfield, Duxbury and Norwell, Mass 1894* (Quincy: J.H. Hogan Company, 1894); *Marshfield Outlook*, 10 December 1898.

5. John Cushing and Jeremiah Hall, to Major General John Thomas, Hanover, 21 April 1775, John Thomas Papers, Massachusetts Historical Society, Boston; Louis Birnbaum, *Red Dawn at Lexington* (Boston: Houghton Mifflin, 1986), 108; Cynthia Hagar Krusell, *Of Tea and Tories* (Marshfield: Marshfield Bicentennial Committee, 1976), 12; L. Vernon Briggs, *History of*

Marshfield Village *(continued)*

Shipbuilding on the North River: Plymouth County, Massachusetts 1640-1872 (Boston: Coburn Bros., 1889), 277.

6. Briggs, 278.

7. MAPT, 26, 182-92; George Leonard, *Marshfield Sixty Years Ago* (Boston: J. Frank Farmer, 1872).

8. Leonard.

9. Eugene Aubrey Stratton, *Plymouth Colony, Its History & People, 1620-1691* (Salt Lake City, Utah: Ancestry Publishing, 1986), 310.

10. MAPT, 39-41; Richards, 1:34-37.

11. Arthur Howland House Study, Historical Research Associates Papers, Historical Research Associates Library, Marshfield Hills (hereafter cited as HRA Library); Plymouth County, Mass., *Plymouth County Registry of Deeds*, 30:221 (hereafter cited as PCRD).

12. Arthur Howland House Study; Plymouth County, Mass., *Plymouth County Probate Records*, 101:218; Docket 19680; PCRD, 1326:545.

13. Arthur Howland House Study.

14. Luther P. Hatch Store and House Study, Historical Research Associates Papers, HRA Library; *Marshfield Mariner*, 3 April 1975, 23 June 1977.

15. Luther P. Hatch Store and House Study; Sarah Rogers Ames House Study, Historical Research Associates Papers, HRA Library.

16. Luther P. Hatch Store and House Study.

17. Sarah Rogers Ames House Study.

18. Jerry Cook, *Roots & Branches* (Boston: New England Methodist Historical Society, 1989).

19. Richards, 1:17-18.

20. MAPT, 8, 16, 59-61; Stratton, 261; Marcia A. Thomas, *Memorials of Marshfield* (Boston: Dutton and Wentworth, 1854), 77-78.

21. Thomas, 78-79; MAPT, 8-9.

22. Stratton, 293.

23. Charles Henry Pope, *The Plymouth Scrapbook* (Boston: C. E. Goodspeed & Co., 1918), 69-71; Nathaniel B. Shurtleff and David Pulsifer, eds., *Records of the Colony of New Plymouth in New England* (Boston: William White, 1855-61.) 1:154.

24. Stratton, 293.

25. MAPT, 174; PCRD, 118:261-62.

26. MAPT, 174; Baker Family Papers, Historical Research Associates Papers, HRA Library.

27. Industries Folder, Historical Research Associates Papers, HRA Library.

28. Ibid.

29. MAPT, 174-79.

30. Ibid., 178.

31. *Marshfield Mariner*, 7 February 1990.

32. Marshfield, Mass., *Town Records of Marshfield* 1 (1659): 70; Thomas, 74.

33. Baker Family Papers.

34. Marshfield, Mass., *Annual Reports of the School Committee*, 1851, 9; Baker Family Papers.

35. Marshfield, Mass., Vital Records, 1850-, card no. 29.

36. Stratton, 259; Thomas, 52-53; *Marshfield's Open Door. Tercentenary Celebration Souvenir Programme* (Boston: Privately printed, 1940); Marshfield, Mass., *Valuation of the Town of Marshfield*, 1941.

37. Stratton, 281-82; Dingley Papers, Betty Magoun Bates, Marshfield.

38. Stratton, 281-82; MAPT, 52.

Marshfield Village *(continued)*

39. MAPT, 12, 24, 29-30.

40. Solomon Hewitt House Study, Historical Research Associates Papers, HRA Library.

41. MAPT, 12; Stratton, 354.

42. *Marshfield Mariner*, 14 September 1983.

43. Marshfield, Mass., *Annual Reports of the Town Officers*, 1989.

44. Charles P. Sinnott, Interview in the *Marshfield Mail*, 28 January 1960.

45. [Evelyn Cecil], "Marshfield Matters", *South Shore Mirror*, 16 September 1965.

46. Marcia A. Thomas House Study, Historical Research Associates Papers, HRA Library.

47. *Boston Sunday Globe*, 11 February 1990.

48. Technical Planning Associates, *Marshfield, Massachusetts Master Plan* (New Haven: Technical Planning Associates, 1962); South Shore Chamber of Commerce, *South Shore Economic Profile 1989-1990* (Quincy, Mass.: South Shore Chamber of Commerce, 1989).

Centre Marshfield Village

1. Marcia A. Thomas, *Memorials of Marshfield* (Boston: Dutton and Wentworth, 1854), 33-34; Marshfield Tercentenary Committee, *Marshfield. The Autobiography of a Pilgrim Town* (Marshfield: Marshfield Tercentenary Committee, 1940), 14 (hereafter cited as MAPT).

2. MAPT

3. Ibid., 64-65.

4. Lucy Mary Kellogg, ed., *Mayflower Families Through Five Generations* (Plymouth: General Society of Mayflower Descendants, 1975), 1:102; Thomas, 33-34.

5. MAPT, 135.

6. Kellogg, 1:155-56.

7. MAPT, 107.

8. L. Vernon Briggs, *History of Shipbuilding on the North River: Plymouth County, Massachusetts 1640-1872* (Boston: Coburn Bros., 1889), 353-54; Kellogg, 1:107.

9. Cynthia Hagar Krusell, "From Pilgrims to Patriots," *Mayflower Quarterly* 42 (1976): 119.

10. Ibid.; Mary Archibald, *Gideon White Loyalist* (Shelburne, Nova Scotia: Shelburne Historical Society, 1975).

11. Plymouth County, Mass., *Plymouth County Probate Records*, 14:190-93.

12. Thomas, 81, 83.

13. Nathaniel Phillips House Study, Historical Research Associates Papers, Historical Research Associates Library, Marshfield Hills.

Sea View Village

1. Richard Warren Hatch, *Leave the Salt Earth* (New York: Covici-Friede, 1933), 25.

2. L. Vernon Briggs, *History of Shipbuilding on the North River: Plymouth County, Massachusetts 1640-1872* (Boston: Coburn Bros., 1889), 285-86; Eugene Aubrey Stratton, *Plymouth Colony, Its*

Sea View Village *(continued)*

History & People, 1620-1691 (Salt Lake City, Utah: Ancestry Publishing, 1962), 318.

3. Little Family Papers, Historical Research Associates Papers, Historical Research Associates Library, Marshfield Hills (hereafter cited as HRA Library).

4. Luther Little, "An American Sea Captain in the Revolution," The Journal of American History 11, no. 3 (1917): 409-20; 13, no. 2 (1919): 217-47.

5. Little Family, Gertrude Lynd Papers, HRA Library.

6. Ibid.

7. Ibid.

8. Massachusetts, *Massachusetts Soldiers and Sailors in the Revolutionary War* (Boston: Wright & Potter Printing Co., 1896), 4:868; Josiah H. Drummond, *John Rogers of Marshfield and Some of His Descendants* (Portland, Maine: Smith & Sale, 1898), 69; Briggs, 286; Cynthia Hagar Krusell, *Of Tea and Tories* (Marshfield: Marshfield Bicentennial Committee, 1976), 18.

9. Little Family.

10. Ibid.

11. Luther Little.

12. Ibid.

13. Lysander Richards, *History of Marshfield* (Plymouth: Memorial Press, 1901), 2:78.

14. Marshfield Tercentenary Committee, *Marshfield. The Autobiography of a Pilgrim Town* (Marshfield: Marshfield Tercentenary Committee, 1940), 215 (hereafter cited as MAPT).

15. Robert M. Sherman and Ruth Wilder Sherman, comps., *The Vital Records of Marshfield, Massachusetts, to 1850* (Warwick, R.I.: Rhode Island Society of Mayflower Descendants, 1983), 137, 395-96; Richards, 2:80.

16. "Reminiscences of William Hall, 9 November 1871," Gertrude Lynd Papers, HRA Library.

17. Sherman and Sherman, 369.

18. MAPT, 151-52; Marcia A. Thomas, *Memorials of Marshfield* (Boston: Dutton & Wentworth, 1854), 80; Briggs, 356-57.

19. MAPT, 151-52.

20. Ibid.

21. Ibid., 181.

22. Briggs, 356-57.

23. Ibid.; William T. Davis, "History of Marshfield," in *History of Plymouth County*, comp. D. Hamilton Hurd (Philadelphia: J. W. Lewis & Co., 1884), 1169-70; Samuel Hall Folder, Gertrude Lynd Papers, HRA Library.

24. Samuel Hall Folder.

25. Ibid.; Davis, 1169-70.

26. Samuel Hall Folder.

27. Ibid.

28. Ibid.

29. Ibid.

30. MAPT, 151.

31. Massachusetts, *The Massachusetts Tax Valuation List of 1771.*

32. MAPT, 215-16.

33. Charles Hatch Jr. Ledger, 1822-30, Marshfield Historical Society Collection, Marshfield Historical Society, Marshfield.

34. Marshfield, Mass., *Annual Reports of the Town Officers*, 1953, 9.

35. MAPT, 180, 292.

36. Richards, 1:186.

Sea View Village *(continued)*

37. Ibid.; Danforth Hall House Study, Historical Research Associates Papers, HRA Library.

38. MAPT, 173; Richards, 1:186.

39. George Leonard, *Marshfield Sixty Years Ago* (Boston: J. Frank. Farmer, 1872), 8.

40. John Ford Jr., surveyor, *Map of Marshfield, Mass. 1838* (Boston, Thomas Moore's Lithography, 1838); Richards, 1:157.

41. MAPT, 183; Richards, 1:152; George Leonard Manuscript, Historical Research Associates Papers, HRA Library.

Marshfield Hills Village

1. Richard Beare House Study, Historical Research Associates Papers, Historical Research Associates Library, Marshfield Hills (hereafter cited as HRA Library).

2. Ibid.

3. Ibid.

4. Ibid.; Plymouth County, Mass., *Plymouth County Probate Records*, docket 20726 (hereafter cited as PCPR).

5. Plymouth County, Mass., *Plymouth County Registry of Deeds*, 92:207-8 (hereafter cited as PCRD).

6. PCPR, docket 15853.

7. Ibid.

8. Ibid., docket 2455.

9. Ibid., docket 30971.

10. Richard Beare House Study; Nathaniel Phillips House Study, Historical Research Associates Papers, HRA Library; Elijah Leonard House Study, Historical Research Associates Papers, HRA Library; Gertrude Lynd Papers, HRA Library.

11. Levi Ford House Study, Historical Research Associates Papers, HRA Library.

12. William Macomber House Study, Historical Research Associates Papers, HRA Library; PCPR, docket 13491.

13. William Macomber House Study; Excerpts from the "William Macomber Account Book 1783-1815," Marshfield Historical Society Collection, Marshfield Historical Society, Marshfield.

14. Richard Warren Hatch, *Leave the Salt Earth* (New York: Covici-Friede, 1933), 106.

15. Lysander Richards, *History of Marshfield* (Plymouth: Memorial Press, 1901), 2:75-76; George E. Bowman, ed., *The Mayflower Descendant: A Quarterly Magazine of Pilgrim History and Genealogy* (Boston: Massachusetts Society of Mayflower Descendants, 1899-1937) 3:188, 8:130-31; William T. Davis, "Genealogical Register of Plymouth Families," part 2 of *Ancient Landmarks of Plymouth* (Boston: Damrell & Upham, 1899), 267; William Macomber Account Book.

16. Edward Rowe Snow, *A Pilgrim Returns to Cape Cod* (Boston: Yankee Publishing Company, 1946), 17.

17. Jonathan Eames House Study, Historical Research Associates Papers, HRA Library.

18. Ibid.

19. Ibid.

20. Ibid.

21. Tilden Ames House Study, Historical Research Associates Papers, HRA Library.

22. Ibid.

23. Ibid.

24. Ibid.

Marshfield Hills Village *(continued)*

25. Elijah Leonard House Study.

26. Ibid.

27. Ibid.

28. Lysander Richards Papers, Trustees-Historical Room Papers, Ventress Memorial Library, Marshfield.

29. Marshfield Tercentenary Committee, *Marshfield. The Autobiography of a Pilgrim Town* (Marshfield. Marshfield Tercentenary Committee, 1940), 97, 103-4 (hereafter cited as MAPT).

30. Elijah Leonard House Study, Historical Research Associates Papers, HRA Library; Sarah E. Leonard and Otis L. Leonard House Study, Historical Research Associates Papers, HRA Library.

31. MAPT, 265.

32. David B. Ford, *Centennial History of the First Baptist Church, Marshfield, Mass. 1788-1888* (Boston: James H. Earle, 1888), 27.

33. Gertrude Lynd Papers.

34. Marshfield, Mass., *Report of the Selectmen on the Financial Affairs of the Town of Marshfield, from April 1, 1865, to Feb. 1, 1866*, 18-23

35. Marshfield, Mass., *Annual Reports of the Town Officers*, 1919 (hereafter cited as MAR).

36. Brian Doherty, "A Proposed Design for Youth Programming in the Arts," Master's thesis, Massachusetts College of Art, 1975, 5-9.

37. MAPT, 107-10.

38. Ibid., 267-68.

39. Richards, 1:158; Gertrude Lynd Papers.

40. Store records of Luther Rodgers, Gertrude Lynd Papers, HRA Library.

41. Danforth Hall House Study, Historical Research Associates Papers, HRA Library.

42. Ibid.

43. Ibid.

44. Ibid.

45. Ibid.

46. Ibid.

47. Hall family genealogy, Gertrude Lynd Papers, HRA Library; MAR, 1960.

48. Levi Ford House Study; PCRD, 132:228-29, 961:549; PCPR, docket 20867; L. Vernon Briggs, *History of Shipbuilding on the North River: Plymouth County, Massachusetts 1640-1872* (Boston: Coburn Bros., 1889), 60-61.

49. Briggs, 60-61; Levi Ford House Study.

50. MAPT, 173-74; Macomber Account Book, 28R.

51. MAPT, 180; Macomber Account Book, 49R.

52. Briggs, 202-13; MAPT, 149-50.

53. MAPT, 150-51.

54. Ibid.

55. Ibid., 145.

56. Isaiah Rogers House Study, Historical Research Associates Papers, HRA Library.

57. Ibid.

58. *Quincy Patriot Ledger*, 17 March 1990; BSC Group, *North River Water Quality Management Plan* (Boston: BSC Group, 1987).

59. Samuel Rogers Papers, Historical Research Associates Papers, HRA Library.

North Marshfield and Two Mile Villages

1. Richard Warren Hatch, *Leave the Salt Earth* (New York: Covici-Friede, 1933), 24.

2. William Phillips Tilden, *Autobiography* (Boston: George H. Ellis, 1891), 34.

3. Ibid., 24.

4. Josiah H. Drummond, *John Rogers of Marshfield and Some of His Descendants* (Portland, Maine: Smith & Sale, 1898), 6; Rogers Family Folder, Betty Magoun Bates, Marshfield.

5. Marshfield Tercentenary Committee, *Marshfield. The Autobiography of a Pilgrim Town* (Marshfield: Marshfield Tercentenary Committee, 1940), 76 (hereafter cited as MAPT).

6. *Marshfield Mariner*, 21 July 1977.

7. Ibid.

8. MAPT, 149-50.

9. L. Vernon Briggs, *History of Shipbuilding on the North River: Plymouth County, Massachusetts 1640-1872* (Boston: Coburn Bros., 1889), 208-9.

10. Drummond, 38; Excerpts from "William Macomber Account Book 1783-1815," Marshfield Historical Society Collection, Marshfield Historical Society, Marshfield; John Rogers House Study, Janet Peterson, Marshfield.

11. MAPT, 180; Marshfield, Mass., *Valuation of the Town of Marshfield, 1907.*

12. *Directory and History of Cohasset, Scituate, Marshfield, Duxbury and Norwell, Mass 1894* (Quincy: J.H. Hogan Company, 1894); *Marshfield Mariner*, 17 August 1983; Excerpts from Marshfield Historical Society Notes, bk. 1 (1913-1919), 74, Marshfield Historical Society Collection, Marshfield Historical Society, Marshfield.

13. MAPT, 76, 181.

14. Ibid., 150-51.

15. Tilden, 9; Lysander Richards, *History of Marshfield* (Plymouth; Memorial Press, 1901), 2:23.

16. Briggs, 36: Commission of Waterways and Public Lands to Selectmen of Norwell, Mass., 12 February 1917, Trustees-Historical Room Papers, Ventress Memorial Library, Marshfield.

17. Cynthia Hagar Krusell, *Plymouth County 1685* (Plymouth: Pilgrim Society and Plymouth County Development Council, 1985), 43-44.

18. Ibid.

19. Ibid.

20. MAPT, 113, 117, 159; Briggs, 211; Hiram Oakman House Study, Historical Research Associates Papers, Historical Research Associates Library (hereafter cited as HRA Library).

21. Hiram Oakman House Study.

22. Henry P. Oakman House Study, Historical Research Associates Papers, HRA Library.

23. Jotham Tilden House Study, Janet Peterson, Marshfield.

24. Richards, 1:155-56; Marshfield, Mass., *Annual Reports of the Town Officers*, 1907; 1920, 75 (hereafter cited as MAR).

25. John Ford Jr., surveyor, *Map of Marshfield, Mass. 1838* (Boston: Thomas Moore's Lithography, 1838); Plymouth County, Mass., *New Topographical Atlas of Surveys Plymouth County Together with Town of Cohasset, Norfolk County Massachusetts* (Springfield: L.J. Richards Co., 1903).

26. *Directory and History 1894*.

27. *Scituate and Marshfield, Mass. Directory 1926* (Boston: Harold Howard Directories, 1926).

North Marshfield & Two Mile Villages *(continued)*

28. Hall-Lincoln Genealogy, Historical Research Associates Papers, HRA Library.

29. Ford; Plymouth County, Mass., *Atlas of Plymouth County 1879* (Boston: George H. Walker & Co., 1879); *New Topographical Atlas* .

30. Richard Warren Hatch, *Curious Lobster* (London: Jonathan Cape, 1940), 11.

31. Samuel Deane, *History of Scituate, Massachusetts, from Its First Settlement to 1831* (Boston: James Loring, 1831), 221.

32. MAPT, 176; Two Mile Folder, Betty Magoun Bates, Marshfield.

33. Plymouth County, Mass., Commissioners, *Plymouth Colony Probate Records*, 1:335-37.

34. MAPT, 179-80; Magoun Family Papers, Betty Magoun Bates, Marshfield.

35. Magoun Family Papers.

36. Ibid.

37. Ibid.

38. Ibid.

39. Ibid.

40. MAPT, 168-69.

41. Richards, 1:156; MAR, 1907, 76.

42. Ephraim Randall House Study, Historical Research Associates Papers, HRA Library.

43. Camp WySibo Material, Cynthia Hagar Krusell Papers, HRA Library.

44. Briggs, 392.

45. Frances Downing Vaughan, "The New Calf," in *The Tulip Planter* (Alfred, N.Y.: Sun Publishing Company, n.d.).

Standish

1. Marshfield, Mass., *Annual Reports of the Town Officers*, 1936.

2. Plymouth County, Mass., "Marshfield Lower Common Lands 1712," In *Plymouth County Registry of Deeds, Plan Book*, 1:132.

3. David B. Ford, *The Centennial History of the First Baptist Church, Marshfield, Mass. 1788-1888* (Boston: James H. Earle, 1888).

4. Ibid.

5. Ibid.

6. Ibid.

7. Ibid.

8. Ibid.

9. Ibid.

10. Isabelle Paulding Magoun, Interview by Betty Magoun Bates, 27 May 1975, Betty Magoun Bates, Marshfield.

11. Ibid.

12. Excerpts from Marshfield Historical Society Notes, bk. 1 (1913-19), Marshfield Historical Society Collection, Marshfield Historical Society, Marshfield; Isabelle Paulding Magoun.

13. Charles McCarry, *Double Eagle* (Boston: Little, Brown and Company, 1979).

14. *Marshfield Mariner*, 1 December 1977.

References

Archibald, Mary. *Gideon White, Loyalist*. Shelburne, Nova Scotia: Shelburne Historical Society, 1975.

Bates, Betty Magoun. Papers. Marshfield.

Baxter, Maurice G. *One and Inseparable: Daniel Webster and the Union*. Cambridge: Harvard University Press, 1984.

Birnbaum, Louis. *Red Dawn at Lexington*. Boston: Houghton Mifflin, 1986.

Boston Sunday Globe. 24 January 1960; 7 January; 11 February 1990.

Bowman, George E., ed. *The Mayflower Descendant: A Quarterly Magazine of Pilgrim History and Genealogy*. 34 vols. Boston: Massachusetts Society of Mayflower Descendants, 1899-1937.

Bradford, Ruth A. "Marshfield and Its Historic Houses." *The New England Magazine*, June 1901, 422-44.

Bradford, William. *Of Plymouth Plantation 1620-1647*. Edited by Samuel Eliot Morison. New York: Alfred A. Knopf, 1966.

Briggs, L. Vernon. *History of Shipbuilding on the North River: Plymouth County, Massachusetts 1640-1872*. Boston: Coburn Bros., 1889.

BSC Group. *North River Water Quality Management Plan*. Boston: BSC Group, 1987.

[Cecil, Evelyn.] "Marshfield Matters". *South Shore Mirror*. 16 September 1965; 23 November 1967.

Church, Thomas. *The History of Philip's War*. Boston: Thomas B. Wait and Son, 1827.

Clark, William B., ed. *Naval Documents of the American Revolution*. Vol.1. Washington: U.S. Government Printing Office, 1964.

Cook, Jerry. *Roots & Branches*. Boston: New England Methodist Historical Society, 1989.

Cushing, John, and Hall, Jeremiah to Major General John Thomas, Hanover, 21 April 1775. John Thomas Papers. Massachusetts Historical Society, Boston.

Davis, William T. "Genealogical Register of Plymouth Families." Part 2 of *Ancient Landmarks of Plymouth*. Boston: Damrell & Upham, 1899.

———. "History of Marshfield." In *History of Plymouth County*, compiled by D. Hamilton Hurd, 1134-72. Philadelphia: J.W. Lewis & Co., 1884.

Deane, Samuel. *History of Scituate, Massachusetts, from its First Settlement to 1831*. Boston: James Loring, 1831.

Diamond Jubilee Seventy-Fifth Annual Marshfield Fair 1941. Marshfield: Marshfield Mail Print, 1941.

Directory and History of Cohasset, Scituate, Marshfield, Duxbury and Norwell, Mass 1894. Quincy: J.H. Hogan Company, 1894.

Doherty, Brian. "A Proposed Design for Youth Programming in the Arts." Master's thesis, Massachusetts College of Art, 1975.

Drummond, Josiah H. *John Rogers of Marshfield and Some of His Descendants*. Portland, Maine: Smith & Sale, 1898.

Fessenden, Helen M. *Fessenden, Builder of Tomorrows*. New York: Coward-McCann, Inc., 1940.

Ford, David B. *The Centennial History of the First Baptist Church, Marshfield, Mass. 1788-1888*. Boston: James H. Earle, 1888.

Hatch, Richard Warren *The Curious Lobster*. London. Jonathan Cape, 1940.

———. *Leave the Salt Earth*. New York: Covici-Friede, 1933.

Historical Research Associates Library. Betty Magoun Bates Papers. Marshfield Hills.

———. Cynthia Hagar Krusell Papers. Marshfield Hills.

———. Gertrude Lynd Papers. Marshfield Hills.

———. Historical Research Associates Papers. Marshfield Hills.

Holton, David Parsons. *Winslow Memorial*. New York: D.P.Holton, 1877.

Jean, Faith. "Storm of 1978." *Brockton Enterprise*, 7 February 1988

Johnson, Richard B., ed. "The Diary of Israel Litchfield." *New England Historic and Genealogical Register* 129 (July 1975): 250-269.

Kellogg, Lucy Mary, ed. *Mayflower Families Through Five Generations*. Vol. 1. Plymouth: General Society of Mayflower Descendants, 1975.

Krusell, Cynthia Hagar. "The Land Where First They Trod." *Mayflower Quarterly* 36 (1970):117-19.

———. "From Pilgrims to Patriots." *Mayflower Quarterly* 42 (1976):115-21.

———. "Plymouth County in 1685: The Land, the Church, the People." Master's thesis, Bridgewater State College, 1984.

———. *Plymouth County 1685*. Plymouth: Pilgrim Society and Plymouth County Development Council, 1985.

———. *Of Tea and Tories*. Marshfield: Marshfield Bicentennial Committee, 1976.

———. "The Winslows of 'Careswell' in Marshfield." In *The Winslows of "Careswell" Before and After the "Mayflower"* by Quentin Coons and Cynthia Hagar Krusell. Marshfield Hills, Mass.: By the authors, 1977.

Lanman, Charles. *The Private Life of Daniel Webster*. New York: Harper & Brothers, 1852.

Leonard, George. *Marshfield Sixty Years Ago*. Boston: J. Frank. Farmer, 1872.

Lewis, Walker, ed. *Speak For Yourself, Daniel*. Boston: Houghton Mifflin Company, 1969.

Little, Luther. "An American Sea Captain in the Revolution." *The Journal of American History* 11, no. 3 (1917): 409-20; 13, no. 2 (1919): 217-47.

Macomber, William. "William Macomber Account Book 1783-1815." Marshfield Historical Society Collection, Marshfield Historical Society, Marshfield.

Marshfield Mariner. 2 August 1973; 3 April 1975; 21 April; 23 June; 21 July; 1 December 1977; 17 August; 14 September 1983; 9-11 May 1989; 7 February 1990.

Marshfield, Massachusetts. *Annual Reports of the School Committee.* 1851-.

———. *Annual Reports of the Town Officers.* 1857-.

———. Records of the Historical Commission.

———. *Report of the Selectmen on the Financial Affairs of the Town of Marshfield, from April 1, 1865, to Feb. 1, 1866.*

———. *Town Records of Marshfield.* 2 vols.

———. *Valuation of the Town of Marshfield* 1857-.

———. Vital Records. 1850-. .

Marshfield Reporter. 28 April 1988; 28 September 1989; 22 February 1990.

Marshfield's Open Door. Tercentenary Celebration Souvenir Programme. Boston: Privately printed, 1940.

Marshfield Tercentenary Committee. *Marshfield. The Autobiography of a Pilgrim Town.* Marshfield: Marshfield Tercentenary Committee, 1940.

Massachusetts. *Massachusetts Soldiers and Sailors in the Revolutionary War.* 17 vols. Boston: Wright & Potter Printing Co., 1896.

———. *The Massachusetts Tax Valuation List of 1771.*

———. *Reports of the Supreme Judicial Court.* .

———. Joint Board Consisting of the Harbor and Land Commissioners and the State Board of Health. *Report of the Joint Board upon the Restoration of Green Harbor in the Town of Marshfield, Mass.* Boston: Wright & Potter, 1898.

McCarry, Charles. *Double Eagle.* Boston: Little, Brown and Company, 1979.

McElroy, George H. "The Fletcher Webster House." In Letters and Poems of Rachel Moorehead, compiled by George H. and John W. McElroy. Trustees-Historical Room Papers, Ventress Memorial Library, Marshfield. .

McGuyre, Ruth C. and Wakefield, Robert S. *Mayflower Families in Progress, Edward Winslow of the Mayflower and His Descendants for Five Generations.* Plymouth: General Society of Mayflower Descendants, 1988.

Melville, Doris Johnson. *Major Bradford's Town: A History of Kingston, 1726-1976.* Kingston: Town of Kingston, 1976.

Metcalf and Eddy Inc. *Marshfield Master Plan.* Boston: Metcalf and Eddy Inc., 1973.

Plymouth County, Massachusetts. *Plymouth County Probate Records.*

———. *Plymouth County Registry of Deeds* .

———. Commissioners. *Plymouth Colony Probate Records.* 4 vols.

Quincy Patriot Ledger. 10 November 1967; 8 December 1989; 9, 29 January; 17 March 1990.

Pool, Maria Louise. *In a Dike Shanty.* Boston: L. C. Page and Company, 1898.

Pope, Charles Henry. *The Plymouth Scrapbook.* Boston: C.E Goodspeed & Co., 1918.

Richards, Lysander. *History of Marshfield.* 2 vols. Plymouth: Memorial Press, 1901.

Raymond, John Marshall. *Thomas Families of Plymouth County, Massachusetts.* Itasca, Ill.: Harlan Carther Thomas, 1980.

Scituate and Marshfield, Mass. Directory 1926. Boston: Harold Howard Directories, 1926.

Scolponeti, Joan. "Assumption Church Latest in Long List of Churches." *Marshfield Mariner,* 10 August 1983.

———. *Daniel Webster Bicentennial Celebration.* Marshfield: Marshfield Historical Society, 1983.

Sherman, Robert M., and Sherman, Ruth Wilder, comps. *The Vital Records of Marshfield, Massachusetts, to 1850.* Warwick, R.I.: Rhode Island Society of Mayflower Descendants, 1983.

Sherrill, Mrs. B. M. *The Story of Rexhame.* Rexhame: Rexhame Country Club, 1915.

Shurtleff, Nathaniel B., and Pulsifer, David, eds. *Records of the Colony of New Plymouth in New England.* 12 vols. Boston: William White, 1855-61.

Snow, Edward Rowe. *Ghosts, Gales and Gold.* New York: Dodd & Mead, 1972.

———. *A Pilgrim Returns to Cape Cod.* Boston: Yankee Publishing Company, 1946.

South Shore Chamber of Commerce. *South Shore Economic Profile 1989-1990.* Quincy, Mass.: South Shore Chamber of Commerce, 1989.

St. George, Robert Blair. *The Wrought Covenant.* Brockton, Mass.: Brockton Art Center, 1979.

Sterry-Cooper, W. *Edward Winslow.* Birmingham, England: Reliance Printing Works, 1953.

Stratton, Eugene Aubrey. *Plymouth Colony, Its History & People, 1620-1691.* Salt Lake City, Utah: Ancestry Publishing, 1986.

Technical Planning Associates. *Marshfield, Massachusetts Master Plan.* New Haven: Technical Planning Associates, 1962. .

Thomas, Marcia A. *Memorials of Marshfield.* Boston: Dutton and Wentworth, 1854.

Tilden, William Phillips. *Autobiography.* Boston: George H. Ellis, 1891.

Vaughan, Frances Downing. "The New Calf." In *The Tulip Planter.* Alfred, N.Y.: Sun Publishing Company, n.d.

Ventress Memorial Library. Trustees-Historical Room Papers. Marshfield.

Waterston, Mrs. R. C. *Adelaide Phillipps.* Boston: A. Williams and Company, 1883.

Webster, Daniel. *The Papers of Daniel Webster: Correspondence.* Edited by Charles M. Wiltse et al. 7 vols. Hanover, N.H: University Press of New England, 1974- .

Willison, George F. *Saints and Strangers.* New York: Reynal & Hitchcock, 1945.

Winslow, Anna Green. Diary 1773. Historic Winslow House, Marshfield.

Winsor, Justin. *History of the Town of Duxbury, Massachusetts, with Genealogical Registers.* Boston: Crosby & Nichols, 1849.

Maps

Ford, John Jr., surveyor. *Map of Marshfield, Mass. 1838.* Boston: Thomas Moore's Lithography, 1838.

Hedge, B., Jr. *A Plan of Plymouth including Bays Harbours Islands Etc.* May 1784. Collection. Pilgrim Society, Plymouth, Mass.

Howland, Charles W. *Villages of Abington, Brant Rock and Green Harbor, Plymouth Co. Mass., September 25, 1879.* Trustees-Historical Room Collection, Ventress Memorial Library, Marshfield.

Map of Winslow Estate, 1822. Collection. Historic Winslow House, Marshfield.

Marshfield, Massachusetts. Marshfield Conservation Commission. *Conservation Map Town of Marshfield Massachusetts*, drawn by Warren Harrington. 1986.

Massachusetts. Joint Board of the Harbor and Land Commission and the State Board of Health. "Plan of Green Harbor the Dike and the Green Harbor Marshes in the Town of Marshfield, Mass." Plan 2 (December 1897). In *Report of the Joint Board upon the Restoration of Green Harbor in the Town of Marshfield, Mass.* Boston: Wright & Potter, 1898.

———. Joint Board of the Harbor and Land Commission and the State Board of Health. "Plan of Green Harbor in the Town of Marshfield, Mass." Plan 3 (December 1897). In *Report of the Joint Board upon the Restoration of Green Harbor in the Town of Marshfield, Mass.* Boston: Wright & Potter, 1898.

Plymouth County, Massachusetts. *Atlas of Plymouth County Massachusetts 1879.* Boston: George H. Walker & Co., 1879.

———. "Marshfield Lower Common Lands 1712." In *Plymouth County Registry of Deeds. Plan Book.* 1:132.

———. *New Topographical Atlas of Surveys: Plymouth County Together with Town of Cohasset, Norfolk County Massachusetts.* Springfield, Mass.: L.J. Richards Co., 1903.

Waterman, Asa. "Plan of Marshfield (Sea Coast) 1785." In *Marshfield the Autobiography of a Pilgrim Town*, by Marshfield Tercentenary Committee. Marshfield: Marshfield Tercentenary Committee, 1940.

Index

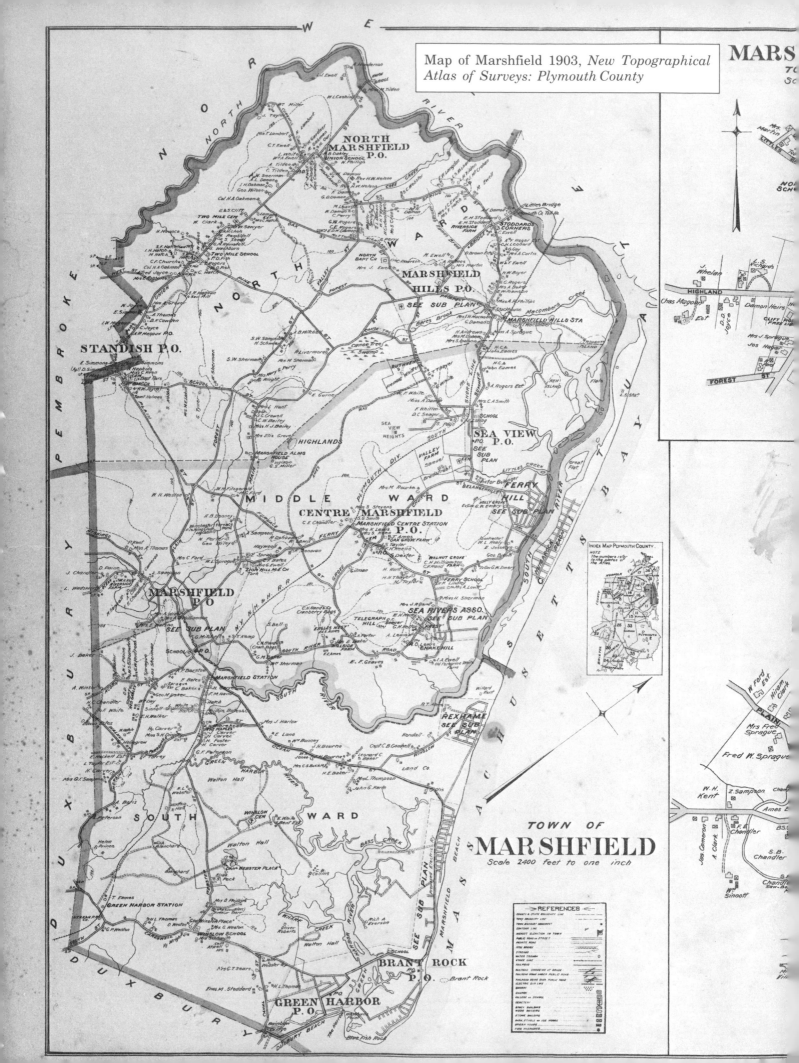

Map of Marshfield 1903, *New Topographical Atlas of Surveys: Plymouth County*

TOWN OF
MARSHFIELD
Scale 2400 feet to one inch